Against the Grain

Parody, Satire, and Intertextuality in Russian Literature

AGAINST THE GRAIN

PARODY, SATIRE, AND INTERTEXTUALITY IN RUSSIAN LITERATURE

EDITED BY

JANET G. TUCKER

Bloomington, Indiana, 2002

SLAVICA

Library of Congress Cataloging-in-Publication Data

Against the grain : parody, satire, and intertextuality in Russian
literature / edited by Janet G. Tucker.
    p. cm.
  Includes bibliographical references and index.
  ISBN: 0-89357-305-1
    1. Russian literature--19th century--History and criticism. 2.
Russian literature--20th century--History and criticism. 3. Parody
in literature. 4. Satire, Russian--History and criticism. 5.
Intertextuality. I. Tucker, Janet G.
    2. Critics--Soviet Union--Biography. 3. Literature and
  folklore. 4. Structuralism (Literary analysis) I. Title.

PG3015.5.P27 A37 2002
891.7'709003--dc21

                                              2002030913

Slavica Publishers   [Tel.] 1-812-856-4186
Indiana University   [Toll-free] 1-877-SLAVICA
2611 E. 10th St.   [Fax] 1-812-856-4187
Bloomington, IN 47408-2603   [Email] slavica@indiana.edu
USA   [www] http://www.slavica.com/

Contents

Janet Tucker

Preface

The present collection of essays grew out of conference panels on parody and satire in Slavic literatures, presented at two successive annual meetings of the American Association of Teachers of Slavic and East European Languages. While originally incorporating the broader treatment of parody and satire in Slavic literatures generally, the focus has shifted. To maintain thematic and chronological consistency, the present collection encompasses only Russian literature from approximately the 1850s, including such diverse writers as Ivan Goncharov and Fedor Dostoevsky from the nineteenth century, Evgenii Zamyatin and Andrei Sinyavsky (Abram Tertz) from the twentieth. The purpose of this collection is to underscore the vital role that parody, satire and intertextuality have played historically and continue to play in Russian literature and culture. Not intended to be a comprehensive treatment, it instead incorporates essays that treat specific writers and works and selected themes. For that reason and because of limitations of space, the collection starts with Ivan Goncharov and extends to the present.

While parody, satire and intertextuality can and often do function as political commentary in nineteenth–century belles–lettres as well as in the literature of the Soviet period and beyond, they also touch significantly on such important non–political concerns as aesthetics, societal foibles, human behavior, and metaphysical dilemmas, questions at once culturally specific and universal in scope. Ideally, therefore, they provide access to larger cultural issues that define a society as a whole, highlighting coincidental concerns or problems. And parody, satire and intertextuality have special aesthetic interest beyond the scope of the particular culture in which they are embedded, giving the present topic widespread appeal not only for Slavists, but for the general reader as well.

The *Slavonic and East European Review* has graciously allowed us to reprint Julie Cassiday's essay on Mayakovsky. My essay "Skaz and

Janet Tucker, ed. *Against the Grain: Parody, Satire and Intertextuality in Russian Literature.* Bloomington, IN: Slavica, 2002, iii–iv.

Oral Usage as Satirical Devices in Isaak Babel's Red Cavalry" originally appeared in *Canadian-American Slavic Studies*, 34, no. 2 (Summer 2000): 201–10 and has been republished here with their gracious permission. I would like to extend special thanks to Caryl Emerson and Jerzy Kolodziej, whose helpful suggestions strengthened the introduction. The recommendations of the anonymous reader improved the collection immensely. I am especially appreciative of the imput of Beth Juhl, Elizabeth McKee, Necia Parker-Gibson, and Donna Daniels of the Mullins University Library at the University of Arkansas, Geoff Husic from the University of Kansas Library, the assistance of Suzanne Smith, Kimberly Chenault and Chad Andrews, and the support, patience and advice of my husband William Tucker and son Robert Tucker. I am particularly greatful to George Fowler, Vicki Polansky, and Timothy Nelson from Slavica Publishers for their patient and able assistance.

The transliteration used in this collection is based on the standard Library of Congress system. However, names commonly known in the West (e.g., Dostoevsky, Gogol, Tolstoy) have been rendered in the text according to accepted practice, except where appended to transliterated Russian texts in endnotes and bibliography.

Introduction: Parody, Satire and Intertextuality in Russian Literature

Universally popular in the West, where a free press is taken for granted, parody, satire and intertextuality have typically functioned in Russian literature, constrained until recently by the censorship, as commentators on societal vices or shortcomings. Nor is this the only role they play. Since Russian literature has drawn on foreign models early on, the references to external texts or situations inherent in parody, satire and intertextuality have figured prominently in the evolution and fluctuation of literary genres and schools. Russia's early debt to Byzantine exemplars set the stage for the later wholesale borrowing characteristic of seventeenth- and, especially, eighteenth-century Russian literature, with the occasionally uneasy synthesis between native and foreign practice encouraging a Russian preoccupation with cultural self-definition, genres and schools. In the Russian context, the doubling or dialogism inherent in parody and intertextuality can endow borrowed texts or genres with a national, indigenous "spin."[1] Given the significance of parody and intertextuality, then, in Russian literature, it is not surprising to find a number of the most important writers of the nineteenth and

---

[1] No single writer more aptly exemplifies this bivalent patterning than the great literary pioneer Aleksandr Pushkin, "one of the first Russian writers to make the tradition conscious of itself as both European *and* other and to teach it to borrow and rework prior sources—often ones that were foreign and therefore in the reading public's eye privileged—in a way that was mature, self-confident, edged with parody, incessantly *dialogic.*" David Bethea, *Realizing Metaphors: Alexander Pushkin and the Life of the Poet* (Madison: University of Wisconsin Press, 1998), 39; emphasis in original. Tynianov comments on the central role of Pushkin as well, noting that nineteenth-century Russian writers were engaged in a "silent struggle with Pushkin...." Iurii Tynianov, *Arkhaisty i novatory* (Priboi, 1929; reprint Ann Arbor: Ardis, 1985), 412.

Janet Tucker, ed. *Against the Grain: Parody, Satire and Intertextuality in Russian Literature.* Bloomington, IN: Slavica, 2002, 1–18.

twentieth centuries, from Dostoevsky and Tolstoy to Zamyatin and Mayakovsky, turning to this mode.[2]

Parody

Parody refers back to a primary text providing the inspiration or impetus for a secondary one that incorporates or echoes it. Familiarity with the primary text is crucial, enabling parody to make its point. Unlike stylization, which simply recalls an original, parody mixes or reverses texts, creating in its wake an effect different or even opposite from the one originally intended by the parodied model.[3] The crucial distinction between parody and stylization lies in the presence or absence of this critical variance between texts. Where stylization underscores similarity, parody stresses difference.[4] Refusing to stay on a semantic fence, parody asserts itself by passing judgment on the original model. It emerges victorious in a contest of semantic rivalry, echoing an earlier utterance and then establishing itself as the new authoritative voice. Parody, notes Gary Saul Morson,

> aims to discredit an act of speech by redirecting attention from its text to a compromising context. That is, while the parodist's ironic quotation marks frame the linguistic form of the original utterance, they also direct attention to the *occasion* (more accurately, the parodist's version of the occasion) of its *uttering.*[5]

The "semantic intention" inherent in parody directly opposes the original one of the primary text,[6] which was deliberately chosen to be famil-

---

[2] Can a later movement be inherently superior to its predecessor? As Linda Hutcheon points out, change does not necessarily mean evolution, which presupposes some sort of improvement. Linda Hutcheon, *A Theory of Parody: The Teachings of Twentieth-Century Art Forms* (New York: Methuen, 1985), 36.

[3] Tynianov, *Arkhaisty i novatory*, 416.

[4] Hutcheon, *Theory of Parody*, 20.

[5] Gary Saul Morson, *The Boundaries of Genre: Dostoevsky's* Diary of a Writer *and the Traditions of Literary Utopia* (Austin: University of Texas Press, 1981), 110–11, 113, emphasis in original; Bethea, *Realizing Metaphors*, 171.

[6] Mikhail Bakhtin, *Problems of Dostoevsky's Poetics*, ed. and trans. Caryl Emerson (Minneapolis: University of Minnesota Press, 1984), 193, cited in

iar—even obvious—to the reader. Not just simple mimicry, since imitation can flatter, parody relies on ironic inversion of an original model to establish a distance between texts.[7] Bakhtin argues that "parody is a double-voiced utterance designed to be interpreted as the expression of two speakers,"[8] a type of satire in which the author imitates an original text to distort and ridicule a literary "victim."[9]

With its inherently dual nature, parody typically functions as a metaliterary vehicle for the development and rise of new schools or movements. Directed against even respected works, the parodic mode operates as an instrument for evolution or modernization[10] (sometimes as a realized metaphor, as when Pushkin equates "parody" with burying the dead and a coffin with a precursor's outmoded practice).[11] Tynianov maintained that literary evolution employed old forms in a new way, producing the comic contrast between new and old typical of parody.[12] Parody enables a writer to stand aloof and comment on an earlier text, precisely the dialogical model central to Bakhtin. Dostoevsky, for instance, at once echoes Gogol and sets up a critical distance from his predecessor.[13] By the time we get to Dostoevsky, Gogol's stammering,

---

Gary Saul Morson and Caryl Emerson, *Mikhail Bakhtin: Creation of a Prosaics* (Stanford: Stanford University Press, 1990), 152.

[7] Hutcheon, *Theory of Parody*, 6, 32. Not that parody should be confused with travesty, which operates outside the stylistic sphere as a character, situation, or notion with comic overtones. See Emil Draitser, *Techniques of Satire: The Case of Saltykov-Ščedrin* (Berlin: Mouton de Gruyter, 1994), 128–29.

[8] Morson, *The Boundaries of Genre*, 108.

[9] Gilbert Highet, *The Anatomy of Satire* (Princeton: Princeton University Press, 1962), 68–69. Caryl Emerson has observed that this model can, perhaps, be reversed, with satire subsumed under parody, which always implies a second voice responding to a first one. Private correspondence.

[10] Margaret A. Rose, *Parody//Meta-Fiction: An Analysis of Parody as a Critical Mirror to the Writing and Reception of Fiction* (London: Croom Helm, 1979), 30.

[11] Bethea, *Realizing Metaphors*, 56–57, n. 96.

[12] Draitser, *Techniques of Satire*, 130. Draitser points out that humor, which lacks a critical distance, differs from satire. *Techniques of Satire*, 29–30, 39.

[13] Iurii Tynianov, "Dostoevskii i Gogol' (k teorii parodii)," *Poetika. Istoriia literatury. Kino* (Moscow: Nauka, 1977), 199. Tynianov here anticipates Hutcheon's critical distance.

humiliated clerk from "The Overcoat" has evolved into the "poet-cock-roach" Captain Lebyadkin in *Demons* (*The Possessed*).

Satire

Forced into political and social commentary in the absence of a free press and loyal opposition, Russian literature has often been compelled to function as a satirical counterweight to established authority. That this authority need not be strictly political—associated with an auto-cratic regime—is readily apparent from an examination of Dostoevsky's *Demons* or Lev Tolstoy's *War and Peace*. The doubling—dialogue—characteristic of parody distinguishes satire as well, especially Menippean satire, and the writer's authority—the only legitimate voice in the context of a given work—undermines the spurious dominance of an external target. With an eye to reform, satire critiques its victim, functioning as "a literary Trojan horse for which polite (or politic) artfulness produces a dissembling form, serving first to contain and conceal, and then to unleash the ... passions of the satirist."[14] If that satirist follows the Juvenalian pattern, he will savagely attack his victim; should he wish instead to be more moderate, he will pattern his satire after Horace's.

Satire and parody have a respected pedigree reaching back to an-cient Greece, with Aristotle categorizing poetry as hymns and pane-gyrics or "invectives" including "satire," "lampoon," or "parody."[15] Satirical media can be broad, taunting or ridiculing literary works or even entire historical epochs. Satire can take the form of narrative fic-tion, such as Voltaire's *Candide*, or, like Aristophanes' *Frogs*, it can be dramatic.[16]

Characterized by a virus-like ability to inhabit other genres, satire need not be aggressive. An offensive tone is not satire's only definitive indicator; it can be playful as well as hostile, with Voltaire's *Candide* a

---

[14] Brian A. Connery and Kirk Combe, "Theorizing Satire: A Retrospective and Introduction," in *Theorizing Satire: Essays in Literary Criticism* (New York: St. Martin's Press, 1995), esp. 2–9.

[15] Robert C. Elliott, *The Power of Satire: Magic, Ritual, Art* (Princeton: Princeton University Press, 1960), 4. Draitser reminds us that the Latin *satura* denotes "a mix of heterogeneous things." Draitser, *Techniques of Satire*, 101.

[16] Highet, *Satire*, 14–15.

case in point.[17] A writer may himself supply a "pedigree," selecting an established satiric theme and labeling a novel or poem a "satire." Ideally, he should depict an absurd predicament, stun or shock the reader, and arouse a "blend of amusement and contempt."[18] Satire needs two basic components: wit and an external victim.[19] Applicable to a readily recognizable historical period and pointing to individuals or situations within a given society, satire then mounts an attack. Most significantly, it must refer to situations or events external to the text, establishing an opposition parallel to the stylistic one encountered in parody. Satirical polarities depicted in their extremes help to achieve maximum tension.[20] The restrictions of a partial dictatorship or totalitarian system, as in pre-revolutionary Russia or the former Soviet Union, tend to give rise to this kind of self-examination, typically communicated indirectly. Along with parody, satire emphasizes the gap between an ideal world and the real one and brings the external world into art, making society fair game for the satirist.[21] While these attacks may be candid during fairly relaxed times, political tyranny calls for a degree of caution and ingenuity, with indirect criticism far safer than blunt censure. Given the historically repressive nature of Russian political systems, the satiric mode in the Russian tradition is "reformative" rather than oppositionist,[22] surely, the safer way to go. While satire can adhere to the Juvenalian pattern and savagely attack its victim,[23] Russian practice typically follows the gentler Horatian model, with literary characters frequently acting as a chorus to explicate events, functioning, according to the traditions of Menippean satire, as mouthpieces for

---

[17] George Test, *Satire: Spirit and Art* (Tampa: University of South Florida Press, 1991), 7–34.

[18] Highet, *Satire*, 15–23.

[19] Northrup Frye, *Anatomy of Criticism* (Princeton: Princeton University Press, 1957), 224–25.

[20] Connery and Combe, "Theorizing Satire," 4–6.

[21] Hutcheon, *Theory of Parody*, 104.

[22] Karen Ryan-Hayes, *Contemporary Russian Satire: A Genre Study* (Cambridge: Cambridge University Press, 1995), 3.

[23] Test, *Satire*, 28, 91.

ideas.[24] Lev Tolstoy's and Dostoevsky's characters illustrate this quite aptly, as do the visitors paying court at the beginning of Goncharov's *Oblomov*.

Intertextuality

In parody, a later text comments on an earlier one through ironic distance. Employing the same dialogical structure present in parody, satire attacks an external situation or institution. Intertextuality is clearly different, presupposing a relationship between different texts and using earlier texts to comment on a contemporary situation. The author of the second text acknowledges a debt to literary tradition instead of attempting to overturn it. Perhaps intertextuality fits in more readily with Tynianov's term "stylization," in which one text can recall another without a critical distance necessarily being present. Evgenii Zamyatin's novel *We* (the subject of Jerzy Kolodziej's essay) is just such a work. Backshadowing to multiple texts—Aleksandr Pushkin's "The Bronze Horseman" and Andrei Bely's novel *Petersburg*—*We* develops the Petersburg theme in the Soviet context. In Iurii Olesha's *Envy* (subject of the editor's essay) competing perceptions of reality, incorporated into visual images, vie for the reader's attention. As Josephine Woll reminds us in her essay, Liudmila Petrushevskaya's sordid vision of Russian life in the late twentieth century—depicted in her novel *The Time: Night*—recalls Dostoevsky's scandals, rows and verbal violence. In all these examples, intertextuality grounds a later text in an established tradition and recalls an earlier or external source to make its point. Similar to both parody and satire in its reliance on external references, intertextuality functions in reverse by stressing similarity instead of difference and by incorporating the earlier text to bolster its case.

The Historical Background

Russian satire can be traced back to short tales of the sixteenth and seventeenth centuries,[25] with satire and parody imported from Western and Central Europe as part of a larger complex of the wholesale borrowing

---

[24] Frye, *Anatomy*, 309. Menippean satire is marked by an "extraordinary freedom of plot and philosophical invention," which makes it a natural choice for Dostoevsky. See Bakhtin, *Problems of Dostoevsky's Poetics*, 114.

[25] Richard L. Chapple, *Soviet Satire of the Twenties* (Gainesville, FL: University Press of Florida, 1980), 1–2.

linked with modernization. In keeping with their traditional role as both critique and amusement, narratives of this period often function as entertainment, not just invective. The association of satire and humor, plus the intimate involvement of the reader, would characterize Russian literature for the next three centuries. In the wry seventeenth-century tale "Frol Skobeev, the Rogue," for instance, the anonymous author treats his protagonist, a contemporary Muscovite social climber, with a healthy degree of contempt, inviting the reader to do the same. "Frol Skobeev" is more than just a thumbnail sketch of the "new man" on the rise. Its anonymous author judges not only the fluctuating social strata of Muscovite society in the late seventeenth century, but, more to the point, skewers the audience whose mores and social practices are distilled in the image of Frol, a superficially amusing yet intrinsically negative character.[26] In chastising readers and protagonists alike and, in effect, stuffing them into the same pigeonhole, "Frol Skobeev" anticipates Denis Fonvizin's comedic masterpieces of the eighteenth century. "Misery–Luckless–Plight," also from the seventeenth century, relies instead on intertextuality, looking backward to the religious literature of the medieval period to underscore change in contemporary society.

Characterized and shaped by wholesale borrowing from Western genres, eighteenth-century Russian literature—most notably satire and parody—turned to classical and French neo-classical models. Verse satire figures in this context not just as a critique of societal mores or conditions but, like parody, plays a role in the evolution of genre. Neo-classical Russian satirists evolved beyond merely producing Russian versions of foreign works to make important original contributions. Antiokh Kantemir followed his translations of Boileau's and Horace's poetic satires with his own Russian versions. An important arbiter of style, Aleksandr Sumarokov was himself the author of eight satires.[27] Their contributions established a foundation that satirical poetry could build on later, in the nineteenth century. Aleksandr Pushkin's "Count Nulin" and "Little House in Kolomna" continued the neo-classical tra-

---

[26] For comments on the role of the reader, see Caryl Emerson, "'The Queen of Spades' and the Open End," *Puškin Today*, ed. David M. Bethea (Bloomington: Indiana University Press, 1993), 32, 35.

[27] Hugh McLean, "Satire," *Handbook of Russian Literature*, ed. Victor Terras (New Haven: Yale University Press, 1985), 385.

dition of amusing verse satire, followed in this vein by Nikolai
Nekrasov's "Who Can be Happy in Russia?" Satirical journals of the
period functioned, however briefly, as critics of the status quo and carried on the venerable classical tradition of exposing an enemy while, at
the same time, they furthered the evolution of satirical prose, itself crucial in shaping and defining prose genres in the eighteenth and, later,
the nineteenth centuries. Emulating Addison's and Steele's *The
Spectator* and *The Tatler*, Fedor Emin and Nikolai Novikov continued
this tradition of journalistic satire.[28] Catherine the Great, no mean
journalist herself, "censored" Novikov by shutting down his journal, *The
Drone*. Novikov's attempted independence illustrates a crucial feature
of the eighteenth century: the emergence of Russian literature as an autonomous voice in its own right. As Russian authority learned belatedly,
the incorporation of Western models also meant exposure to Western
values. Because parody and satire are, by definition, inherently critical,
Russian literature imported the substance along with the form.

     The great eighteenth-century playwright Denis Fonvizin humorously
lampooned societal shortcomings in his ever-popular comedies *The
Minor* and *The Brigadier*, his double-edged dramas catching characters
and audience alike in the same net. Fonvizin focused on his contemporary bifurcated society, characterized by an uneasy amalgamation of
native plus partially digested foreign influences, his plays anticipating
the conflicts between Slavophiles and Westernizers that emerged early
in the nineteenth century. The earlier tradition of employing humor to
chide the larger community—including the reader—was continued in
the nineteenth-century theatre by such gifted dramatists as Aleksandr
Griboedov in *Woe from Wit*, Nikolai Gogol in *The Inspector General*,
and Aleksandr Sukhovo-Kobylin in his *Trilogy*. Griboedov documented
the vices, petty and otherwise, of early nineteenth-century Moscow
society. His reader/audience is at once hunter and prey, responsive to
Griboedov's criticisms, yet the target of his invective. Griboedov's character Skalozub (Grinner) encapsulates this double-edged sword within
his very name. Nor can the overall importance of Gogol in the development of Russian satire be underestimated.[29] His drama *The Inspector*

---

[28] McLean, "Satire," 384–85.
[29] Leslie Milne considers *Dead Souls* the first Russian picaresque novel to
achieve a universal reputation as a "satirical panorama." Leslie Milne, "Satire,"

General is a scathing indictment not only of the limitations of contemporary Russian society, but of human shortcomings generally (including, of course, the audience's). Gogol freezes the action at the end of the final scene, not only dehumanizing his personae by rendering them inanimate, but also emphasizing the timelessness of his enterprise. Sukhovo-Kobylin opposes the writer's principled authority to the miscarriage of justice endemic in the Russian autocratic state.[30] *Krechinsky's Wedding*, first of the *Trilogy*, follows the French tradition of Eugène Scribe and the *pièce bien faite* (the well-made play), the intricately plotted, suspenseful comedy popular in contemporary Paris.[31] In his middle play, *The Case*, the author shifts from comedy to a drama with tragic overtones, a classic confrontation between good and evil.[32] *The Death of Tarelkin*, last of the *Trilogy*, draws on vaudeville elements of Parisian boulevard theatre and the Russian puppet theatre (combining thereby Western and Russian conventions). Because of its structure, this final piece lent itself well to experimental staging under the avant-garde director Vsevolod Meyerhold in 1922.[33]

Aleksei Konstantinovich Tolstoy and his cousins the Zhemchuzhnikov brothers thrust parody to its logical extreme by inventing an author, Koz'ma Prutkov. Not only does Prutkov himself parody contemporary literature in his verse, his *poshlye* (banal) poetic themes mock the elevated status of the Romantic poet and any reader who might take him seriously. Prutkov enables his creators to take potshots at their targets in relative safety and, in effect, parodies literature, literary creation, and other authors. As a literary fabrication, his

---

Malcolm V. Jones and Robin Feuer Miller, ed., *The Cambridge Companion to the Classical Russian Novel* (Cambridge: Cambridge University Press, 1998), 86–89.

[30] See Harriet Murav, *Russia's Legal Fictions* (Ann Arbor: University of Michigan Press, 1998), 15–54.

[31] Harold Segel, "Introduction," *The Trilogy of Sukhovo-Kobylin* (New York: Dutton, 1969), xxiv–xxvii.

[32] Elizabeth Stenbock-Fermor reminds us that "the problem of Good and Evil lies at the bottom of any *Menippean* satire." Elizabeth Stenbock-Fermor, "*The Master and Margarita* and Goethe's *Faust, Slavic and East European Journal* 13, no. 3 (Fall 1969): 310. Emphasis in original.

[33] Segel, "Introduction," xxxvii–xlvii.

twentieth-century echo is Andrei Sinyavsky's literary alter ego Abram Tertz, the subject of Caryl Emerson's essay.

Following the reign of the reactionary Tsar Nicholas I (1825–55), Russian literature and, especially, civic criticism began to make gingerly attempts to expose and correct major societal problems. Almost immediately after the publication of Goncharov's *Oblomov* in 1859, therefore, critics responded to the novel as a social document. Nikolai Dobrolyubov's essay "What is Oblomovism?" ("Chto takoe oblomovshchina?"), which appeared in the same year, represents only the first of many such reactions. But Goncharov was not simply a "critical realist" bent on a detailed examination of societal ills; he was a brilliant parodist as well. Amy Singleton Adams' essay on *Oblomov* explores this aspect of Goncharov's genius. Throughout the novel, *The Odyssey* figures simultaneously as a backdrop and an echo of Russian "Homers," especially Antonii Pogorelsky (pen name of Aleksei Perovsky, who enjoyed enormous popularity early in the nineteenth century) and the literary idylls of the previous century.[34] Odysseus' return—hampered by numerous misadventures—is the focus of *The Odyssey*, echoed in the homecoming theme in *Oblomov*. But Goncharov's protagonist lacks Odysseus' heroic stature. Where *The Odyssey* is an epic, *Oblomov* functions as mock-epic, Oblomov's "return" to his miniature estate spoofing Odysseus' great quest. Goncharov's parodic masterpiece creates a "dialogue" (the essence of parody and satire) between Homer's original and contemporary texts, and functions as a satiric commentary on the idiosyncracies and flaws peculiar to Russian society on the eve of the liberation of the serfs, in 1861.

Mikhail Saltykov-Shchedrin (Saltykov) is one of the dominant satirists of nineteenth-century literature. A Juvenalian satirist, Saltykov savaged Russian bureaucracy and the failings of Russian culture and society in *Provincial Sketches*, *Pompadours and Pompadouresses*, and *The Story of a Town*.[35] Despite denials to the contrary, he castigated Russian historians and historiography, themselves powerful shapers of the national image. That Russia had no formal tradition of historiogra-

---

[34] Robert A. Maguire, "The City," Jones and Miller, eds., *The Cambridge Companion to the Classic Russian Novel*, 29.

[35] Chapple, *Satire*, 1–2.

phy is significant here, since literature then had to step into the breach,[36] and Saltykov's town of "Glupov" ("Foolsville") drives this point thoroughly home. Echoing Koz'ma Prutkov's ingenuous foolishness, Saltykov's parody doubles back on itself in anticipation of Sinyavsky's later intricacy.

Bakhtin's conviction that parody is "double-voiced" is particularly apt for Dostoevsky, who frequently uses one character to double and undermine another in, for example, *Crime and Punishment*, *The Brothers Karamazov*, and, most significantly for our purposes here, *Demons*. Deborah Martinsen's essay examines Dostoevsky's treatment of Lebyadkin (in *Demons*) as a parodic double of his brother-in-law Stavrogin. Conflicts between these characters force the society tale—inherited from English and French literature—to its furthest realization, in effect exploding a genre too limited for the Russian context. Dostoevsky's ruthless parody opens up the novel to the metaphysical questions lying behind the physical details and the immediate social issues that constitute the framework of the traditional novel. These confrontations highlight the very center of Dostoevsky's work: the larger questions of God's existence and man's place in the universe relative to God.

Central to Lev Tolstoy's castigation of societal foibles, satire, distinguishing his work from *Sebastopol' Sketches* to *War and Peace* and *Hadji Murad*, is the subject of Derek Maus's essay. Tolstoy's satirical tone flows quite naturally from his narrator, the supreme authority always ready to debunk or disparage characters who fail to measure up to his elevated standards. His assertion that his work is "true to life" gives Tolstoy enormous stature.[37] The more exalted a character's position in society and the greater the power he holds, the more likely he is to incur Tolstoy's invective. Negative traits vary according to the work, with cowardice skewered in his *Sebastopol Sketches* and self-mythology (especially Napoleon's) in *War and Peace*. The false values of Russian society provide a prime target in *Hadji Murad*.

---

[36] Svetlana Evdokimova, *Pushkin's Historical Imagination* (New Haven: Yale University Press, 1999), 1.

[37] George Steiner, "A Reading Against Shakespeare," *No Passion Spent: Essays 1978–1995* (New Haven: Yale University Press, 1996), 116–21.

The October Revolution of 1917, a watershed in Russian history and culture, established a great rift between the entrenched system that finally collapsed and a new one, initially identified with revolution itself, that would eventually deteriorate into stagnation interrupted periodically by stark terror. After October, parody and satire (and art in general) embarked down a dangerous path into unfamiliar terrain and found itself in the anomalous position of criticizing a system which, while not ideal, was assumed to be on the road to perfection. The role literature in general was expected to play throughout Soviet history produced an especially precarious environment for the (*un*official) parodist and satirist, whose work had traditionally touched on societal and political issues. The new Soviet regime, which allowed only a single official voice, undermined the dialogical structure basic to parodic and satirical writing by insisting on a monological apprehension of reality.

Official satire and parody, however, were champions of state control from the very beginnings of the Soviet rule, when pro-regime writers mass-produced satirical feuilletons for newspapers and magazines.[38] The Soviet journal *Krokodil* (*The Crocodile*), for example, took aim at such safe targets as "sleepy street sweepers, drunken plumbers, and inefficient factory guards,"[39] targeted as impediments to the realization of a perfect society. In its primary role as a "corrector of morals," "official" Soviet satire was more closely akin to the classical tradition than to the experimental literature of the Silver Age.[40] Official satire was directed against the *dis*empowered rather than the empowered, the standard satirical pattern. At this early stage of Soviet culture, satire, like Cubo-Futurism and Constructivism, was an enthusiastic partisan of the new regime, and official parody and satire complied with the monological model inherent in the new system.[41] *Un*official satire of the

---

[38] Chapple, *Satire*, 3–4.

[39] Draitser, *Techniques of Satire*, 34.

[40] I am grateful to the anonymous reader for this insight. Abram Tertz (Andrei Sinyavsky) also maintains that socialist realism was much closer to the eighteenth century than the nineteenth. Abram Tertz (Andrei Sinyavsky) "Chto takoe sotsialisticheskii realizm?" *Fantasticheskii mir Abrama Tertza* (Paris: Inter-Language Literary Associates, 1967), 431.

[41] For a discussion of the monological limitations of Soviet Marxism, see my *Revolution Betrayed: Jurij Oleša's* Envy (Columbus, OH: Slavica Publishers, 1996).

nineteen-twenties climaxed with Mikhail Zoshchenko's immensely popular short stories and Il'ia Il'f and Evgenii Petrov's picaresque novels *The Twelve Chairs* and *The Little Golden Calf*.[42] Evgenii Zamyatin's *We* alludes to earlier texts and artifacts associated with the culture displaced by the revolution, creating a dystopia that castigates the contemporary system. The most important subtext in *We* is the Petersburg motif, dominant in the work of such nineteenth-century writers as Pushkin, Gogol, Lev Tolstoy and Dostoevsky and resurfacing in the twentieth century in Andrei Bely's eponymous novel *Petersburg*, which captures the explosiveness of Russian society on the eve of the 1905 Revolution while anticipating the upheavals of 1917. Bely echoes major writers who preceded him: from Pushkin, Gogol, and Dostoevsky to Tolstoy and Chekhov. His misquotes of Pushkin and allusions to Tchaikovsky's opera librettos based on Pushkin's originals set up complex, additional intertextual paradigms with parodic overtones. As Gary Saul Morson reminds us, an anti-genre (parodic genre) parodies a target genre that operates as a subtext.[43] But Bely turns parody on its head in *Petersburg* and, like Bitov in *Pushkin House*, instead uses a subtext to deflate the (apparent) hegemony of contemporary authorities, be they governmental or revolutionary (both identified with Peter the Great, who functions in the novel as a form of self-parody). The very paradigm of text/subtext is built into the city of Petersburg: an uneasy amalgam of authority and rebellion, of Russian tradition versus the West, marked Petersburg from its very beginnings in 1703. This uncomfortable, essentially, untenable combination is reproduced in the parodic dialogue of the novel and, Jerzy Kolodziej notes, dominates in *We*.

In *Red Cavalry*, Isaak Babel' employs *skaz* and oral usage as satirical devices to undermine the dubious aims of the new Soviet order. Babel' focuses on the traditional culture of the illiterate and semi-literate masses and, through his imagery—a twisted echo of the Russian folk tale—he provides a critical examination of the horrific impact that the October Revolution and subsequent civil strife created in Soviet Russian society. Babel' explodes the very foundations of the revolution by alluding to its fatal impact on those very masses in whose name it had been made.

---

[42] Ryan-Hayes, *Contemporary Russian Satire*, 2.
[43] Morson, *Boundaries of Genre*, 115–16.

Iurii Olesha, whose novel *Envy* is the subject of the editor's essay, focuses on the primacy of the visual image and the imagination as counterweights to contemporary political dominance and authority. Olesha divides his characters into two camps that reflect each other through the visual imagery of the novel: visionaries unable to act, and actors devoid of any vision. The shift in narrators—completely antithetical to Lev Tolstoy's practice—between parts 1 and 2 results in a mirrored structure, itself a form of self-parody. By teasing, nudging, and chiding his readers, Olesha recalls Pushkin, anticipates Sinyavsky/Tertz, and reminds us of the creative intricacy and playfulness characteristic of parodic and intertextual literature.

Zamyatin's imaginative evocation of a future dystopia is echoed later in Mayakovsky's dramas *The Bedbug* and *The Bathhouse*, which Julie Cassiday treats in her essay. Both plays were directed by Vsevolod Meyerhold and followed on the success of Mayakovsky's revolutionary miracle-play, *Mystery-Bouffe*. The staging of these later pieces met with resistance on the part of the political establishment,[44] at least in part because, by the end of the first revolutionary decade, the new regime felt uncomfortable with satire and parody. Meyerhold's and Mayakovsky's experimental theater would also have been distasteful to a government that increasingly favored either realism—modelled on Lev Tolstoy's practice but soon to degenerate into socialist realism—or the propaganda art that flourished in the twenties. Mayakovsky, who incorporated a critical sketch of life under NEP (the New Economic Policy) during the nineteen-twenties in *The Bedbug* and *The Bathhouse*, anticipated a sterile future closely patterned on the unappetizing dystopia of Zamyatin's *We*.

Aesthetic concerns important in the nineteenth century also figure significantly in the twentieth, with such writers as Arkhangel'sky and Sinyavsky (Tertz) stressing literary issues. Arkhangel'sky's parodies on Mikhail Zoshchenko are a case in point. Inspired in his turn by Gogol, Zoshchenko was the prolific author of numerous amusing yarns. A foremost humorist/satirist of the nineteen-twenties, his work inspired not only imitators, but also parodists. Arkhangel'sky's later stories "unmask" Zoshchenko's parody and focus in a cunning way on the limi-

---

[44] Edward J. Brown, *Russian Literature Since the Revolution* (New York: Collier Books, 1963), 64.

tations of Zoshchenko's readers, as well as on the strictures of contemporary criticism. Arkhangel'sky brought out a collection of parodies in 1930, with the infamous critic Leopold Averbakh providing the introduction for this volume. The elusiveness of his parody probably accounts for its survival even during the increasingly tense and dangerous conditions of the nineteen-thirties.

Satire and parody suffered under socialist realism, the only officially acceptable form of art from 1934 until recent changes under *glasnost'* and *perestroika*. Yet, even in this cultural wasteland, they survived and continued to thrive underground, with the absurd extremism of socialist realism providing fertile ground. The most prominent parodist who continued to work into the nineteen-thirties was the great absurdist Daniil Kharms (Yuvachev). Along with Aleksandr Vvedensky, Konstantin Vaginov, and Nikolai Zabolotsky, among others, Kharms was a member of OBERIU (*Ob"edinenie real'nogo iskusstva*, The Association for Real Art), an avant-garde Leningrad group that flourished in the late nineteen-twenties. Committed to experimentation, Kharms and his fellow Oberiuty (OBERIU members) soon ran into trouble. Kharms, who was initially arrested in 1931, several years before the beginnings of the Great Terror, eventually perished of starvation in a camp ten years later.[45] His parody, intimately connected with aesthetics as well as politics, was metaliterary as well as social in its thrust. Perhaps Kharms engaged, to at least an extent, in the self-mockery that figures in the work of his great avant-garde predecessor Andrei Bely.[46]

Officially-sanctioned satire re-entered literature during World War II as a part of the war effort and served as propaganda directed against the Nazis—only to be eclipsed once more with the end of the conflict in 1945.[47] The death of Stalin (March 1953) eased constrictions in all facets of Soviet life, with the arts benefitting enormously from this relaxation. Circumscribed yet tangible freedom transformed literature, and limited official criticism of the system reappeared openly after a hiatus of over

---

[45] Henryk Baran, "Kharms, Daniil Ivanovich," *Handbook of Russian Literature*, ed. Terras, 221.

[46] For self-mockery in Bely, see Robert A. Maguire and John E. Malmstad, "Notes," Andrey Bely, *Petersburg*, trans. Robert A. Maguire and John E. Malmstad (Bloomington: Indiana University Press, 1978), n. 316.

[47] Peter Henry, *Modern Soviet Satire* (London: Collet's, 1974), ix–x.

two decades. In 1956, the Twentieth Party Congress and Nikita Khrushchev's secret speech brought about a striking transformation. Once Khrushchev had denounced Stalin's excesses and condemned the "Cult of Personality," writers could be more open in their censure of the system.[48] Harkening back to the nineteen-twenties and drawing especially on the work of Mayakovsky, Zoshchenko, Bulgakov, and Il'f and Petrov,[49] satire and parody flourished in the more liberal atmosphere that prevailed following Stalin's death (albeit with alternating repressive intervals), and writers frequently paid only lip service to the tenets of socialist realism.[50]

The final essays of the present collection, on Sergei Dovlatov, Andrei Sinyavsky (Abram Tertz) and Liudmila Petrushevskaya, deal with this era. Dovlatov flourished during the period of stagnation (*zastoi*) that characterized the later days of the Soviet regime under Brezhnev. And while his ironic satire is directed to some extent against an aging and bankrupt political system, Alexander Prokhorov and Helena Goscilo contend in their essay that Dovlatov's scope is larger. His is a comprehensive assault, perhaps similar to what we find in Anton Chekhov's works, on the oddities and shortcomings of the human condition. Dovlatov indulges in ironic asides and drops hints to the reader, stressing the basic absurdity of human behavior: the ridiculous situations that we create for ourselves and those visited upon us by a fate with a paradoxical sense of humor.

Dovlatov's use of irony was typical for parody in general and for the *zastoi* in particular, since irony can underscore the "critical distance of parody."[51] "A collapse of hopes and loss of faith brought the turn to irony in the literature of the 1970s," Anatoly Vishevsky stresses, noting that "sociopolitical processes create a dominant taste, a special approach to literary and cultural texts... In the time of disillusionment and

---

[48] Deming Brown, *Soviet Russian Literature Since Stalin* (Cambridge: Cambridge University Press, 1979), 4.

[49] Ryan-Hayes, *Contemporary Russian Satire*, 1–2.

[50] As the anonymous reader reminded me, by this point socialist realism was observed more in the breach than in actual practice.

[51] Ryan-Hayes, *Contemporary Russian Satire*, 7.

despair of the 1970s, people were especially attuned to irony...,"[52] with irony clearly central to Dovlatov's *Ours*. Like Chekhov's characters, Dovlatov's in *Ours* are typical of the larger society in which they (dys)function. Dovlatov's ironic smile is especially wry when considered in the context of a collapsing system, resembling Chekhov's own reaction during an earlier (and comparable) period of social and political disintegration.

With Sinyavsky/Tertz we have self-directed parody defined by narratorial shifts and focused on the aesthetic theme established earlier by Prutkov, Olesha, and Arkhangel'sky. Parody in Sinyavsky/Tertz is frequently internal and, Caryl Emerson reminds us, is a bifurcated entity critiquing itself and, in the process, questioning the established conceptions that a culture holds about itself and its most sacred values. The very divisions between subject and critic, orthodoxy and iconoclasm, propriety and naughtiness underscore a basic schism in human behavior in general and within Russian culture in particular. As Sinyavsky/Tertz gently instructs us, parody and satire basically exist to remind us that the reality we think we see and comprehend slides out of our grasp, larger than any single political system or literary method.

In his brilliant novel *Pushkinskii dom* (*Pushkin House*), Andrei Bitov looks back to Bely's remarkable achievement in *Petersburg*. Like Bely, Bitov stresses Pushkin's central and abiding role in Russian culture. Bely's references to earlier writers, most notably Pushkin, underscore the emptiness of his own revolutionary era. How much more barren by comparison is the world of Bitov's novel, with Pushkin reduced to a bust in a museum and his values subordinated to the very societal opportunism he detested. By demonstrating how far standards have fallen in the mediocre banality of contemporary Russian society, Bitov recalls Iurii Tynianov's argument that almost all Russian writers of the nineteenth century carried on a "silent struggle" with Pushkin.[53]

Liudmila Petrushevskaya's caustic excoriation of contemporary Soviet and post-Soviet society echoes themes touched on in Dostoevsky's works and brings us, in a sense, full circle, back to her

---

[52] Anatoly Vishevsky, *Soviet Literary Culture in the 1970s: The Politics of Irony*, (Gainesville, FL: University Press of Florida, 1993), 5–6.

[53] Tynianov, *Arkhaisty i novatory*, 412. My thanks to the anonymous reader for the suggestion to comment on *Pushkinskii dom*.

great nineteenth-century predecessor. Women populate the laboratory
where Petrushevskaya conducts her experiments. The weakness of their
position parodies Dostoevsky's protagonists and symbolizes a society in
disintegration. In her essay on Liudmila Petrushevskaya, Josephine
Woll proposes that Dostoevsky's internal "drawing room" scenes are
microcosms of tensions and dilemmas found in the larger society and
hint at the most important social and philosophical questions dominant
in his time. Petrushevskaya focuses on individuals—specifically women,
and their relationships with one another and the men and children in
their lives—as a way of addressing vital contemporary issues. The fault
lines running through the fragmented families in her works echo stresses
underlying the entire society, with its loss of a center, its harsh everyday
reality, its hopelessness and pessimism. The towering political apparatus
that progressively overwhelmed writers in the course of the Soviet period and loomed over Zamyatin's and Olesha's works has now disappeared. Balanced at the edge of the black hole that has replaced the
previous oppressive state, Petrushevskaya's post-Soviet citizens peer
into the void. The societal wreckage resulting from Soviet political oppression, ominously present in the form of a vacuum, is echoed by the
distant powerful wind scouring her work. Her biting parody, lacking the
playfulness that distinguishes Sinyavsky/Tertz, serves as a reminder of
the perilous state of Russian affairs at the end of the twentieth century
and the beginning of an uncertain future.

Amy Singleton Adams

𝒯𝓌𝓸

The Russian Homer: Goncharov's *Oblomov* and the Mock Epic

From his perpetually reclined position, the eponymous hero of Ivan Goncharov's novel *Oblomov* (1859) so perfectly epitomizes indolence and stasis that, even within the narrative itself, he invites comparisons with the paralyzed Russian folk hero Il'ia Muromets. Yet, by using Homer's *The Odyssey* as a parodic subtext in *Oblomov*, Goncharov transforms his apparent monument to immobility into an ironic reworking of the heroic homecoming mythos. As such, Oblomov's journey from his unkempt city apartment to the more comfortable and truer domesticity of his house in Vyborg becomes an Odyssean homecoming in miniature. Viewing Vyborg as a diminished version of Oblomov's childhood home (Oblomovka), readers of Goncharov's novel generally credit this symbolic return to the characteristic inertia of the hero, as Oblomovism (*oblomovshchina*) is widely defined. However, the narrative stance toward Oblomov exhibits an ambivalence that suggests that his homecoming is not simply the result of some kind of existential idleness. The tension between the epic invocation and novelistic form that characterizes the narrative point of view simultaneously celebrates and parodies Oblomov's upbringing within the traditional world of Russia's landed gentry. Oblomov endures a series of mock-epic trials wherein his ironic capabilities as well as his comic limitations come to light. Ultimately, the Homeric subtext measures the distance between the modern mind and the epic past while it expresses a poignant nostalgia for the meaning and values of the mythic mode, in which Oblomov lives and by which he returns home.

In his short autobiographical sketches, Goncharov describes Homer as an early influence.[1] The epic expansiveness and frequent allusions to Homeric motifs throughout Goncharov's work have earned the author

---

[1] I. A. Goncharov, *Sobranie sochinenii* (Moscow: Khudozhestvennaia literatura, 1953), 8: 222. All citations from Goncharov will be taken from this edition and will be referred to by volume and page number.

Janet Tucker, ed. *Against the Grain: Parody, Satire and Intertextuality in Russian Literature.* Bloomington, IN: Slavica, 2002, 19–36.

the sobriquet of the Russian Homer.[2] Certainly "Homer worship," as
Griffiths and Rabinowitz describe it, was a "sustained fashion" among
nineteenth-century writers and critics alike.[3] From the Little Russian
tales of Pogorelsky and Gogol and the early romanticism of Odoevsky
to the masterpieces of Tolstoy, Dostoevsky, and Chekhov, literary invo-
cations of epic motifs glorified Russia's perceived past and heralded a
heroic future. So pervasive was the Homeric in Russian prose that, by
the middle of the century, critic Vissarion Belinsky famously declared
that "[t]he epic of our time is the novel" (*Epopeia nashego vremeni est'
roman*).[4] Borrowing his parodic method from Gogol, Goncharov in-
flates the quotidian with Homeric motifs, emphasizing the comically
diminished proportions of Oblomov's life with the sheer magnitude of
the Odyssean *mythos*.[5] Goncharov describes the ridiculous in terms of
the sublime as he shows how the ordinary company gathered in the
drawing room in "Oblomov's Dream" ("Son Oblomova") "laughs long,
warmly, *ineffably*, like the Olympic gods."[6] Again, in a description of
the Vyborg kitchen that mimics epic catalog, the narrator insists that it
would take another Homer to list in detail the contents of the "shrine"
(*kovcheg*) to domestic life.[7]

However, Goncharov's particular use of the Homeric subtext in
Oblomov suggests that he was as ambivalent about his own place in
Russia's epic prose tradition as he is about his hero. The epic immortal-
izes the distant (and inaccessible) past while it establishes national
identity in the present. These dual functions combine in the ability of
the epic to bestow cultural significance on those who invoke its forms.

[2] See, for example, Dmitrii Merezhkovskii, "Gomer russkoi pomeshchich'ei
zhizni," in *Polnoe sobranie sochinenii* (St. Petersburg, 1912), 1: 237–46 and A.
G. Tseitlin, *I. A. Goncharov* (Moscow: Akademiia nauk, 1950), 9.

[3] Frederick T. Griffiths and Stanley J. Rabinowitz, *Novel Epics: Gogol,
Dostoevsky, and National Narrative* (Evanston, IL: Northwestern University
Press, 1990), 8.

[4] Vissarion Belinsky, *Sobranie sochinenii v 3-kh tomakh* (Moscow:
Khudozhestvennaia literatura, 1948), 2: 38.

[5] On the comic in Gogol's work, see Dmitry Chizhevsky, "Gogol: Artist and
Thinker," *Annals of the Ukrainian Academy of Arts and Sciences in the U.S.* 4
(1952): 269.

[6] Goncharov, *Oblomov*, in *Sobranie sochinenii*, 4: 135; Goncharov's emphasis.

[7] Goncharov, *Sobranie sochinenii*, 4: 483.

"Epic tradition enables a culture that perceives itself as somehow new, or that expresses itself in a yet unestablished literary language [...] to claim spiritual authority."[8] But Goncharov's self-mocking use of the Homeric questions its validity as the talisman of Russia's search for national identity. Also, *Oblomov* paints in epic hues the dying world of traditional Russia rather than the emerging shapes of its modern age. Doing so, the novel signals the end of both the epic age in Russia and the usefulness of the Homeric mode itself. However, even as a target of his parody, Goncharov's gesture toward *The Odyssey* breathes new life into the dead epic. This double-edged functioning of the mock epic is essential to the nostalgic relationship between the text and subtext in *Oblomov*.

Perils on the Open Sea

Like *The Odyssey*, *Oblomov* begins *in medias res* with a comic allusion to Odysseus' captivity on Calypso's island. In the twelve years since Oblomov has seen his native Oblomovka, his pursuit of "peace" has caused him to withdraw from friends, work, and society until he is quite stranded in his Gorokhovaia Street apartment. Here, lying in bed, Oblomov receives a string of visiting acquaintances who "swim" (*kupat'sia*) in the sea of bustling life that surrounds Oblomov's "island."[9] Impervious to his visitors' attempts to draw him into this *vita activa*, Oblomov remains prone. On the street below, St. Petersburg comes alive with the sounds of merchants hawking their wares, barking dogs, and, curiously, a sea monster (*zver' morskoi*) on display.[10] Although at times he loses himself in the "flood" (*priliv*) of life's worries,[11] or, with his thoughts racing like "waves on the ocean" (*kak volny v more*), imagines the "great deeds" (*podvigi*) he will perform,[12] Oblomov does not act on his ideas. He merely turns over in bed.

Although most of Goncharov's implied comparisons between Oblomov and Odysseus are comic, not every one is truly ironic. In the same way that the pleasures of Calypso's island cannot distract

---

[8] Griffiths and Rabinowitz, *Novel Epics*, 7.

[9] Goncharov, *Sobranie sochinenii*, 4: 44.

[10] Goncharov, *Sobranie sochinenii*, 4: 78.

[11] Goncharov, *Sobranie sochinenii*, 4: 18.

[12] Goncharov, *Sobranie sochinenii*, 4: 69.

Odysseus from thoughts of home, the comfortable inactivity of Oblomov's Petersburg existence does not represent his domestic ideal. In St. Petersburg, Oblomov is a stranger among strangers. He longs for his childhood home, which is presented in a series of dreams and daydreams throughout the novel. "What a life!" Oblomov says, realizing the vast difference between his present reality and his dream of "eternal summer, eternal happiness, and sweet, sweet idleness (*len'*)." "This city noise is disgraceful! When will the heavenly life I want begin? When will I return to my native fields and woods?"[13]

Something prevents Oblomov from living the life he longs for; it is, he thinks, as if a "heavy stone had been thrown on the narrow and pitiful path of his existence."[14] In *The Odyssey*, Odysseus is unaware that Poseidon has condemned him to a treacherous homeward journey. Oblomov's fate, too, rests with a "secret enemy" (*tainyi vrag*) who, having "laid a heavy hand on him at the start of his journey," prevents him from pursuing, "under full sail of mind and will," a "clear-cut human purpose." Here, the parallels between Oblomov and Odysseus emphasize their comic dissimilarity. The miniscule dimensions of life's events overwhelm Oblomov. He cannot navigate them but is "tossed to and fro by them, as if from wave to wave"[15] as Odysseus is left to flounder in the open sea. But Oblomov is not bravely clinging to the remains of his wrecked ship; he is in bed. And, when looking for the source of his woes, Oblomov does not appeal to the gods or to fate. He ducks under the covers.

From there he embarks on an Odyssean descent into the underworld in "Oblomov's Dream." This episode, written a decade earlier as the launching point for Goncharov's novel, most clearly demonstrates the ambivalence of the narrative voice toward the mythic world of the hero's childhood. The proportions of the dream's Arcadian Oblomovka are so small that the sky seems to hug the earth. The peasants who haul grain to the Volga regard their journey as an outing so dangerous that the narrator compares it to an expedition to the Pillars of Hercules. The comic mode of "Oblomov's Dream" is further intensified by the ironic disjunction between Odysseus' peril in the netherworld and Oblomov's

---

[13] Goncharov, *Sobranie sochinenii*, 4: 80.

[14] Goncharov, *Sobranie sochinenii*, 4: 100.

[15] Goncharov, *Sobranie sochinenii*, 4: 101.

oneiric visions of his overprotected upbringing. In the first of several dream vignettes describing Oblomovka, the young Oblomov ("Iliusha") wakes to see his mother. Here, the sleeping Oblomov sheds tears, as Odysseus does when he encounters his own mother in Hades. "Seeing his long-dead mother, Oblomov even in sleep trembles from joy and passionate love for her. Two warm tears slowly appeared out from under his sleeping eyelashes and remained motionless."[16] The comparison ends here, however, as Oblomov's mother frets over him as a small child, rather than an epic hero.

In one sense, though, the differences between Oblomov and Odysseus are bridged by the function the visit to the underworld plays in each hero's life. In both instances, the descent confirms the absolute identification of the hero with his destiny. In *The Odyssey*, the prince of Thebes emerges from the ranks of the dead and foresees the circumstances of Odysseus' death. In *Oblomov*, Oblomov's mother and his two elderly aunts together play the role of soothsayer. These three women, busily sewing in the dim candlelight of the sitting room, introduce the image of the ancient Fates into the "strange and uncanny world" of "Oblomov's Dream."[17] But while the revelation of Odysseus' future underscores the wholeness and finality that mark the epic hero, Oblomov's encounter with the images that shape both his past and future emphasizes the essential duality of his nature.[18]

In addition to creating comic rifts between the text and subtext, Goncharov's allusions to the Homeric underworld in "Oblomov's Dream" bring to light Oblomov's own mixed feelings about his "return" home. In the dream, Oblomovka becomes at once a childhood paradise Oblomov longs to access and an anxiety-provoking land of the dead. The Oblomovkan way of life represents a mythic kingdom, which finds further reflection in the fairytales of Oblomov's nanny. "With the simplicity and good-naturedness of Homer" the old woman tells "Iliusha" about an "unknown land" (*nevedomaia storona*) where rivers of milk

---

[16] Goncharov, *Sobranie sochinenii*, 4: 100.

[17] Milton Ehre, *Oblomov and His Creator: The Life and Art of Ivan Goncharov* (Princeton: Princeton University Press, 1973), 168.

[18] Mikhail Bakhtin, "Epic and Novel," in *The Dialogic Imagination*, ed. Michael Holquist, trans. Caryl Emerson and Michael Holquist (Austin: University of Texas Press, 1981), 3–40.

and honey flow and where "nobody does anything all year long." There, the nanny says, an enchantress chooses a quiet, unassuming boy like Iliusha ("in other words," the ironic narrative voice adds, "a lazy-bones"), feeds him, clothes him in "ready-made garments," and then marries him to a rare beauty, Militrisa Kirbit'evna.[19]

The parallel between life at Oblomovka and that described in the nanny's fairytale is not difficult to imagine. In the Oblomovs' remote "little corner" (*ugolok*), the endless repetition of daily gestures and the ritual observance of birth, marriages, deaths, and seasonal holidays renders time immutable.[20] To describe the Oblomovs' understanding and treatment of time, readers often refer to Mircea Eliade's studies of myth.[21] With the effect of delineating the world spatio-temporally into zones of the sacred and profane, the mythic in Eliade's understanding expresses a belief in cyclical time, wherein each generation can access the "Great Time" of its progenitors and, thus, regenerate and refresh the sense of the sacred. Although the epic, too, depicts what Bakhtin calls the world of "fathers, of beginnings, and peak times," it is essentially different from the mythic—a degeneration of the mythic, according to Eliade.[22] Rather than providing a means of "eternal return" to the absolute past, *in illo tempore*, or the sacred "center" of the mythic world, the epic exists on an inaccessible "time-and-value plane," distanced and completed, a "congealed and half-moribund genre."[23] And so, Oblomov can no sooner generate the epic mode in his life than the narrator of Goncharov's novel can approach Oblomov's heroism with-

---

[19] Goncharov, *Sobranie sochinenii*, 4: 120.

[20] On timelessness in *Oblomov*, see Ehre, *Oblomov*, 169–72; Ellen Jane Harrison, *Aspects, Aorists and the Classical Tripos* (Cambridge: Cambridge University Press, 1919); Kenneth Harper, "Text Progression and Narrative Style," *American Contributions to the Eighth International Congress of Slavists, Zagreb and Ljubljana, September 3–9, 1978*, ed. Victor Terras (Columbus. OH: Slavica Publishers, 1978), 2: 223–35; Christine Borowec, "Time After Time: The Temporal Ideology of *Oblomov*," *Slavic and East European Journal* 38, no. 4 (1994): 561–73.

[21] Among those who cite Eliade are: Alexander and Sverre Lyngstad, *Ivan Goncharov* (New York: Twayne Publishers, 1971), 83; Ehre, *Oblomov*, 173; and Borowec, *passim*.

[22] Bakhtin, *The Dialogic Imagination*, 14.

[23] Bakhtin, *The Dialogic Imagination*, 14.

out comic irony. What is sincere is Oblomov's mythic mindset, which helps him symbolically destroy the historical progression of modern time that, like Poseidon's curse, impedes his return home.

Because Oblomov is a product of both "Great Time" and present time, his dream reveals a similar duality in his attitude toward a home-coming of any sort. A return to a "Great Time" through ritual signifies rebirth, renewal, and regeneration.[24] The timelessness of Oblomovka, however, does not result from the perceived stasis of constant regenera-tion, as a spinning wheel appears to stand still, but from the stillness of death. In addition to invoking the imagery of Odysseus' visit to Hades, the narrative consciousness characterizes "the quiet and imperturbable peace" of Oblomovka as "a deathly silence,"[25] hinting that the meadows where young Iliusha plays are more like Elysian Fields. In one scene, Iliusha is free to wander only when the rest of the Oblomovkans succumb to the overwhelming force of sleep on a hot summer day. The world around the boy turns into a world of the dead. The deathly atmo-sphere suggested by the sleeping bodies lying about the house and grounds echoes the eerie stillness of the natural surroundings:

> It was sultry at midday; there was not a cloud in the sky. The sun stood motionless overhead and burned the grass. The air stopped flowing and hung without movement. Not a tree or the water rus-tled. Above the village and field lay an immutable silence—ev-erything was as if dead.[26]

At noon, the residents of Oblomovka surrender to the "all-consuming, insurmountable sleep, a true likeness to death." In this world "all is dead," disturbed in Gogolian fashion only by "various snores of all tones and harmonies."[27] Iliusha alone is immune to the soporific effects of the noon heat. He explores his environment "as if he were the only person in the entire world" and, indeed, he seems to be the only *living* person in this dream underworld.[28] Iliusha's unique perspective reveals

---

[24] Mircea Eliade, *Cosmos and History: The Myth of the Eternal Return*, trans. Willard R. Trask (New York: Harper, 1959), 79–84.

[25] Goncharov, *Sobranie sochinenii*, 4: 107.

[26] Goncharov, *Sobranie sochinenii*, 4: 115–16.

[27] Goncharov, *Sobranie sochinenii*, 4: 116.

[28] Goncharov, *Sobranie sochinenii*, 4: 117.

the fundamental split in Oblomov's feelings about his childhood home. Although Iliusha avoids complete integration into the sleeping realm of the dead, the adult (and sleeping) Oblomov finds himself "unwillingly" (*nevol'no*) drawn to that "land" (*storona*) that promises a carefree existence of restful amusement.

The Goddess Appears

As Oblomov wakes from his dream, his childhood friend Shtol'ts—a successful businessman and incessant traveler—arrives. Poggioli's assessment of Shtol'ts' role as a kind of crisis manager who appears on the scene, puts Oblomov's affairs in order, and leaves until he is needed again would support the characterization of Shtol'ts as a parodic Hermes, Odysseus' helpful messenger and the god of roads and commerce.[29] Inducing Oblomov to leave the Gorokhovaia Street apartment and reluctantly to rejoin St. Petersburg society, Shtol'ts is responsible for introducing his friend to Ol'ga Ilinskaia. Some regard Ol'ga as the failed eternal feminine who, despite her vigilance and intuitive wisdom, cannot overpower Oblomov's passivity.[30] Others see her as a passionate and sometimes dangerous creature whose consciousness develops so rapidly under the influence of love that she surpasses not only Oblomov but also her teacher, Shtol'ts.[31] The ambiguity of Ol'ga's relationship with Oblomov may account for the divergent interpretations of her characterization. Oblomov mistakenly identifies Ol'ga with his ideal of the past—a real life Militrisa Kirbit'evna—while Ol'ga falls in love with what she imagines a future Oblomov to be.

As in "Oblomov's Dream," the Homeric motifs that encode the Ol'ga-Oblomov love story elucidate his underlying ambivalence toward Ol'ga. Oblomov initially sees her as the incarnation of the passionless and generous women at the center of his vision of home. But Ol'ga's portrayal as Siren, Charybdis, and goddess suggests that she will become

---

[29] Renato Poggioli, *The Phoenix and the Spider* (Cambridge: Harvard University Press, 1957), 41.

[30] Poggioli, *Phoenix*, 40–42; Lyngstads, *Goncharov*, 93; Vsevolod Setchkarev, *Ivan Goncharov: His Life and Works* (Würzburg: Jal-Verlag, 1974), 43, 153; Nathalie Baratoff, *Oblomov: A Jungian Approach: A Literary Image of the Mother Complex* (Berne: Peter Lang, 1990), 75–93.

[31] Indeed, A. Tseitlin theorizes that Ol'ga would eventually leave Shtol'ts. *Goncharov*, 180–84.

an obstacle rather than a pathway to Oblomov's domestic idyll. The Odyssean subtext defines Oblomov's Lilliputian point of view (he sees the world from a child's height or from a reclined position) and emphasizes Ol'ga's power over him; she frequently places herself beyond or above him. The association of Ol'ga with the supernatural dangers of the ancient world also lends poignancy to Oblomov's sense of loss when he realizes that a life of passion, duty, and activism with Ol'ga would threaten rather than expedite his homecoming.

Oblomov's first meeting with Ol'ga comically suggests Odysseus' encounter with the Sirens, a confrontation the Ithacan king survives by plugging the ears of his crewmen with beeswax. In Oblomov's first conversation with Ol'ga, he insists that he is indifferent to music, saying that, at times, he even "stops his ears to Mozart." Ol'ga's singing, however, affects Oblomov like a Siren's song. "His heart was pounding, his nerves trembling, and his eyes shone and filled with tears from the words, the sound, from that pure, strong, maidenly voice." The intensity of his reaction instills in him both vitality and fatalism. "At one and the same moment he felt that he could die, never waking from the sounds, and now again his heart thirsted for life." Oblomov experiences a sense of expanded capability and feels "prepared for an heroic deed."[32] The ironic distance between the Homeric allusion and Oblomov is abruptly revealed when it becomes clear once again that Ol'ga is merely a young woman singing drawing room romances and that Oblomov's idea of an "heroic deed" is a trip abroad.

The Odyssean motif of the whirling, bottomless Charybdis surfaces in the Ol'ga-Oblomov love story to suggest, as does the image of the Siren, that Oblomov is drawn to Ol'ga while still vaguely aware of the danger she represents. In part 1 of the novel Oblomov concertedly avoids the "whirlwind of life,"[33] unable to find the center "around which it all revolves."[34] But he is mesmerized by the vortex of emotion that Ol'ga inspires. In her presence "[h]is thoughts flew in a whirlwind, and he looked at her as if into an endless distance, into a bottomless

---

[32] Goncharov, *Sobranie sochonenii*, 4: 202–03.

[33] Goncharov, *Sobranie sochinenii*, 4: 88.

[34] Goncharov, *Sobranie sochinenii*, 4: 179.

abyss."[35] When Ol'ga seems to return his love, Oblomov is fearful and
ecstatic, saying "Lord! What a maelstrom I've fallen into!"[36]

As Goncharov qualifies his idyllic portrayal of Oblomovka by invoking the Homeric underworld, so too does he express the equivocal nature of the Ol'ga-Oblomov relationship with ironic allusions to
Odysseus' captivity by Calypso and Circe. In part 2, Oblomov finds himself in the "magic circle of love"[37] in which their story unfolds. Like the
islands of Homer's goddesses, the country parks beyond Petersburg
where Ol'ga and Oblomov spend the summer become what Ehre calls
"a realm of experience beyond the usual arena of human complica-
tion."[38] With a network of ephemeral images—light, song, lilacs—
Goncharov creates the unearthly atmosphere that pervades the geography of the romance. As the goddess who presides over this "circle of
love," Ol'ga, too, takes on supernatural attributes. When angered, she is
transformed in Oblomov's eyes into an "offended goddess of pride and
rage [...] with lightning in her eyes."[39] She is also so closely associated
with the short-lived images of summer that she seems on the verge of
losing corporeality.[40]

Ehre attributes the airy and unreal qualities of Oblomov's summer
romance to Goncharov's stylistically poetic prose. In the case of Ol'ga's
characterization, some consider her otherworldliness a narrative flaw.[41]
Ol'ga appears suddenly in *Oblomov*; Goncharov does not describe her
past as he does with Oblomov and Shtol'ts. Pisarev argues that the weak
attempt to explain Ol'ga's origins reflects Goncharov's failure to clearly
define the roots of her character. In his criticism of Ol'ga's abrupt
introduction, Pisarev nevertheless detects her unearthly aura.
Comparing her spontaneous materialization to the birth of the fully-
formed Pallas Athena from out of Zeus's head, Pisarev says: "From her
first appearance on the scene, Ol'ga emerges from the author's head

---

[35] Goncharov, *Sobranie sochinenii*, 4: 206.
[36] Goncharov, *Sobranie sochinenii*, 4: 225.
[37] Goncharov, *Sobranie sochinenii*, 4: 248.
[38] Ehre, *Oblomov*, 183–84.
[39] Goncharov, *Sobranie sochinenii*, 4: 271.
[40] Ehre, *Oblomov*, 183.
[41] For example, Setchkarev, *Goncharov*, 142.

perfectly formed, in full armor."[42] While Pisarev's exaggerated simile is meant to detract from Goncharov's narrative style, it better reflects Oblomov's perception of Ol'ga as a superior being. In one instance, when Oblomov spies Ol'ga climbing a hill in the distance, he likens her to "an angel ascending into the heavens." Oblomov realizes the great distance between Ol'ga and himself. It seems to him that "she hardly touched the grass and in fact it was as if she would take flight."[43]

The images that surround Ol'ga—fire, music, flowers—symbolize her regenerative powers and, perhaps as a result of this inner life force, her unrealizable relationship with Oblomov who, on an equally symbolic level, has emerged from the Oblomovkan "underworld." The lilac, the "flower of life," represents Ol'ga and her love for Oblomov.[44] And, in the same way Calypso wants to grant Odysseus immortality, Ol'ga dreams of giving Oblomov eternal wakefulness. She imagines how she would "bring him back to life." "She would realize this miracle, [she would be] the architect of this transformation!"[45] Ol'ga's efforts are at first well directed; Oblomov is "resurrected" (*voskres*) from his indolence. "Life, life has opened up to me again," he says,[46] but the images of Oblomov's reawakening are fleeting and, with the fading of the lilac and summer sun, the romance ends. As winter sets in, Oblomov's view of Ol'ga as his passionless ideal fades, and, feeling increasingly trapped, he starts to withdraw from the circle of love.

The Homeward Journey

At the beginning of part 3, Oblomov finds himself in a situation reminiscent of his predicament in the opening of part 1. Once again obliged to tend to the neglected Oblomovka and to locate a new apartment in St. Petersburg, Oblomov complains about the frenzied pace of workaday city life and longs for the "poetry of life" (*poeziia zhizni*) that he imagines for himself. "What is this all about?" he asks himself, "Is this

---

[42] D. I. Pisarev, "Zhenskie tipy v romanakh i povestiakh Pisemskogo, Turgeneva, Goncharova," *Russkoe slovo* 12, no. 2 (1861): 16.

[43] Goncharov, *Sobranie sochinenii*, 4: 285.

[44] Goncharov, *Sobranie sochinenii*, 4: 242.

[45] Goncharov, *Sobranie sochinenii*, 4: 212.

[46] Goncharov, *Sobranie sochinenii*, 4: 242.

what I promised myself? Is this really life?"[47] In part 1, a doctor friend assures Oblomov that social activity and travel will alleviate the physical effects of a sedentary life.[48] In part 3, Ol'ga's task of awakening Oblomov is compared to that of a doctor trying to save a hopeless patient.[49] She also urges Oblomov to live a life of constant activity. Oblomov, who imagines marriage as an expression of "timid affection and quiet, sleepy joy," is disturbed by Ol'ga's perpetual motion. Gradually, he equates her not with his ideal of home and family life, but with its antithesis: Shtol'ts. "It is," Oblomov says, "as is she has no dreams, no need to sink (*utonut'*) into deep thought! Go register the marriage, go find an apartment—just like Andrei [Shtol'ts]!"[50]

When Oblomov finds himself trapped on a rowboat on the Neva after Ol'ga has lured him to an improperly clandestine meeting, he clearly demonstrates his new perspective of her. Richard Peace shows how the symbolism of this chilly autumn scene inverts the "poetry" of married life that Oblomov earlier described to Shtol'ts: a boat ride on a hot summer night on a peaceful river with his wife at the oars.[51] Representing Oblomov's retreat from Ol'ga in another way, the imagery of this rendez-vous becomes a parodic reenactment of Odysseus' escape from the islands of the female immortals. Ol'ga insisted on a boat ride and "ran, dragging him along" while he "held back and grumbled." Ol'ga wants to prevent any sudden retreat on Oblomov's part by trapping him on the boat. Only when the boat reaches the middle of the river will Ol'ga explain the deception of her unchaperoned appearance. She prefaces her answer to his questions with a "sly" (*lukavo draznila ona*) admission, to which Oblomov reacts fearfully (*so strakhom*): "How should I tell you? Now I can. You won't escape from here. But there," she says, referring to the shore," you would run away." When Oblomov hears how Ol'ga sent her footman home under false pretenses, he orders the boatman to return to the shore and, when Ol'ga contradicts him, becomes insistent. "'Hey, boatman,' he shouts, 'back to shore (*k beregu*)!'

---

[47] Goncharov, *Sobranie sochinenii*, 4: 302.

[48] Goncharov, *Sobranie sochinenii*, 4: 88.

[49] Goncharov, *Sobranie sochinenii*, 4: 212.

[50] Goncharov, *Sobranie sochinenii*, 4: 302, 304.

[51] Richard Peace, *Oblomov: A Critical Examination of Goncharov's Novel* (Birmingham: Birmingham Slavonic Manuscripts, 1991), 49.

'No need, no need!' [Ol'ga] orders the boatman. 'Back to shore,'" Oblomov demands.[52]

Oblomov's retreat from the rowboat/island marks the beginning of his return to the conditions of his childhood home, which he recreates at the Pshenitsyn house in Vyborg. Although the regressive movement of Oblomov's escape is not initiated by heroic action but by passive resistance, it is as powerful and languid as the slow forces of nature by which Oblomov's withdrawal from life is described.[53] Preferring the peace and idleness of Vyborg to the myriad tasks that his impending marriage to Ol'ga entails, Oblomov devises reasons not to go across the Neva River in St. Petersburg to visit her. The new geography of the love story does not unite the couple in an ethereal "circle of love" but, rather, separates them on either side of a river that Oblomov is unwilling to cross. The passivity that prevents Oblomov from fording the waters is as powerful as Odysseus' own determination to return home, although Oblomov's "heroics" are of a lower sort. As winter sets in, the bridges over the Neva are temporarily removed to allow for freezing. Given the opportunity to let the river "catch" him (*zakhvatit'*) in St. Petersburg for a few days, Oblomov opts instead to stay in Vyborg. And, after wooden foot bridges are installed and Ol'ga's servant arrives with a note, Oblomov hides from him, "afraid that he may be required to cross over to the other side."[54]

Ol'ga proves to be no match for Oblomov's inaction. Indeed, her attempts to maintain the level of activity to which she had motivated him during the summer months only serve to sharpen Oblomov's growing realization that Ol'ga is not the incarnation of his ideal but an obstacle to it. In response to Oblomov's continued absence, Ol'ga writes to him that she has spent a night in tears. The impassioned tone of Ol'ga's note, like Shtol'ts's constant movement, falls outside the parameters of life and love for Oblomov. In a familiar refrain, he says, "And what kind of life is this, all agitation (*volneniia*) and worry! When will I have peaceful happiness and tranquility?"[55]

---

[52] Goncharov, *Sobranie sochinenii*, 4: 340, 342.

[53] Goncharov, *Sobranie sochinenii*, 4: 385–98.

[54] Goncharov, *Sobranie sochinenii*, 4: 349–50.

[55] Goncharov, *Sobranie sochinenii*, 4: 348.

In a scene ironically reminiscent of Odysseus' escape from Calypso's island, Ol'ga finally concedes that her efforts to wake Oblomov to an active life are futile, paving his way to a life of "rest and peace" (*otdykh i pokoi*). With the "supernatural calm" of the Homeric goddess, Ol'ga tells Oblomov that although she "will not grow old, will never stop living," he is hopelessly mortal.[56] "I thought," she says, "that I would revive (*ozhivit'*) you, that you could live on for me. But you had already died long ago." As different as man and immortal, neither Oblomov nor Ol'ga can live in the world of the other. Ol'ga's need for constant growth and progress ("Vpered, vpered! Vyshe, vyshe!") would be stifled by Oblomov's imagined ideal. "[W]e would go to bed thanking God that the day had passed quickly, and in the morning we would wake with the wish that today would resemble the day before ... that is our future, is it not? Is that really life? I would wither away and die."[57] Like the fading lilac that heralds the end of the summer romance, the image of Ol'ga "withering away" signifies her final break with Oblomov.

Eternal Return

Soon after he arrives at the widow Pshenitsyn's house in Vyborg, Oblomov senses a familiar rhythm in the daily household routine. Surrounded by the sounds, sights, and smells of his childhood he says, "They remind me of the country, of Oblomovka."[58] Conforming to Bachelard's concept of the "oneiric house," Oblomov reinhabits Oblomovka through dream and memory.[59] In Vyborg, Oblomov eats heartily "as at Oblomovka" and works lazily "as at Oblomovka"; he again falls asleep to the sound of sewing and snapping thread, once more the passive center of tireless attention.[60] Regarding his present life as an extension of the Oblomovkan existence, Oblomov "inwardly rejoices" that he has realized his goal of that "immense, ocean-like, and imperturbable peace of life, the picture of which was imprinted indelibly

---

[56] Goncharov, *Sobranie sochinenii*, 4: 380.

[57] Goncharov, *Sobranie sochinenii*, 4: 379, 380.

[58] Goncharov, *Sobranie sochinenii*, 4: 323.

[59] Gaston Bachelard, *The Poetics of Space* (New York: The Orion Press, 1964), 14.

[60] Goncharov, *Sobranie sochinenii*, 4: 484–94.

on his soul in childhood, under his father's roof."[61] Oblomov ultimately manages to return to the "Great Time" of his childhood through ritual imitation, although the Vyborg house represents only a debased version of the Oblomovkan ideal.[62] Because the significant cultural gestures established at Oblomovka are recreated to such an extent in Vyborg, Oblomov ultimately perceives the two households as one. "He regarded his present way of life as a continuation of that Oblomovkan existence, only with a different local color."[63]

The sacred archetypes of a mythic "Great Time" are defined for Oblomov by his nanny's fairy tale about Militrisa Kirbit'evna. To the modern mind—that of Shtol'ts and the narrator, for example— Oblomov's equation of Vyborg, an "undistinguished" (*nevedomaia*) side of St. Petersburg, with the mythic land of milk and honey deepens the irony of his homecoming. To Oblomov, however, the merging of his present and past through the imitation of rituals and domestic patterns is a reality that informs his ideal of home and self. In a state that Goncharov describes as something akin to a "hallucination" or "*déjà vu*," Oblomov "returns" to his parents' drawing room:

> He saw the large, dark living room of his parents' home, lit by a tallow candle. His mother and her guests are seated at the round table. They are sewing silently. His father paces silently. The present and the past flowed together and were indistinguishable.[64]

The scene repeats Oblomov's dream vision of his childhood home, only now Oblomov's waking mind merges Vyborg and Oblomovka with the world of his nanny's fairy tale. "He was dreaming that he had arrived in that promised land, where rivers of milk and honey flow and where everyone ate unearned bread and dressed in silver and gold."[65] In Vyborg, Oblomov's main garment—the threadbare *khalat* that his landlady, Agaf'ia Matveevna, mends and washes for him—becomes a parodic emblem of his homecoming. The tireless hands that "clothe and shoe

---

[61] Goncharov, *Sobranie sochinenii*, 4: 394.

[62] Peace, *Oblomov*, 60–64.

[63] Goncharov, *Sobranie sochinenii*, 4: 487.

[64] Goncharov, *Sobranie sochinenii*, 4: 493.

[65] Goncharov, *Sobranie sochinenii*, 4: 493.

him [and] put him to bed"[66] belong not to a princess, but to the simple and unrefined Agaf'ia Matveevna. Despite such obvious discrepancies, the traditional ontology of repetition allows Oblomov to transcend the ironic disjuncture between myth and reality. In his daydreams, Agaf'ia Matveevna and Militrisa Kirbit'evna become one: "He could hear the telling of dreams and omens and the ringing of dishes and clatter of knives. He pressed against his nanny, listening to her ancient, trembling voice. 'Militrisa Kirbit'evna!' she said, showing him the image of [Agaf'ia Matveevna]."[67]

Oblomov's confusion of Vyborg with Oblomovka serves his ultimate purpose: to withdraw from life while ensuring himself "imperturbable peace" (*nevozmutimyi pokoi*).[68] To Shtol'ts, Oblomov's goal of "peace" is a death wish. An "abyss" (*bezdna*) opens and a "stone wall" is thrown up between the two friends when Shtol'ts realizes that Oblomov's marriage to his landlady Agaf'ia Matveevna marks his demise. Stunned by the news that Oblomov and Agaf'ia Matveevna have a son, Shtol'ts feels "like someone who, hurrying with excitement to see a friend after a long separation, finds out that [the friend] has already been gone for a long time, that he has died."[69] The narrator, who describes Oblomov as a hermit who, living in isolation in the wilderness, digs his own grave, echoes Shtol'ts's sentiment. "Little by little he quietly laid himself out in a simple and wide coffin of his own making."[70]

"My life," Oblomov tells Shtol'ts, "began at sunset,"[71] a fatalism reflected in the funereal atmosphere of his childhood home of "Oblomov's Dream." Despite the efforts of Shtol'ts and Ol'ga to draw Oblomov into an active life, he eschews the modern world, preferring to return symbolically to the deathly stillness and peace of the Oblomovkan way of life. In keeping with the parodic scheme of *The Odyssey*, Oblomov's symbolic return to a home that, while representing

---

[66] Goncharov, *Sobranie sochinenii*, 4: 395.

[67] Goncharov, *Sobranie sochinenii*, 4: 493.

[68] Goncharov, *Sobranie sochinenii*, 4: 487.

[69] Goncharov, *Sobranie sochinenii*, 4: 497.

[70] Goncharov, *Sobranie sochinenii*, 4: 488.

[71] Goncharov, *Sobranie sochinenii*, 4: 190.

a "promised land" for him, is characterized as a living death, inverts the traditional epic sequence of birth-death-rebirth.[72]

A reading of *Oblomov* through the parodic subtext of *The Odyssey* measures the degree of narrative irony and ambivalence toward Oblomov and his ideal of home. Yet, although the gap between the glory of the mythic past and the actuality of the debased present is clearly delineated, faint echoes of the heroic ideal resound in the depiction of Oblomov as the triumphant Odysseus as he arrives home in Ithaca. When Oblomov banishes the conniving Tarant'ev, the scene recalls Odyseus's banishing of the suitors. The figure of the hobbled Oblomov in his tattered *khalat* calls up the image of Odysseus disguised as a lame, rag-clad old man. While the comic invocation of Homeric motifs may highlight Oblomov's shortcomings, the judgment of the narrative voice is tempered by the possibility that, even in Oblomov's narrow existence, certain values have been preserved. The mock-epic may express an illicit nostalgia for the lost world of its own targeted text.[73]

Oblomovism Revisited

Oblomov ultimately represents an ironic heroism that, while admitting the wide discrepancy between the mythic past and the present, still recognizes efforts of even the smallest dimensions. While Oblomov celebrates his ability to avoid life's "battlefield" as a solemn victory, even Shtol'ts cannot but perceive nobility, value, and strength in his friend's passive resistance: "I have never came across a heart more pure, clear, and simple. Let an entire ocean of rot and evil surge (*volnovat'sia*) around him, let the whole world be poisoned and turned inside out. Oblomov will never bow down to the idol of falsehood. His soul will always be pure, clear, and honest."[74]

Oblomov's symbolic homecoming is achieved only when he overcomes a succession of mock epic trials that illustrate his inability to adapt to the demands of modern life. Within the framework of

---

[72] Helen Chavis Othow, "*Roots* and the Heroic Search for Identity," *College Language Association Journal* 26, no. 3 (1983): 314.

[73] See Roger B. Salomon, *Desperate Storytelling: Post-Romantic Elaborations of the Mock-Heroic Mode* (Athens, GA: University of Georgia Press, 1987); Ulrich Broich, *The Eighteenth-Century Mock-Heroic Poem* (Cambridge: Cambridge University Press, 1990).

[74] Goncharov, *Sobranie sochinenii*, 4: 480.

Goncharov's parodic invocation of Homer's *The Odyssey*, the tension between Oblomov's low-level adventures and his obvious limitations represents the forces of epic expansion and containment, the combination of superhuman deeds and human mortality that imbue the hero's name and exploits with meaning.[75] Oblomovism, then, may be understood as a mode of ironic self-discovery that describes the dynamic play between Oblomov's comic capacities, represented by the Odyssean subtext, and his failure to cope with the most innocuous aspects of daily life. Subtly reworking the mythos of homecoming by which Oblomov returns home, Goncharov shows a critical empathy for Oblomov's nostalgia for the traditional modes of domesticity and self-knowledge irretrievably lost in the "transition from one epoch of Russian history to another."[76] And, while Goncharov's parodic treatment of Oblomov's life as odyssey does not constitute an apology for the lived passivity of Russian patriarchal life, it does ultimately mitigate the popular condemnation of his hero's idleness.

---

[75] See Thomas Greene, "The Norms of Epic," *Comparative Literature* 13 (1961): 196–99.

[76] Goncharov, *Sobranie sochinenii*, 8: 72.

Three

Deborah A. Martinsen

Identity via Parody: Captain Lebyadkin, Poet-Cockroach

Parody presupposes an original which it imitates and reduces, thereby provoking a comparison. Parody also invites hyperbole and is frequently comic. An author can parody a literary work or a character or both. In *Demons* (*The Possessed*), one of Dostoevsky's most parodic and satiric novels, Dostoevsky creates a character, Lebyadkin, who not only serves as a parody of other characters but also quotes literary works in a parodic manner. In portraying him as a parodic imitator of both life and literature, Dostoevsky amplifies the tragic dimensions of comic narcissism.

   Before investigating Lebyadkin as parodic imitator of Nikolai Stavrogin and parodic echo of Stepan Verkhovensky, I shall examine one sentence that demonstrates how Dostoevsky uses Lebyadkin as a figure of parody. Throughout, Lebyadkin's enforced anonymity (as Stavrogin's brother-in-law) gives rise to a sense of urgency impelling him to reveal himself—both in speech and on paper. Not by chance does he use every possible means to express himself verbally: he authors five poems, spates of letters (mostly anonymous), and claims to have written a last will and testament; he also recites his poetry and delivers speeches whenever possible. In one of these speeches, Lebyadkin consciously quotes a famous ode by Derzhavin, modifying it to fit the occasion: "I am a slave, I am a worm, but not a god, that's the only way I differ from Derzhavin."[1] Unbeknownst to Lebyadkin, his declaration parodically encapsulates the novel's essence and makes him an imitator of Dostoevsky, who situates the novel's serious metaphysical thematics in a tragicomic and satiric political context.

   In the parodied ode, Derzhavin invokes his own "wondrous" powers as a human being to identify himself as God's creation:

---

[1] Fedor Dostoevskii, *Polnoe sobranie sochinenii* (Leningrad: Nauka, 1972–90), 10: 213. When two page numbers are given [vol: page; page], the second refers to F. M. Dostoevsky, *Demons*, trans. R. Pevear and L. Volokhonsky (New York: Vintage Classics, 1994).

Janet Tucker, ed. *Against the Grain: Parody, Satire and Intertextuality in Russian Literature*. Bloomington, IN: Slavica, 2002, 37–54.

But, wondrous as I am
Whence come I?—It's unknown.
Yet I cannot exist by myself.
Your creation am I, Creator...

No, buduchi ia stol' chudesen,
Otkole proisshel?—Besvesten.
A sam soboi ia byt' ne mog.
Tvoe sozdan'e ia Sozdatel'...[2]

Lebyadkin's source thus touches on the metaphysical thematics of
Dostoevsky's novel—the question of God's existence and man's relationship to God as a source of morality. The context in which Lebyadkin
invokes his poetic forebear, however, is a political one. Attempting to
retain Stavrogin's patronage and, more importantly, to obtain his protection from Peter Verkhovensky, Lebyadkin informs Stavrogin of all
the resources for political blackmail that Peter has at his disposal. He
confesses to having distributed subversive literature and counterfeit
money. Given Peter's knowledge of his activities, Lebyadkin justifiably
fears for his life and requests Stavrogin's help. In quoting his source,
Lebyadkin thus emphasizes his lowly status ("I am a slave, I am a
worm") and modifies Derzhavin's line both consciously ("but not a
god"), and unconsciously—omitting the first element of Derzhavin's
famous line: "I am a tsar."

Both what Lebyadkin emphasizes and what he modifies reverberate
with the novel's thematics, demonstrating Dostoevsky's tight structural
control of his material. Lebyadkin's self-identification as a "slave" links
him with the nine-tenths of the population that Shigalev's theory identified as "slaves," and his self-identification as a worm (*cherv'*) anticipates
Peter Verkhovensky's declaration to Stavrogin—"I am your worm"
(*cherviak*).[3] Furthermore, Lebyadkin's omission ("I am a tsar") is a proleptic avoidance of competition with Stavrogin, whom Peter Verkhovensky later declares to be the political pretender "Ivan-Tsarevich."[4]
Finally, Lebyadkin's disavowal ("but not a god") calls to mind Kirillov,
a man likewise obsessed with his identity, who finally declares himself to

[2] Gavriil Derzhavin, *Sochineniia* (Moscow: Pravda, 1985), 54.
[3] Dostoevskii, *PSS*, 10: 324.
[4] Dostoevskii, *PSS*, 10: 325.

be the "God-man" and who offers to donate his metaphysically-motivated suicide as a cover for subversive political activity.

Lebyadkin's declaration also echoes the novel's literary thematics. Significantly, Lebyadkin does not renounce his status as a poet ("that's the only way I differ from Derzhavin"), placing him among the large number of characters with creative ambitions in *Demons*. His identification with Derzhavin is also important for an understanding of Lebyadkin in two ways. First, Derzhavin's ornamental style and his willingness to mix high and low language and imagery make him a worthy literary model for Lebyadkin. Second, Derzhavin's low social origins, his elevation through military service, and his poems in praise of Catherine the Great draw attention to the uneasy relationship between poet and political patronage, one of Lebyadkin's sore spots. Lebyadkin's next line—"But my means, what are my means!"[5]—emphasizes the financial dilemma faced by poets.

This example demonstrates how Dostoevsky uses a minor character to draw comic attention to his novel's major thematics. Even in an apparently digressive speech, Dostoevsky's character never strays from his creator's preoccupations. Lebyadkin links the question of personal identity to questions of social, national, and metaphysical identity. His quotation of Derzhavin reduces the original, making it a comic declaration of personal identity, but then, in this new context, it "activates the potentialities of meaning in the original,"[6] heightening and expanding the social and metaphysical dimensions of Derzhavin's poem. Every word in Lebyadkin's parodic quotation of Derzhavin's ode both finds an echo in Dostoevsky's own text and draws attention to issues in the Russian literary tradition. Furthermore, this example not only focuses on Captain Lebyadkin's own personal hobbyhorse—his obsession with his identity—but comically articulates one of the novel's major thematics: the question of its characters' personal, social, and political identities. I will continue to examine the dynamics of parody in Dostoevsky's novel by focusing on Lebyadkin's identity crisis as articulated by Lebyadkin himself in one speech about his last will and testament to Stavrogin and

---

[5] Dostoevskii, *PSS*, 10: 213.

[6] Joan Hartwig, *Shakespeare's Analogical Scene: Parody as Structural Syntax* (Lincoln: University of Nebraska Press, 1983), 6.

in one speech and one poem to those in Varvara Stavrogina's drawing room.

When Lebyadkin is granted permission to enter her drawing room, readers have heard of him once and encountered him twice. We know that Lebyadkin and his sister are living in the house of Filippov on Epiphany Street, a location associating them with the novel's thematics of impostorship and revelation.[7] Though the narrator refers to him as "Captain" throughout the novel, his first two mentions of Lebyadkin make it clear that the title is one Lebyadkin has assumed, not earned. First, in describing Lebyadkin's initial visit to town, the narrator claims that Lebyadkin "wasn't even a retired junior captain as he entitled himself. He only knew how to twirl his mustache, drink, and blather the most uncouth nonsense imaginable."[8] Fifty pages later, as Lebyadkin returns to town, we learn from Liputin that Lebyadkin is now calling himself "a retired captain; earlier he only called himself a junior captain...."[9] "Captain" Lebyadkin is thus one of the novel's assorted impostors, a comic heir to Gogol's Khlestakov and Major Kovalev.

Lebyadkin's readiness to adopt titles and roles demonstrates his belief that his real identity is somehow inadequate. In Varvara Stavrogina's drawing room, and thus out of his normal milieu, he reveals his consciousness of the gap between his apparent and ideal identities. Frustrated by his enforced anonymity, constrained by his new clothing, and anxious to prove himself to two women he has little chance of meeting otherwise, Lebyadkin quickly forgets his place (both his literal place—a chair by the door—and his figurative place as social inferior) and launches into a speech that shifts the blame for the gap between his actual and ideal identities from himself onto his country of birth:

> Madam, ... I, perhaps, might wish to be called Ernest, but instead am forced to bear the coarse name of Ignat,—why's that, what do you think? I might wish to be called Prince de Monbars, yet I'm only Lebyadkin, from lebed', the swan—why's that? I am a poet, Madam, a poet in my soul, and I could be getting a thousand

---

[7] Richard Peace, *Dostoevsky: An Examination of the Major Novels* (Cambridge: Cambridge University Press, 1971), 171–72.

[8] Dostoevskii, *PSS*, 9: 29.

[9] Dostoevskii, *PSS*, 9: 78.

rubles from a publisher, yet I'm forced to live in a washtub, why, why? Madam! In my opinion, Russia is a freak of nature, nothing more![10]

Lebyadkin's speech, which aims to prove to Varvara Petrovna that he is a worthy (though anonymous) relative and to Liza Tushina that he is a worthy suitor, reveals a lot about him. His peroration of comparisons makes it clear that even his name, this most basic fact of his actual identity, distresses him, reminding him of his lower-class origins and the arbitrariness of life. He expresses his desire for a different name and a different financial position, as well as for recognition of his verbal talent. Though the first two oppositions on his list are equivalents (Ernest/Ignat, Prince de Monbars/Lebedev), his next ones are comically dissonant (his writing ambitions/his living quarters). Though seemingly alogical, this dissonance demonstrates the peculiarly literary cast of Lebyadkin's mind, as cramped living space and creative genius are often conjoined in the Romantic imagination. Lebyadkin's dissonant comparison and his concluding slander of Russia reveal his belief that his troubles (with his identity, vocation, social status) are rooted in the fundamental Russianness of his birth.

Lebyadkin's speech also highlights some of the novel's literary thematics. By expressing the desire to bear the name of a Frenchman who was an actual historical figure as well as the hero of several literary works, Lebyadkin reveals his desire to be a recognized and admired other—to be a member of the upper class, a European, a hero. He also demonstrates his blurring of the boundaries between life and literature, proving himself a consumer of Romantic fictions. Interestingly, the semi-fictional Monbars more resembled Stavrogin (and Shakespeare's Prince Hal) than Lebyadkin. Noble by birth, Monbars is equally at home in drawing room and tavern; he is handsome and well-dressed; he makes the ladies swoon and his enemies quake. Monbars' move to the Antilles (where he took the name "Exterminator" to demonstrate his resolve to wipe out the Spaniards oppressing the natives) and Stavrogin's early travels can be seen as flights from their historical situations, attempts to do something with their talents. While still young, they both attain notoriety: Monbars—military notoriety for such exploits as the sacking of Maracaibo and the capture of Vera Cruz,

---

[10] Dostoevskii, *PSS*, 10: 141; 175.

Stavrogin—social notoriety for his scandalous behavior in Russia. Monbars acts as a Romantic hero, however, while Stavrogin acts sometimes as a perverse, sometimes as an impotent Romantic hero. Lebyadkin, who aspires to be like Monbars and emulates Stavrogin, comically imitates, thus parodying, both literature and life.

The components of Lebyadkin's stated self-image in this speech, that he is 1) a poet, 2) who desires monetary recompense for his talent, and 3) who has the misfortune of being born in Russia—evoke the image of Pushkin, Dostoevsky's favorite poet. The image of Lebyadkin as poet is parodic, as he is a poetaster who produces pekoral (unintentionally comic or stylistically incompetent pieces of writing by "would-be" but untalented poets).[11] Nonetheless, Lebyadkin's comic woes have serious counterparts in Pushkin's life and writing. Pushkin struggled with the advantages and limitations of political patronage, the exigencies of the literary market place, and the difficulties facing a man of talent in Russia (see his May 1836 letter to his wife: "[T]he devil got it into his head to have me be born in Russia with a soul and with talent! It's amusing, there's nothing to be said!")[12] Lebyadkin's laments about talented men's lack of outlets and recognition in Russia echo actual concerns in Russian life (as in the case of Pushkin) which are mimetically, though parodically, reproduced in Dostoevsky's novel (in the figure of Stepan Verkhovensky).

Lebyadkin's Prince de Monbars speech thus raises questions explored throughout Dostoevsky's novel: questions of personal and national identity, the role of men of talent in Russia, and the relationship of literature to life. Lebyadkin's "Zaveshchanie," his last will and testament, elaborates on these questions in an even more comic manner. In a late-night conversation with Stavrogin, when Lebyadkin is trying to reestablish himself in his patron's good graces, Lebyadkin announces that he is writing a will. Stavrogin, incredulous, asks him: "Whatever are you leaving and to whom?" Lebyadkin responds:

> To the fatherland, to mankind, and to students. Nikolai Vsevolodovich, in the newspapers I read a biography about an American.

---

[11] Margaret A. Rose, *Parody: Ancient, Modern, and Post-Modern* (Cambridge: Cambridge University Press, 1993), 68.

[12] A. S. Pushkin, *Polnoe sobranie sochinenii v desiati tomakh* (Leningrad: Nauka, 1979), 10: 454.

He left his whole huge fortune to factories and for the positive
sciences, his skeleton to the students at the academy there, and
his skin to make a drum so as to have the American national anthem drummed on it day and night. Alas, we're pygmies compared to the soaring ideas of the North American States; Russia
is a freak of nature, but not of mind. If I were to try and bequeath
my skin for a drum, to the Akmolinsk regiment, for example,
where I had the honor of beginning my service, so as to have the
Russian national anthem drummed on it every day in front of the
regiment, it would be regarded as liberalism, my skin would be
forbidden ... and so I limited myself only to the students. I want
to bequeath my skeleton to the academy, on condition, however,
that a label be pasted to its forehead for ever and ever, reading:
"Repentant freethinker." There, sir![13]

Lebyadkin's last will and testament clearly parodies a last will and testament that Dostoevsky has parodied before in his "Village of
Stepanchikovo"—Gogol's.[14] In *Demons*, Dostoevsky returns to the
language and images of Gogol's "Zaveshchanie" ("Testament") in order
to continue his dual parody of literature and life. As a false captain,
Lebyadkin reminds readers of Gogol's literary characters, the impostors
Khlestakov and Major Kovalev. His title and the suffix of his surname
also invoke the memory of Gogol's lower class military hero Captain
Kopeikin. As a generator of hyperbolic prose, however, Lebyadkin
echoes Gogol himself. Even his name, like Gogol's, derives from a
bird's name.

Both Lebyadkin's and Gogol's bequests reveal their authors' obsession with identity, fear of being misunderstood, and yearning for public
recognition. Stavrogin picks up on Lebyadkin's desire for acceptance
and suggests that he wants credit for mere designs during his lifetime:
"So you intend to make your will public in your lifetime, and get re-
warded for it?"[15] This observation can be understood as a dig at Gogol,
but it also anticipates Tikhon's remark that Stavrogin wants recognition

---

[13] Dostoevskii, *PSS*, 10: 209; 264.

[14] See Iu. Tynianov, "Dostoevskii i Gogol': k teorii parodii," in *O Dostoevskom: Stat'i*, ed. Donald Fanger (Providence: Brown University Press, 1966), 153–96.

[15] Dostoevskii, *PSS*, 10: 209; 264.

for publishing his confession during his lifetime, thus underscoring Lebyadkin's status as a parody of Stavrogin.

Lebyadkin's self-identification as a "Repentant Freethinker" likewise both refers to his Gogolian source and finds parodic resonances within Dostoevsky's novel. The epithet "Repentant Freethinker" parodies the reactionary views articulated in Gogol's late work. It is also self-plagiarism from Lebyadkin's anonymous letter to Governor von Lembke, which draws further attention to Lebyadkin's political crimes. In Dostoevsky's *oeuvre*, the epithet "freethinker" (*vol'nodumets*) has associations with Enlightenment beliefs, particularly atheism.[16] As Lebyadkin confesses to Stavrogin, he has distributed subversive political pamphlets calling for the closing of churches, the annihilation of God and inheritance laws, the disruption of marriage, and the taking up of knives. In both his confession to Stavrogin and his letter to von Lembke, Lebyadkin repents his association with atheism and revolution and affirms his fealty to Russia. Given this context, Lebyadkin's self-identification as "repentant freethinker" also prefigures Stepan Verkhovensky's deathbed change of heart towards God and Russia. (Given Belinsky's view of Dostoevsky's post-exilic political conversion, Dostoevsky is probably indulging in a little self-parody as well. As he well knew, radical critics viewed Dostoevsky himself as a repentant freethinker.)

The reductive element of parody makes itself particularly felt when comparing Lebyadkin's and Gogol's last wills and testaments. While Gogol bequeaths his literary works, particularly his *Selected Passages*, to his fellow countrymen, Lebyadkin leaves his skeleton—a parodic reduction of the sublime (words) to the ridiculous (bones). Nonetheless, Lebyadkin's emphasis on his body (skin, skeleton) parodically echoes Gogol's obsession with his own body and his fear of being buried alive. (Lebyadkin circumvents this option by keeping his remains above ground.) Furthermore, Lebyadkin's list of legatees—the fatherland, humanity and students—include Gogol's—his fellow countrymen. Finally, both leave their bequests for the "use" of their countrymen, though Dostoevsky degrades Gogol's focus on spiritual utility to Lebyadkin's focus on physical utility.

---

[16] See Dostoevskii, *PSS*, 14: 261.

Lebyadkin's putative will is not merely a parody, however. It contributes to the novel's satiric side as well. Despite their humorous presentation, Lebyadkin's continual laments that his country of birth has greatly hindered his options serve as serious social criticism. Lebyadkin twice claims that "Russia is a freak of nature," thus an arbitrary force. By adding "but not of mind" in his testament, Lebyadkin provides a mordant criticism of Russia's system of censorship. While in Varvara Stavrogina's drawing room, Lebyadkin claims to be a poet in his soul, but unrecognized—presumably because he lives in Russia, which robs its citizens of any outlets for their talents. While this is clearly untrue of Lebyadkin, whose raggedly metered verses that prize sound over sense receive exactly the fame they deserve, this note of social criticism nonetheless echoes throughout the novel in the portrayal of superfluous men, young and old alike. Stepan Verkhovensky never truly applies his talents—either to teaching, research, or writing—but constantly retreats from the socio-political sphere, all the while blaming the political situation in Russia for his lack of fame. Stavrogin complains more indirectly that he has tried to exercise his talents, but in vain (see his farewell letter to Dasha). However disparate these three figures—Lebyadkin, Stepan Verkhovensky and Stavrogin—they are all "uprooted" (*otorvannye*), i.e. they have lost a sense of vital connection to Russia, their country of birth, and to the Russian people. Lebyadkin's criticism of Russia parodically echoes Stepan Verkhovensky's overt and Stavrogin's indirect censure, thus linking the three and diminishing the parodied characters. Furthermore, since Lebyadkin constantly demands recognition as a poet, which reminds the reader of his difference from real poets such as Pushkin and Derzhavin, Stepan Verkhovensky and Stavrogin by analogy are also compared negatively to these servitors of the Russian state and the Russian people.

Lebyadkin's most comic criticism of the social, political, and metaphysical order occurs in his unintentionally satiric doggerel masterpiece, "The Cockroach." One can best appreciate this poem by placing it in the context of the Captain's explicit self-images. Throughout *Demons*, Lebyadkin supplies the reader with lists of his self-images, both negative and positive. In his letter to Liza, he calls himself "an unlearned at a debate," "nothing," and "an infusorium" (the last two also cribbed from Derzhavin's ode "God"). At Varvara Petrovna's, he proclaims himself "nothing" and "an insignificant link." To Stavrogin, he refers to himself indirectly as a louse, and, in the example discussed earlier, declares: "I am a slave, I am a worm."[17] On the positive side, he reminds Stavrogin that he has been his "Falstaff." He also asserts that he is now living "like Zosima. Sobriety, solitude, and poverty—the vow of the knights of old,"[18] and claims "I am renewing myself like a snake."[19]

But Lebyadkin's most consistent positive self-image is that of poet. The first time the narrator meets him, Lebyadkin bursts into verse ("To a Star-Amazon"). He declares his love for Liza in verse ("To the Perfection of the Maiden Tushin") and calls his marriage proposal to her a poem ("The letter from the infusorium is to be understood in verse"). To Stavrogin Lebyadkin justifies his marriage proposal to Liza with his swan song ("In Case If She Broke Her Leg"), which he compares to Gogol's "Farewell Story." He equates himself with Derzhavin. He composes a poem for the fête ("To the Governess"). And he answers Varvara Petrovna's query about Mar'ia's relationship to her in verse fable ("The Cockroach"). This last creation, a parody of Miatlev's "Fantastic Tale" composed by Dostoevsky in his notebooks for his non-realized story of Captain Kartuzov, perhaps best sums up Lebyadkin's dilemma: Lebyadkin claims that the cockroach "does not grumble," but his poem about the cockroach (his self-image) is itself a grumble. Lebyadkin's recitation of "The Cockroach" follows almost immediately upon his Prince de Monbars speech. He claims that it will answer Varvara Petrovna's question about why he cannot reveal Mar'ia's identity.

> "On this earth a cockroach dwelt,
> A roach from infancy,
> And then into a glass he fell
> Full of fly-phagy ..."

> "Lord, what is this?" Varvara Petrovna exclaimed. "It's in the summertime," the captain hurried, waving his arms terribly, with the irritated impatience of an author whose recitation is being hindered, "in the summertime, when lots of flies get into a glass, then fly-phagy takes place, any fool can understand that, don't

[17] Dostoevskii, *PSS*, 10: 213; 269.

[18] Dostoevskii, *PSS*, 10: 207; 261.

[19] Dostoevskii, *PSS*, 10: 209; 264.

interrupt, don't interrupt, you'll see, you'll see…" (he kept waving his arms).

"The cockroach took up so much room
The flies began to grumble.
'A crowded glass, is this our doom?'
To Jupiter they rumbled.
But as the flies did make their moan
Along came Nikifor,
The no-o-blest old man…"

"I haven't quite finished here, but anyway, in plain words!" the captain rattled on. "Nikifor takes the glass and, in spite of their crying, dumps the whole comedy into the tub, both flies and cockroach, which should have been done long ago. But notice, madam, notice, the cockroach does not grumble! This is the answer to your question, 'Why?'" He cried out triumphantly. "The cock-roach does not grum-ble! As for Nikifor, he represents nature," he added in a quick patter, and began pacing the room self-contentedly.[20]

Lebyadkin clearly wants praise for his doggerel. In choosing the fable as genre, he endows his verses with a noble literary heritage. He even hyperbolically claims that it is a "fable of Krylov" (basni[a] Krylova) written by an acquaintance but admits his own authorship when pressed. While it is typical to represent humans in animal form in fables, Lebyadkin reveals his own sense of insignificance in choosing to imitate Miatlev's poem and thus to represent himself not as an animal (such as a bear), but as an insect (Miatlev's is a poet-cockroach). Furthermore, his choice of insect, the cockroach, reveals Lebyadkin's sense of physical size and awkwardness (in his notebooks, Dostoevsky stressed the physical awkwardness [nelovkost'] of Captain Kartuzov, the model for Lebyadkin). By representing the rest of humanity as flies, Lebyadkin further reveals his own sense of social immobility (flies fly; cockroaches, though they have wings, usually crawl). Finally, in the fable, he represents himself as an outcast—persecuted for his superficial differences. Nonetheless, Lebyadkin portrays the cockroach as morally superior. Like the flies, the cockroach finds himself in an untenable position, but,

---

[20] Dostoevskii, PSS, 10: 141–42; 176.

unlike the complaining majority who are busy eating one another alive (political satire), he remains silent. His image of fly-phagy anticipates the claim in his letter to von Lembke that in looking for a culprit the people are destroying one another. It also takes up Mme. Epanchina's prophesy in *The Idiot* that "… vanity and pride have so eaten you up, that in the end you will eat one another up…."[21]

Lebyadkin's answer to the political disorder represented by "fly-phagy" is to have Nikifor dump the whole socio-political mess into the tub, "which should have been done long ago." Nikifor, who "represents nature" or the divine order, has both a servant's name and a servant's job, emphasizing his role as servitor of divine will. Lebyadkin thus comically represents the socio-political order (man-made) as a chaotic mess and nature (divinely-created) as a paradoxically destructive force of order. Furthermore, he singles out for praise the Jobbean cockroach, who, despite the chaos and the protests of those around him, "does not grumble!" But Lebiakin is not Job. He claims that he does not grumble, thus intimating that he accepts the order of the universe. Yet he emphasizes the cockroach's silence and even demands that the cockroach be praised for it: "Madam, your magnificent halls might belong to the noblest of persons, but the cockroach does not grumble! Notice, yes, notice finally that he does not grumble, and cognize the great spirit!"[22]

Lebyadkin's choice of the verb "grumble" (*roptat'*) provides readers with a further sense of how Dostoevsky reworks his sources to fit their new context. Lebyadkin's poem parodies I.P. Miatlev's "Fantastic Tale" (*Fantasticheskaia vyskazka*). Since it is short, I shall translate it here (trying to preserve its anapestic monometer):

The cockroach
As in a cup
Will land up—
Will perish;
On the glass,
It's so steep
No escape.
Such am I:
For my life

---

[21] Dostoevskii, *PSS*, 8: 238.
[22] Dostoevskii, *PSS*, 10: 142; 177.

Has faded
Has fled by,
I'm captive,
I'm in love,
But with who?
Not a thing
Will I say,
I will grieve,
While my God
Does not rob
Me of strength;
That I might
Cease to love,
And forget,
No, never;
Forever
I sadly
Won't escape
Evil grief;
I cannot
Run Away,
Cannot stop
This loving—
I will live
And I'll grieve.
The cockroach
As in a cup
Will land up—
Will perish;
On the glass,
It's so steep
No escape.[23]

From Miatlev, Lebyadkin lifts the image of a cockroach fallen into a cup from which he cannot escape. The source poem also depicts grieving love, which would appeal to Lebyadkin because of his unrequited love

---

[23] I. P. Miatlev, *Polnoe sobranie sochinenii* (St. Petersburg: Apollon Fridrikson, 1857), 1: 121–22.

for Liza Tushina. Furthermore, Miatlev's image of silent loyalty certainly inspires the impostor captain, for he uses his own poem to answer
Varvara Stavrogina's question about why he can not reveal his sister's
(and thus his own) identity.

Lebyadkin's creator, however, transforms Miatlev's Romantic, elegiac poem of melancholy love and solitude into social and metaphysical
satire. While initially both cockroaches are passive victims of fate,
Miatlev's lyric poet finds himself alone and grieves in solitude.
Lebyadkin's cockroach, by contrast, not only finds himself in a social
roil but is also the object of others' disgruntlement. Miatlev's poet-cockroach mourns his past life and love. Dostoevsky's poet-cockroach,
Lebyadkin, has no time to reflect on anything. First scapegoated by the
cup's other inhabitants, he then becomes a victim of God's servitor,
Nikifor. Alone, Miatlev's poet focuses on his own thoughts and feelings.
Thrown together with others, Lebyadkin emphasizes the differences between himself, "a cockroach from infancy," and his neighbors, flies engaged in "fly-phagy." Furthermore, despite its lowly origins, the cockroach remains silent while the disgruntled and murderous flies cry out to
the heavens in complaint.

Lebyadkin's addition of Jupiter as well as his choice of the verb "to
grumble" (*roptat'*) add a metaphysical dimension not present in the
Miatlev poem. Lebyadkin's verses, though a parody of Miatlev's, were
first written by Dostoevsky as the creation of his non-realized character
Captain Kartuzov. In Dostoevsky's first version (Kartuzov's), there is
no mention of Jupiter ("*Razom zakrichali*"[24] becomes "*K Iupiteru zakrichali*" [Lebyadkin]). Ludmila Koehler's argument that the change
evidences Dostoevsky's desire to further degrade Lebyadkin by adding
a violation of stress misses the point.[25] Dostoevsky's modification reflects both Lebyadkin's comic and the novel's serious concerns with
metaphysics. Lebyadkin contrasts the meekness of his poetic "I" with
the flies' metaphysical rebelliousness. A look at the parodic source confirms this emphasis. Miatlev's lyric "I" uses the verb "to grieve"
(*protuzhit'*, *tuzhit'*). Lebyadkin/Kartuzov's lyric "I," by contrast,
employs the verb "to grumble" (*roptat'*/*vozroptat'*), thereby invoking the

---

[24] Dostoevskii, *PSS*, 11: 38.
[25] Ludmila Koehler, "The Grotesque Poetry of Dostoevskij," *Slavic and East
European Journal* 14, no. 1 (Spring 1970): 17.

Biblical figure of Job and images of metaphysical rebellion. Though the verb "to grumble" does not occur in the Russian Bible account of Job, it figures in Dostoevsky's accounts of Job's story. In *The Brothers Karamazov*, Zosima uses it in his sketch of Job's story where he has the devil say to God, "Hand him [Job] over to me and you shall see that your servant will begin to grumble (*vozropshchet*) and will curse your name."[26] Once he associates the verb "to grumble" with the story of Job, Dostoevsky uses it again as a shorthand for metaphysical rebellion. In describing Alyosha's grief and the doubts raised in him by the corruption of Zosima's body, the author notes: "He loved his God and believed in Him unwaveringly, even though he suddenly grumbled (*vozroptal*) against Him for a moment."[27]

By having Lebyadkin invoke Job, Dostoevsky the author highlights the contrast between his character Lebyadkin and the Biblical Job. Lebyadkin is not a righteous man who first earns his good fortune by hard work and devotion to God but a liar and a parasite who daily beats the sister who supports him. Nor does Lebyadkin quietly accept his humble place on this earth, but rails against heaven and earth at the perceived injustices against him. He does not passively endure his anonymous status as Stavrogin's brother-in-law but does everything he can to let others know of it. He gladly misrepresents himself (as silent cockroach) to earn others' praise and recognition. Lebyadkin is not a humble believer but a shame-ridden, materialistic, vain, and rebellious individual who will do anything for personal recognition.

So what are Dostoevsky's purposes in portraying Lebyadkin as an imitator of life and literature largely unconscious of his parodic status? First, one must look to Dostoevsky's interest in the relationship between literature and life. In declaring himself Stavrogin's Falstaff or comparing himself to Derzhavin, Lebyadkin acts like most of the characters in *Demons*, who take literary characters or real-life figures as models for themselves or others and behave accordingly (the list is fairly inclusive). Lebyadkin proves himself but one variation on the theme of Romantic imitator who fervently desires to be other. His status as a liar (*vrun*) enhances his imitative self-fashioning: when believing his own lies, he largely acts as though he already were other. Lebyadkin acts the

---

[26] Dostoevskii, *PSS*, 14: 264.

[27] Dostoevskii, *PSS*, 14: 307; 340.

way he reads: in reading Derzhavin, he conflates the poet and his lyric "I." He thus serves to warn Dostoevsky's readers of two things: 1) the error of conflating an author and his characters, and 2) the dangers posed by unselfconsciously adopting a role that does not fit reality. Dostoevsky's unrealized Captain Kartuzov never for a moment forgets the social gap between himself and his beloved. Captain Lebyadkin acknowledges the gap verbally but ignores it actually. He sincerely believes that his status as Stavrogin's brother-in-law raises him socially, despite his actual social origins. Consequently, once he receives a small estate from Stavrogin, he believes that he has every right to propose to the aristocratic Liza.

This brings us to the second, related point. Dostoevsky was interested in the Russian national character. In an 1873 *Diary of a Writer* article, he hyperbolically identified a specific kind of lying (*vran'yo*) as that which characterizes Russian social interactions.[28] Dostoevsky also links lying and a sense of identity, arguing that all Russians lie because they are ashamed of their true selves and want to be other. Finally, he connects lying and a disregard for truth, contending that Russian liars are more concerned about appearances than reality. Lebyadkin is a Dostoevskian liar with a naive faith in the power of money and words to change reality. He believes that the acquisition of property and aristocratic relations obliterates the social differences between himself and the upper class and represents himself as other in the hope that he will actually become so. By changing words—his title, his sister's name, his self-label— Lebyadkin hopes to alter his actual identity. He thinks that by dressing as a suitor, he will become one, by achieving rhyme, he will achieve poetry, by changing his name, he will transform his essence (shades of Chichikov!). Yet it is comically and often painfully clear to the reader that clothes do not make a man, rhyme does not make a poem, a name does not always express a person's essential character (although a name often does so in Dostoevsky). By stressing the gap between source and parody, Dostoevsky underscores this point for the reader.

Third, Lebyadkin as a parody of both Stavrogin and Stepan Verkhovensky serves to highlight thematics associated with them— identity and social role. As an imitator and echo, Lebyadkin draws at-

---

[28] Dostoevskii, *PSS*, 21: 119.

tention to those he imitates (Stavrogin) and echoes (Stepan Verkhovensky). By obsessing about marrying a potentially lame woman, Lebyadkin makes readers consider Stavrogin's motives for marrying an actual lame woman. Furthermore, Lebyadkin's plans to publish his will make us question Stavrogin's motives (in the unpublished chapter) to publish his confession. Likewise, in blaming Russia for his lack of public recognition, Lebyadkin parodies Stepan Trofimovich, who does the same. Lebyadkin's self-identification as a "repentant freethinker," i.e., someone who has reconsidered his past relationship with his country, also prefigures Stepan Verkhovensky's deathbed change of heart toward Russia. It thus provides readers with a second model for understanding characters' changes of heart, neither of which is primarily political. If we see the label "repentant freethinker" as Dostoevsky's self-parody (in addition to being a parody of Gogol and Stepan Verkhovensky), then we must re-evaluate the view that *Demons* is primarily a political text.[29]

Fourth, Lebyadkin's status as a Dostoevskian liar makes him a perfect vehicle for parody. Parody presupposes an original with which it provokes comparison. Lebyadkin invokes the images of Derzhavin, the Prince de Monbars, Gogol, Krylov, Miatlev's cockroach, and Job (to mention only those discussed in this essay). Once he names or hints at his sources, we compare his words and images to theirs, thus setting up a dialogue that forces us to reconsider both source and parody. Lying (*vran'yo*) works in a similar manner. In attempting to conceal the gap between Russian ideals and reality, it signifies the cover up. The lie usually represents an ideal (comic or serious) that makes us consider the reality it is trying to improve on and usually signals the gap between the two. When Lebyadkin calls himself a poet and decries his debased circumstances, for example, the reader conjures up images of real poets and finds him wanting. Nonetheless, Lebyadkin's parodic plaints evoke, albeit comically, the actual dilemmas faced by men of talent in Russia.

Finally, Lebyadkin as a minor character serves as a vehicle for social commentary. Through him, Dostoevsky demonstrates the tragic side of the political comedy being enacted. A comic impostor in a novel about serious impostorship, Lebyadkin moves from social embarrassment to

---

[29] Olga Meerson, *Dostoevsky's Taboos* (Dresden: Dresden University Press), 1997.

political sacrifice. Lebyadkin (with his sister Mar'ia and their servant) becomes the innocent victim of the political machinations of Dostoevsky's Khlestakov of the sixties, Peter Verkhovensky.[30] Lebyadkin's death also demonstrates the potential tragedy of the non-correspondence between the ideal and the actual. He conceives of his identity as Stavrogin's brother-in-law as a model—a source of social status and potential wealth, steppingstone to a new life, a marriage into wealth. He spends the entire novel trying to make public this family tie, to realize the ideal by gaining the recognition of others. In reality, the connection kills him. His real identity as social embarrassment ensures his death. Lebyadkin, the impostor captain, must die in order for Verkhovensky, the impostor revolutionary, to realize his plan to enthrone an impostor Ivan-Tsarevich, Stavrogin.

The comic Gogolian world of the impostor Khlestakov takes a tragic turn in the political climate of late 1860s Russia. Lebyadkin composes comic swan songs of love and dies tragically, throat cut by the blade of a peasant turned criminal through the negligence of a nobleman father (Stepan Verkhovensky) and turned murderer through the machinations of a revolutionary son (Peter Verkhovensky). Lebyadkin's benefactor (Stavrogin) turns aside indifferently as his wife and brother-in-law are brutally murdered. Throughout the novel, Lebyadkin parodically refracts the narcissistic grandiosity and self-absorption of his social superiors, startling Dostoevsky's readers. His death testifies to the socio-political consequences of the psycho-spiritual illness infecting all of the novel's characters, himself included. Nonetheless, he remains a low character, a reminder of what he is as well as of what he is not. Lebyadkin lives and dies, not a poet-prophet, but a poet-cockroach.

---

[30] Deborah Martinsen, "Dostoevsky and the Temptation of Rhetoric" (Ph.D. diss., Columbia University, 1990), 53.

Four

Derek Maus

Satirical Subtlety in Lev Tolstoy's *Sebastopol Sketches, War and Peace* and *Hadji Murad*

Satire was certainly not a literary convention unfamiliar to Lev Tolstoy. His late novel *Resurrection*, for example, is a critical account of late nineteenth-century Russian government, society, and religion whose satirical power (if not necessarily its ideology) rivals the work of Nikolai Gogol and Mikhail Saltykov-Shchedrin, a pair of authors roughly contemporary with Tolstoy[1] who are more frequently associated with satire. However, Tolstoy was a master at incorporating satirical elements into his less-didactic novels as well.[2] From his earliest writings through the short fictional works he produced near the end of his life, Tolstoy's descriptions of individual characters are almost always tinged with some sort of subtle narrative bias, usually related to his personal opinion about the traits he ascribes to his creation. Such authorial manipulation lends itself not only to controlling the reader's mental image of the character but also to conveying the moral perspective that the author intends the reader to adopt in relation to that particular figure. Without

---

[1] Even though Gogol died just as Tolstoy was beginning his career and had not produced a major work in several years at the time of his death, he was influential in creating the artistic renaissance that A. N. Wilson notes Tolstoy was born into: "Tolstoy [...] belonged to the first generation in Russia to have been born into a full, vigorous literary and intellectual inheritance; to have been born into a Russia which not only received western intellectual writings, but which also now produced such writings themselves, writings of a kind which rivalled and outshone their western equivalents." See A. N. Wilson, *Tolstoy* (London: Hamish Hamilton, 1988), 76.

[2] William Rowe (among several others) has noted that *Resurrection* is "moralistic and didactic novel ... [that] condemns virtually all the established institutions of church and state." While most of Tolstoy's work contains some elements of this characteristic teaching/preaching, few of them are as heavy-handed or as unified in their criticism as *Resurrection*. See William W. Rowe, *Leo Tolstoy* (Boston: Twayne, 1986), 106.

Janet Tucker, ed. *Against the Grain: Parody, Satire and Intertextuality in Russian Literature*. Bloomington, IN: Slavica, 2002, 55–80.

writing the sorts of farcical or darkly comic works most often associated (and often incorrectly[3]) with satire, Tolstoy guides the reader— sometimes gently, sometimes brusquely—into sharing his ethical perspective through the accretion of satirically charged narration.

At times, Tolstoy uses this technique to prevent the reader from judging too harshly a character he wants to present as likable or, at least, deserving of sympathy. More often, though, Tolstoy will employy this method when making negative comments about characters he wishes to disparage. Only occasionally does he step into the frame and offer an outright denunciation of a particular character. He generally prefers the satirist's more indirect approach: presenting a character in such a way that his own words and actions, rather than the protestations of an intrusive author/narrator, make him seem ridiculous and unworthy of the reader's respect. In his *Satire and the Transformation of Genre*, Leon Guilhamet describes the way in which modal satire of this sort functions:

> The basic difference between the satiric and the comic is that the satiric reinterprets the ridiculous in an ethical light. The satiric employs comic techniques of ridicule, but discovers harm and even evil in the ridiculous. The ridiculous that is proper to satire cannot be reconciled to the good at the conclusion of a comic plot.[4]

This sort of subtextual derision recurs throughout the body of Tolstoy's work, ranging from a rather light-hearted, almost paternally scolding

---

[3] The ongoing (more than 130 years after its inception) critical debate over whether Gogol was a satirist, a realist, a hyper-realist, a fabulist, or some combination of all these, is an example of the difficulty in pinning down satire's distinctive characteristics. I would argue that Tolstoy rarely receives the title of satirist, despite his large-scale adoption of the mode, because his style of writing is, in general, more easily accepted as realism than Gogol's, and realism and satire have traditionally been viewed as somewhat incompatible. See the opening chapter to Karen Ryan-Hayes, *Contemporary Russian Satire: A Genre Study* (Cambridge: Cambridge University Press, 1995), for a good revision of this viewpoint.

[4] Leon Guilhamet, *Satire and the Transformation of Genre* (Philadelphia: University of Pennsylvania Press, 1987), 8.

tone[5] to the occasional near-Jeremiads of *Resurrection* or "The Devil." When Tolstoy wishes to spare a character from the full force of his indignation, he allows the satiric to evolve back into the comic, usually by showing how that character has learned from the mistakes that were scorned in him/her previously. Essentially, these characters are allowed catharsis despite their missteps. The unreconciled ridicule that Guilhamet contends is the identifying mark of satire is reserved for those characters whose actions and beliefs are consistently immoral in Tolstoy's view.

Gary Saul Morson analyzes the role of parody at length in *Boundaries of Genre*, and many of his ideas are useful in the identification of Tolstoy's satirical technique. While parody and satire are by no means interchangeable terms, parody can be an indispensable element of satire whose goal is the exposure of meaninglessness beneath a seemingly significant surface. As Morson notes concerning parody's function:

> Parody aims to discredit an act of speech by redirecting attention from its text to a compromising context. That is, while the parodist's ironic quotation marks frame the linguistic form of the original utterance, they also direct attention to the *occasion* (more accurately, the parodist's version of the occasion) *of its uttering*. The parodist thereby aims to reveal the otherwise covert aspects of that occasion, including the unstated motives and assumptions of both the speaker and the assumed and presumably sympathetic audience.[6]

Tolstoy's narratives frequently include "act[s] of speech" (whether quoted conversations, interior monologues or narration that affects a particular attitude) by characters he wishes to satirize made ridiculous by the disparity that Tolstoy perceives between meaning and context. In this way, Tolstoy uses parody effectively to uncover "the divergence be-

---

[5] His attitude towards Pierre Bezukhov, for example, during the early chapters of *War and Peace*, illustrates this form of satirical treatment.

[6] Gary Saul Morson, *The Boundaries of Genre: Dostoevsky's Diary of a Writer and the Traditions of Literary Utopia* (Evanston, IL: Northwestern University Press, 1981), 113. Emphases in original.

tween professed and unacknowledged intentions—or the discovery of naiveté, the difference between belief and disconfirming evidence."[7]

Morson's study explicitly links this technique with Dostoevsky's *Diary of a Writer*, and examples in Dostoevsky's work are plentiful from both his early liberal period and his later more conservative years. R. L. Busch extensively examines Dostoevsky's parodic technique in *Crime and Punishment*, claiming that an elaborate system of character foils provides both a parody of Chernyshevskian rhetoric and a derisive satire of the ideas contained within it:

> Closely relatable in function to irony are the parodic figures of Lebezyatnikov, Luzhin and Svidrigailov. Significant characterological parallels exist between them and Raskolnikov and thereby lower both him and what he represents.[8]

The ideas expressed by each of these characters are discredited not only by their respective reprehensible actions but also by the incongruity between their high-minded theoretical rhetoric and the decrepit situation of the Marmeladov family. Although both Raskolnikov and Lebezyatnikov represent ideas that Dostoevsky reviles, their satirical portrayal leaves room for redemption that is not afforded to Luzhin or Svidrigailov: "Like Raskolnikov, Lebezyatnikov stands for a sharp break with the past, but both are subverted in this by their own natures and by the weight of tradition."[9] Lebezyatnikov's ambivalence is largely confined to his exposure of Luzhin's false accusation of theft against Sonya. Even in this instance, though, Dostoevsky parodies Lebezyatnikov's language and logic, despite their positive function. The scattered good deeds that Lebezyatnikov and Raskolnikov perform when their moral natures briefly overcome their ideologies actually serve to further Dostoevsky's satirical agenda, since they underscore the ways in which both men fail to take "disconfirming evidence" against their ideologies truly to heart. Raskolnikov's spiritual renewal, achieved only after he abandons his old beliefs through Sonya's example, reconciles the satirical viewpoint from which he has been consistently depicted into a cautiously hopeful, if not

---

[7] Morson, *Boundaries of Genre*, 113.

[8] R. L. Busch, *Humor in the Major Novels of F. M. Dostoevsky* (Columbus, OH: Slavica Publishers, 1987), 33.

[9] Busch, *Humor in the Major Novels*, 33.

a happy, ending. Tolstoy's fiction is filled with similar scenarios in which single-minded characters (at least those who are single-minded in the "wrong" way) are satirized into meaninglessness, while characters deemed capable of moral edification are chided for their mistakes but also allowed to repent.

Since most of the surprisingly sparse critical evaluation of Tolstoy's satire has treated the moralizing and often rather severe works in the vein of *The Kreutzer Sonata* or *Resurrection* (neither of which is likely to be confused with comedy),[10] I shall limit myself in this essay to discussing examples of Tolstoy's more subtle satirical mode in one of his early works (*The Sebastopol Sketches*), one of his last works (*Hadji Murad*), and perhaps his finest and most notable work (*War and Peace*), all of them involving the Russian military and military operations. I shall focus on the ways in which Tolstoy fuses his authorial opinions with his descriptions of recurrent character types, such as the overly ambitious military officer, in an attempt to retain didactic control over his readers' interpretations of his works.

❖   ❖   ❖

Consisting of three rather dissimilar stories (in narrative form, if not in content), *The Sebastopol Sketches* (1855) allow Tolstoy to express a full range of emotions and opinions concerning the nature of war and, more notably, the nature of humans involved in war. A richly diverse assortment of characters populates Sebastopol throughout the three stories and nine months of the book. Tolstoy uses his satirical tone on numerous occasions to make commentaries on certain members of this cast, many of whom are representative of persons he encountered first-hand during his military service in the Crimean War. In his essay, "A Project

---

[10] Whether the paucity of detailed critical examination of Tolstoy explicitly in terms of satire stems from a misapprehension of satire as necessarily humorous (which admittedly few of Tolstoy's works are) or from categorization of satirical elements within different hermeneutics (moralistic satire can easily be classified as religious instruction by example if removed from a literary context) is unclear. Tolstoy's satire, especially in his zealous anti-vice writings, is perhaps unusual for the radical religious moralism that underlies it, but it bears significant formal resemblance to the darker sections of Saltykov-Shchedrin's *The Golovlyovs*, which is among the most commonly mentioned Russian satires of the nineteenth century.

for Reorganizing the Army," published roughly contemporaneously with *The Sebastopol Sketches*, Tolstoy enumerates the six "main vices" of the Russian military:

1) Meagre rations.
2) Lack of education.
3) Barriers to the promotion of capable men.
4) An air of oppression.
5) Seniority.
6) Extortion.[11]

In this essay, he goes on to explain briefly how each of these factors is detrimental to the effectiveness of the military, but it is in the fictional work of the three tales in *The Sebastopol Sketches* that one finds the elaboration bringing the weight of these issues home. Personifications of each of these "vices" can be found in the characters of these stories (especially the latter two, "Sebastopol in December" and "Sebastopol in May") and their negative effects are demonstrated through the satirical *reductio ad absurdum* that Tolstoy undertakes with regard to the characters that embody them.

Few, if any, characters in these stories are spared from Tolstoy's contempt, although not all are indicted as being personally responsible for the traits that he finds so distasteful. The officer class, especially the higher-ranking officers, receives the brunt of Tolstoy's animosity,[12] with rank-and-file soldiers or junior officers often having any such taints excused as proceeding from the faults of their superior commanders. For example, in "Sebastopol in May," the relatively affable lieutenant-captain Mikhailov[13] exhibits some characteristics that Tolstoy personally

---

[11] Lev Tolstoy, "A Project for Reorganizing the Army," in *I Cannot be Silent: Writings on Politics, Art and Religion, by Leo Tolstoy* (Bristol, U.K.: Bristol Press, 1989), 30.

[12] This trend would continue throughout most of Tolstoy's work and is an example of the conflicted self-loathing—Tolstoy himself being an officer—that Berlin and others have attributed to him. See Sir Isaiah Berlin, *The Hedgehog and The Fox: An Essay on Tolstoy's View of History* (New York: Simon and Schuster, 1953).

[13] For the sake of continuity with the editions used for reference, Russian names are spelled here as they are in the English texts from which quotes are taken, rather than in Library of Congress transliteration style.

found objectionable—he is something of a defeatist,[14] occasionally given to mild fits of cowardice,[15] and a bit of a tippler—and he receives some rather mild chiding from the author because of them. However, the real invective in this story is saved for characters like Prince Galtsin or Baron Pest, who "command" the battle largely from the relative safety of their townhouses or from the heavily fortified and wine-filled lodgings on the bastions. When Tolstoy describes these characters and their motivations, it is usually using the derisive language of satire.

To wit, after a lengthy scene in which Mikhailov and his manservant Nikita go through a somewhat melodramatic, yet affectingly genuine, scene of parting and foreboding before the former's departure for his "thirteenth time on the bastion,"[16] Tolstoy immediately switches scenes to the quarters of Adjutant Kalugin where Galtsin, Pest, and two other staff officers have gathered for tea and conversation in the midst of the fighting. This episode (chapter 5 of "Sebastopol in May"), in which Tolstoy recounts the narcissistic attitude of the officer class, comprises a mere six of the nearly 150 pages of *The Sebastopol Sketches*. Setting a precedent that he would follow intermittently for the remainder of his career, Tolstoy uses a concise satirical depiction to cast aspersions on the group of people he believes to be responsible for the problems in the army and for the wasteful slaughter at Sebastopol.

Prior to the explicit depiction of the officers' way of thinking, though, Tolstoy foregrounds his criticism by noting the falseness and vapid behavior surrounding perceptions of the word "aristocrat" ("even though," Tolstoy points out, "death hangs over the heads of *aristocrats*

---

[14] A better designation for him would perhaps be "realist," given the Russian military's situation at Sebastopol in May of 1854.

[15] Mikhailov's "cowardice" only manifests itself as an understandable trepidation that certainly is not as reprehensible to Tolstoy as Pest's bombastic charge down the redoubt.

[16] Lev Tolstoy, "Sebastopol in May," in *The Sebastopol Sketches*, trans. David McDuff (London: Penguin Books, 1986), 70. The specific mention of the ordinal number of Mikhailov's trip to the bastion is portentous, giving him a *chёrtova diuzhina* (devil's dozen). Mikhailov's more plebian background (compared with Galtsin, Pest, et al.) makes his trepidation at the negative prospects of this trip understandable, since he would presumably be more attuned to such popular superstition.

and *non-aristocrats* alike"[17]). He sternly denounces the self-serving motivation behind their actions: "Vanity, vanity, all is vanity—even on the brink of the grave, and among men who are ready to die for the sake of a lofty conviction!"[18] The chatter in the officers' quarters that Tolstoy subsequently relates reads like (and alludes to) that of the salons of Petersburg, a culture Tolstoy repeatedly derides throughout his works. For example:

> "I say, you never finished telling me about Vaska Mendel," said Kalugin, who had taken off his greatcoat and was sitting in a soft, comfortable armchair by the window, unbuttoning the collar of his clean, starched linen shirt. "How did he get married?"
>
> "My dear fellow, you'd simply die laughing! *Je vous dis, il y avait un temps où on ne parlait de ça à Peterbourg,*" said Prince Galtsin, laughing and jumping up from the piano at which he had been sitting. He resettled himself on the window seat, next to Kalugin. "You'd die laughing! I know the whole story," and he quickly launched, with much wit and humour, into an account of a love affair which we shall omit as it is of no interest to us.[19]

The banal subject matter Prince Galtsin discusses not only serves as a counterpoint to Mikhailov's brooding one chapter earlier on the very real possibility of his own imminent demise, but also marks Galtsin's speech as incongruous with the serious setting. No one in Sebastopol is dying of laughter,[20] but plenty are dying. Furthermore, his use of French, while standard among the Russian aristocracy, is especially out of place in this situation, given that the French are the very ones shelling the city and killing Galtsin's countrymen. The officers' speech is made plainly incongruous with the setting, thus becoming a perfect example of

---

[17] Tolstoy, "Sebastopol in May," 65. Emphasis in original.

[18] Tolstoy, "Sebastopol in May," 66.

[19] Tolstoy, "Sebastopol in May," 73.

[20] The English translation actually makes the irony more explicit here than it is in the original, turning the Russian "*umora, bratets*" into "you would die laughing," thereby giving a cause to the figurative death (laughter, rather than the real death caused by being too near a French shell). The Russian original, however, does not carry this figurative meaning. See *Polnoe sobranie sochinenii L'va Nikolaevicha Tolstogo* (Moscow: I. D. Sytina, 1912), 2: 204.

parody as Morson defines it. There is a degree of *poshlost'*[21] in both the artificiality of the salon atmosphere within a besieged city and the emptiness of the conversation among the officers, a fact that is not overlooked by the narrator in stating that he will omit Galtsin's tale "as it is of no interest to us" (since "we" are presumably more interested in the surrounding events).

The entire scene is reminiscent of Tolstoy's later critical descriptions of Petersburg salon society, especially the chapters of *War and Peace* that center around Anna Scherer's coterie of acquaintances. As such, his comment that "all these gentlemen who had made themselves comfortable in various parts of the room" were in their element in this isolated apartment in wartime Sebastopol is highly ironic: "They seemed to have lost all the absurd haughtiness and snobbery with which they addressed the infantry officers; here they were among their own kind, and they revealed themselves as charming, high-spirited and good-hearted young men."[22] Sebastopol in May 1854, was most certainly *not* a salon. Rather, it was a place where "the angel of death ... hovered ceaselessly" for six months,[23] and Tolstoy exhibits his extreme resentment at the introduction of this superficial subculture into the terrible environment of wartime through his satirically tinged portrayal of these characters.

Given the innumerable privations and hardships (both mental and physical) that Tolstoy presents to the reader in these stories, the conversation among these "charming, high-spirited and good-hearted" men is not only inappropriate (it points out their lack of understanding of the military situation,[24] as well as their lack of sympathy with the troops they command) but also duplicitous, given their demonstrated behavior towards their subalterns throughout the tale. When the officers actually discuss the troops, their conversation alludes to almost all of Tolstoy's six vices within the course of a few lines:

---

[21] *Poshlost'* is a largely untranslatable term, roughly equivalent to "banality that goes unrecognized by the possessor, who mistakes it for refinement." See Vladimir Nabokov's *Nikolai Gogol* (New York: New Directions, 1961), for a full treatment of the term.

[22] Tolstoy, "Sebastopol in May," 73.

[23] Tolstoy, "Sebastopol in May," 59.

[24] The fact that Galtsin sits on a windowsill in a city being shelled, thus needlessly (and apparently, unknowingly) exposing himself to live fire, points out this lack of understanding still more explicitly.

"It's a strange thought," said Galtsin, when he had taken his glass and was on his way back to the window-seat again. "Here we are in a town that's under siege, tickling the ivories and having tea and cream in the sort of flat I for one would be proud to own in St. Petersburg."

"Well, all I can say is it's just as well," said the old lieutenant-colonel, who was never satisfied with anything. "Otherwise this constant waiting about for something to happen would be intolerable.... Just think what it would be like if we had to live surrounded by this never-ending slaughter day after day up to our necks in mud, without any creature comforts."

"But what about our infantry officers?" said Kalugin. "They have to live in the bastions with the rest of the men and have to eat the same borshch they're given in the casements. What about them?"

"There's something I don't understand," said Prince Galtsin. "I have to confess, I don't really see how men in dirty underwear, suffering from lice and not even able to wash their hands, can possibly—be capable of bravery. You know what I mean, *cette belle bravoure de gentilhomme*—it's simply not on."

"Well, they don't understand *that* kind of bravery," said Praskukhin.[25]

Kalugin does manage a somewhat positive rejoinder to the toadying Praskukhin's jibe, but his assertion that the infantry officers are "heroes, wonderful people" excuses only him (and not entirely at that) among the officers from Tolstoy's satirical glare. The "bravery of the gentleman" that Praskukhin and Galtsin refer to is ultimately useless and false, as both Praskukhin's inglorious death on the ramparts and Pest's ineffectual, foolishly courageous and almost totally misremembered charge serve to illustrate.

In case it has still eluded the reader, Tolstoy makes the difference between Praskukhin and Mikhailov evident by comparing the way each reacts to the stimulus of having a shell fall in his vicinity while on the ramparts. Donna Tussing Orwin does not specifically identify Tolstoy's

---

[25] Tolstoy, "Sebastopol in May," 74.

technique in this regard as satirical, although the effect she describes clearly imparts satirical ridicule to Praskukhin and his kind:

> Like the others, Mikhailov has feelings of fear and ambition; he may have felt all the emotions that visit Praskukhin in the seconds before his death; but he *overcomes* his fear and other feelings to force himself to check up on Praskukhin back where the battle rages, because "it's my *duty*."
>
> Praskukhin, like the other officers at headquarters, is a creature of *amour propre*. He thinks only of himself, and yet his self-esteem depends entirely on what others think of him. His gaze remains directed outside himself and toward the world of men…. Praskukhin's *amour propre* diminishes his reality, both for himself and for Tolstoy's readers. He is more a shadow than a man.
>
> Mikhailov looks inside himself to God…. His self-esteem, also important to him, depends on what God, not men, thinks of him. Asking for forgiveness of sins, he conceives of himself as an independent individual capable of moral responsiblity[….] One can say of Mikhailov, then, as one cannot of Praskukhin, that he has fixed inner principles, or ideas, as well as an active inner life.[26]

Orwin sees Tolstoy's depiction of Praskukhin's death as part of the author's "unflinching realis[m],"[27] but I contend that it is rather a distinctly satirical commentary on the way in which the lack of "moral responsibility" makes an individual "more a shadow than a man." Orwin's distinction between Praskukhin's diminished reality in comparison with Mikhailov does, however, reinforce the impression that the characters satirized by Tolstoy rarely rise above stock types. In contrast, the more fully developed (i.e., more "real") characters are either spared satirical treatment entirely or, like Mikhailov, behave in ways that demonstrate intrinsic virtue, thus mitigating prior satirical description. As Tolstoy repeatedly asserted about himself, no individual is perfect, but one should be able to learn from one's mistakes and live an upright life if he so chooses.

---

[26] Donna Tussing Orwin, *Tolstoy's Art and Thought, 1847–1880* (Princeton: Princeton University Press, 1993), 25. Emphases in original.

[27] Orwin, *Tolstoy's Art and Thought*, 25.

Tolstoy's lament about the ultimate purpose of the fighting at Sebastopol opens this story and sets the mood that retroactively frames the three stories collectively:

> Six months have now passed since the first cannonball came hurtling over from the bastions of Sebastopol…
>
> During this time, thousands of individual personal vanities have been insulted, thousands have been gratified and thousands have gone to rest in the arms of death. How many military decorations have been pinned on, how many stripped off, how many St. Anne Ribbons and orders of St. Vladimir have been awarded, how many pink coffins and linen palls have gone to the grave…?
>
> One of two things appears to be true: either war is madness, or, if men perpetrate this madness, they thereby demonstrate that they are far from being the rational creatures we for some reason commonly suppose them to be.[28]

None among vainglorious Pest (who thinks of the battle "with a sinking heart" even as he "don[s] his cap at a rakish angle and march[es] out of the room with loud, firm steps"[29]), doomed Praskukhin or imperceptive Galtsin give any evidence to disprove this contention. Mikhailov's initial characterization also supports this idea, but his small affirmation of the role of duty (a concept both religious and military) and individual responsibility near the end of the story provides the simple positive (for Tolstoy) alternative to the madness of war and the irrational culture of the officers. Tolstoy stops short of making Mikhailov into a heroic figure for his actions, though, and even shows him relapsing into the vanity (and language) of his last quoted speech:

> *"Est-ce que le pavillion est baissé déjà?"* enquired Prince Galtsin, who had resumed his customary haughty manner, surveying the lieutenant-captain's cap and addressing no one in particular.
>
> *"Non pas encore."* replied Mikhailov, anxious to show that he too could speak French.[30]

---

[28] Tolstoy, "Sebastopol in May," 60.
[29] Tolstoy, "Sebastopol in May," 75.
[30] Tolstoy, "Sebastopol in May," 104.

Tolstoy even goes so far as to conclude the sketch with the assertion that "[a]ll the characters are equally blameless and equally wicked," leading him to assert that "the hero[,] ... who has always been, is now and will always be supremely magnificent, is truth."[31]

His approach in "Sebastopol in December" is somewhat less hostile to the military, although the second-person address of this reportage does still take an occasional swipe at "vain, petty and mindless emotions" as it extols the qualities of Sebastopol's defenders, the enlisted soldiers.[32] This piece, which (unlike the other two) Tolstoy wrote before the fall of Sebastopol, maintains something of a positive outlook on the war,[33] even as it chronicles some of the horror.

On the other hand, "Sebastopol in August" takes the harshest stance among the three stories towards the wastefulness and corruption among the army as it documents the experiences of the Kozeltsov brothers in and around Sebastopol as the city succumbs to the French attack. Tolstoy's criticism of both the conduct of the officer class and of war in general reaches a peak in this story, as does the negative reaction of the censors and critics: "... [T]he censor cut from the text numerous insinuations that the Russian officers were pampered cowards, greedy for personal glory. Even so, the published versions of these stories reflect Tolstoy's sad conviction that even the bravest men were dying in vain."[34] In all, *The Sebastopol Sketches* served as an apprenticeship for Tolstoy's satirical voice, one that he would put to good use in the creation of his monumental novel *War and Peace*.

❖   ❖   ❖

In the course of its intricate story, *War and Peace* (1865–68) introduces a cast of characters which numbers almost as many as the thousand-plus pages of the book. This group includes those characters created from

---

[31] Tolstoy, "Sebastopol in May," 109.

[32] Lev Tolstoy, "Sebastopol in December," in *The Sebastopol Sketches*, 56.

[33] The first story gained the admiration of Alexander II and of Russians in general, giving a "grimly inspirational" account of the defense of Sebastopol rather than describing "cowardice, glory and the senseless tragedy of military combat." See Rowe, *Tolstoy*, 5, 34.

[34] Rowe, *Tolstoy*, 35.

whole cloth by Tolstoy[35] (such as the myriad Rostovs, Pierre Bezukhov, or Prince Andrei Bolkonsky), those who are thinly-disguised stand-ins for historical personages (Denisov, for example, is largely modeled on folk-hero Denis Davydov), and "actual" historical figures (like Napoleon or General Kutuzov), over all of whom Tolstoy exerts a considerable authorial/editorial control. None of these classes of characters are exempt from Tolstoy's satirical tendencies, although the last group is especially susceptible,[36] as are those characters in the other two groups who are more types than fully-realized individual characters.

Again, though, Tolstoy's satire does not take on the quality of simple parody or burlesque, both because this novel is, at heart, realistic (if not entirely believable at all times) and because his satire is intended as a part of his didacticism and must therefore serve a greater purpose than to simply make Napoleon seem like a clown. Tolstoy's characterization of Napoleon as a crass, somewhat ignorant and wholly egomaniacal figure is not intended for mere comic effect, but to point out the fallacy in the established historical writing, which asserts that Napoleon was a military genius and a statesman of the first order. Furthermore, Tolstoy's depiction of Kutuzov as a wise old man surrounded by a military hierarchy composed largely of incapable and self-absorbed sycophantic foreigners (neither part of which is more than partially accurate), assists him in promulgating his opinion that the "natural" wisdom of Russians like Kutuzov or Platon Karataev is superior to that which is generally considered estimable by historical opinion. Tolstoy's satire is aimed at correcting the mistakes that he believes have been made by history and historians in valuing men like Napoleon, Murat, Ermolov or Miloradovich over those like Kutuzov or Bagration, who go about the admittedly grim business of war in a way that does not seek self-aggrandizement (or even shuns it) while still accomplishing the goal of victory.

As John Bayley points out in his *Tolstoy and the Novel*, Tolstoy accomplishes this correction of historical vision by utilizing "coincidence,

---

[35] It should be noted, though, that several critics have correctly pointed out similarities between these characters and Tolstoy's relations, by birth and by marriage. However, they are still distinct enough to stand alone without the autobiographical linkage.

[36] This tendency should not come as much of a surprise, given Tolstoy's larger goal (as stated most directly in the second epilogue) of correcting historians' notion that individuals guide the course of history.

oversimplification and even his early mania for types."[37] The last of these is most important for an analysis of his satirical technique, since satire often relies heavily on associations with archetypes to achieve its effects. Bayley discusses some of the satirical types that Tolstoy employs in depicting the general staff: "It is natural that Miloradovitch, who is later compared to Murat, the epitome of stupid military panache, should represent the absurdity of mere pugnacity for its own sake...." As Bayley describes Kutuzov's real-life mentor Suvorov:

> He belonged to no Tolstoyan category; neither to the cold, vain Don Juan-like war-lovers, like Napoleon, nor to the pathetic and dedicated purists, like Weyrother and Pfuel, nor to the boasters and strong men, like Murat and Miloradovitch.[38]

That Tolstoy can reduce a monolithic historical figure like Napoleon to such a type, yet maintain his viability as a realistic character within his novel, is a testament to his skill at understated satire.

Tolstoy constantly deflates Napoleon's attempts at self-mythology, parodying the language of gallantry and bravura that Napoleon used to amplify his reputation. When taken together with Tolstoy's explicit critique of historical recollection, this parody also attempts to invalidate the claims made by those who bought into such myths. Tolstoy's description of Napoleon at Austerlitz is one example that Bayley cites as indicative of the author's attitude towards the "greatness" of the French leader: "'his face wore that special look of confident, self-complacent happiness that one sees on the face of a boy happily in love'—the tone is overtly objective, satirical, [and] even disgusted."[39]

Still, there are entire episodes which are written by Tolstoy with comic effect to satirize certain traits of social life, mostly that of the Petersburg courtiers. The marriage of the icy Vera Rostova and the climber Berg (one of the most status-obsessed characters in Tolstoy's *oeuvre*, rivaling even Aleksei Karenin) is one example out of many.

---

[37] John Bayley, *Tolstoy and the Novel* (London: Chatto and Windus, 1966), 167.

[38] Bayley, *Tolstoy*, 170. Additionally, Bayley sees Suvorov's relative absence from the novel's version of Kutuzov's background as a failure on Tolstoy's part, although he acknowledges that it is a necessary one for the maintenance of Tolstoy's positive recasting of Kutuzov.

[39] Bayley, *Tolstoy*, 74.

Others include Pierre's attempts to decipher and utilize the numerology of Freemasonry, Hippolyte Kuragin's near-idiotic attempts at social conversation[40] and the morbid and *comme il faut* courtship of Julie Karagina and Boris Drubetskoy, which concludes with a statement illustrative of the superficial basis for their engagement:

> There was no need to say more: Julie's face shone with triumph and self-satisfaction; but she forced Boris to say all that is said on such occasions—that he loved her and had never loved any other woman more than her. She knew that for the Penza estates and Nizhegorod forests she could demand this, and she received what she demanded.[41]

Neither of these characters receives much positive description, with Julie conforming to the familiar type of the controlling Petersburg society women that Tolstoy disliked (and portrayed negatively often in his works[42]) and Boris essentially mirroring the careerist officers who inhabited the drawing rooms of Sebastopol in the earlier stories.[43]

In all, Tolstoy's control over the reader's perspective in this novel is masterfully executed, almost so lightly as to make its presence invisible to less-sophisticated readers. His narrator does not intrude so far as to make his voice distinct within the story as a character—except, of course, when the narrator is in fact Tolstoy himself, holding forth on history, morals, etc.—choosing instead to guide the opinion of the reader

---

[40] Tolstoy's entire portrayal of the Kuragin family is so negatively tinged as to almost transcend satire and move on to savage lampooning (especially his portrait of Hélène, whose physicality, scheming and dabblings in Jesuit religion draw some of Tolstoy's harshest criticism), mitigated only by occasional humanizing scenes, such as Anatole's death.

[41] Lev Tolstoy, *War and Peace*, trans. Aylmer Maude, Louise Shanks Maude, and George Gibian (New York: W.W. Norton and Co., 1996), 490.

[42] Cf. Hélène Kuragina or Princess Betsy Tverskaya in *Anna Karenina*. Even the similarity of Julia Karagina's last name to that of the loathsome Kuragins points out this typology to some degree.

[43] Although, afforded the narrative freedom of this expansive novel, even Boris occasionally shows hints of overcoming this typology, a characteristic perhaps unavoidable with this form of satirical presentation. Developed characters are not as simple as literary types, making Tolstoy's satire less effective when characters are more fully fleshed out and their possible motivations can be understood, if not necessarily accepted as worthwhile or desirable.

by filtering the presentation of various characters and their action through a smoky lens of satirical inferences. Almost all of these spring from Tolstoy's personal agenda concerning history and society. As Ernest Simmons notes, "The revelation of personality in real life comes about over a period of time by slow accretion, by the accumulation of much detailed information and understanding through innumerable small actions and intimacies ... and a close approximation of it is pursued in Tolstoy's novels."[44] A close approximation, yes, although not one that is necessarily free of prejudice on the part of the provider of these "small actions and intimacies," namely, Tolstoy.

The "heroes" of *War and Peace* most often make themselves identifiable as such through their righteous actions. However, they can also be separated by the manner in which Tolstoy spares them, for the most part, from his mockery when they go astray. None of the foursome who emerge by novel's end as Tolstoy's chosen exemplars for the future (Natasha, Pierre, Nicholas and Mary) progress through the novel without some thoughts or behavior that is presented by the narrator as distasteful or even downright bad. A lack of faults would change them from being relatively complete characters into being simple specimens of a type: the saintly innocent. Not only could such a beatific type invite satire in return,[45] but it also lacks the verisimilitude that this essentially realistic (if idealistic and heavily biased) novel demands. The happy (in a Tolstoyan moral sense) ending that comes to this group of four is representative of the comic resolution of ridicule that Guilhamet mentions. Had these characters remained static like Berg or Hippolyte Kuragin, the ridicule would have remained in the realm of the satiric, since they would have been incapable of realizing the error of their past ways.

Minor characters, especially those like Tushin and Karataev, are allowed to flirt with saintliness, but only as allegorical models for Tolstoy's incalculably more complex "central" characters and, by extension, his readers. Furthermore, these ancillary figures behave as they do without any conscious recognition on their part of the possibility that they might be saintly, since that would be unbecomingly hubristic in Tolstoy's view. Tolstoy refrains from outright condemnation when his

---

[44] Ernest J. Simmons, *Introduction to Russian Realism* (Bloomington, IN: Indiana University Press, 1965), 161.

[45] After all, even Father Zosima stank after death.

heroes stumble, usually presenting them either as youthfully ignorant and inexperienced or as the victims of connivance by those characters whom he does condemn.[46] Tolstoy, as in *The Sebastopol Sketches*, reserves his real venom for those characters who are deserving of it within his scheme of things, as dictated by his personal philosophy and by the ax he has to grind with historians. These characters repeatedly are subject to the inclusion of small details or brief scenes that cast aspersions on their behavior, adding up over the course of the novel to place them clearly on the side opposite that which Tolstoy wishes to extol.

❖   ❖   ❖

Nearly four decades pass between the publication of the final installment of *War and Peace* and that of the elegantly crafted novella *Hadji Murad*, which was composed off-and-on between 1896 and 1904 but remained unpublished until after Tolstoy's death. If *War and Peace* is the "large loose baggy monster..." that Henry James so questionably claims it to be, then this work, which picks up many of the same themes that had been covered in Tolstoy's younger writing, is as tight a summation of his mature philosophy as is extant in the author's *oeuvre*.

Vastly different from the moralistic and proselytizing tracts and stories that Tolstoy had produced for thirty years since the publication of *Anna Karenina*, this work returns Tolstoy to the Russian frontier (specifically Chechnya) and also marks a return to his examination of war and human behavior in relation to it. His adroit satirical commentary also returns, not in the form of thinly-veiled invective that it took in *Resurrection*, but in the more measured tones found in the works already discussed. *Hadji Murad* is a story about honor and bravery, both as the term is understood by Tolstoy's Russian contemporaries and as he himself comprehended it, and the satirical thrusts of the novel again are aimed towards those who do not share Tolstoy's revised version of the "truth."

The story of the real-life Hadji Murad is one that Tolstoy had known since his youth, referring to it both in an 1861 essay entitled

---

[46] Pierre's "seduction" *en masse* by the Kuragins and Dolokhov's hustling (albeit an easy one) of Nicholas at cards are two examples of many that come easily to mind.

"Schoolboys and Art"[47] as well in the frame narration that opens this novella, in which he states that the story was "partly seen [by him]self, partly heard from eye-witnesses, and in part imagined."[48] The third part of this statement is the one which allows him to transform this tale from a simple retelling of a war-story into a meditation and subsequent lecture about morality. Through the introduction of characters like Chernyshov, the elder Vorontsov and Poltoratsky (some of whom, again, are drawn from real figures), Tolstoy is able to use satire to turn such officially celebrated personages (they are, after all, representative of the Russian military commanders who eventually subdued the Chechen insurrection) into foils, against whom the "true" dignity and goodness of a character like the Hadji Murad he creates is immediately recognizable.

The most striking example of this treatment occurs after Hadji Murad has surrendered himself to the younger Vorontsov and is taken to meet with the elder Vorontsov, a representative of the Tsar. Tolstoy here satirizes the superficiality of Russian high society by reversing the technique he employed in "Sebastopol in May." Rather than bringing the mountain of Russian high society to the Muslims of Chechnya, Tolstoy chooses to place Hadji Murad, the embodiment of all the virtues that he sees in the Chechen mountaineers, directly into that society and to contrast the values of the two directly. Tolstoy utilizes his trademark technique of *ostranenie*[49] to survey the scene from Hadji Murad's unconditioned perspective. Before Hadji Murad arrives in Tiflis, he is the topic of a heated dinner-table discussion among Vorontsov's coterie. Once he arrives, he becomes a first-hand participant (and commentator) on an evening in the company of this group,

---

[47] See Lev Tolstoy, *I Cannot be Silent* (Bristol, U.K.: Bristol Press, 1989).

[48] Lev Tolstoy, *Hadji Murad*, in *Great Short Works of Leo Tolstoy* (New York: Harper and Row, 1967), 549.

[49] Variously translated as "estrangement" or "making strange," this concept is central to the early Formalist theories of the critic Viktor Shklovsky. Before Shklovsky gave a name to this technique of presenting everyday experience from a different or foreign—hence the Russian root *stran*—perspective, Tolstoy had used the technique extensively, perhaps most notably in the section of *War and Peace* in which Natasha goes to her first opera. The narrative voice describes this scene largely through her unfamiliarized eyes.

with both scenes providing opportunities for Tolstoy to comment depre-
catingly on the Russian elites.

As Hadji Murad is discussed at a sumptuous dinner, a general
speaks of his personal experience regarding the Chechen leader:

> "Why it was he, if your excellency will please remember," said
> the general, "who arranged the ambush that attacked the rescue
> party in the 'Biscuit' expedition."
>
>   What the brave general spoke of as the "rescue" was the affair
> in the unfortunate Dargo campaign in which a whole detachment,
> including Prince Vorontsov who commanded it, would certainly
> have perished had it not been rescued by the arrival of fresh
> troops. Everyone knew that the whole Dargo campaign under
> Vorontsov's command had been a shameful affair, and therefore,
> if anyone mentioned it in Vorontsov's presence they did so only
> in the aspect in which Vorontsov had reported it to the Tsar—as
> a brilliant achievement of the Russian army.[50]

Vorontsov is essentially caught in a lie in the relation of this seemingly
small detail, but Tolstoy makes sure to point out that almost everyone
else participates in this lie so that Vorontsov may retain his honor despite his failure. The author wishes to compare this false honor with the
actual integrity of Hadji Murad and inserts the brief corrective comment
about the truth of the Dargo campaign in order to cast aspersion on
those who distort reality.

This narrative "correction" of the official report of a military action
echoes almost exactly the manner in which Tolstoy's narrator sets
straight the account that Baron Pest gives of his comportment under fire
in "Sebastopol in May":

> [...] Pest proceeded to describe how he had ended up in com-
> mand of his entire company, how his company commander had
> been killed, how he, Pest, had bayoneted a Frenchman and how,
> had it not been for him, the day would have been lost, and so on,
> and so forth.

---

[50] Tolstoy, *Hadji Murad*, 588.

> The principal elements of this story were factually true; in recounting its details, however, the cadet boasted and made things up.[51]

And again, in a slightly later passage:

> Baron Pest had also come up to the Boulevard. He was telling a long story about how he had been present when the truce was signed, and had spoken with the French officers, one of whom had apparently said to him: *"S'il n'avait pas fait clair encore pendant une demi-heure, les ambuscades auraient été reprises,"* and how he had replied: *"Monsieur! Je ne dit pas non, pour ne pas vous donner un démenti,"* and what a good rejoinder it had been, and so forth.
>
> While it is true that he had been present at the signing of the truce, he had not managed to say anything particularly clever. It had only been later, on his way to the boulevard, that he had thought up the French ripostes with which he was now entertaining everyone.[52]

The dismissive use of the phrase "and so forth" (*i tak dalee*, in the original Russian) in both these passages pointedly demonstrates the insignificance and meaninglessness of Pest's words—they do not even merit full reproduction, since they are only dissembling attempts at saving face rather than actual events.

Overt narrative identification of instances in which characters willingly distort the truth for their own self-aggrandizement remains a consistent feature throughout Tolstoy's writing.[53] In a largely unconcealed manner, Tolstoy is engaging in what Morson calls "the etiology of utterance": "[The parodist] does not ... quote 'out of context,' as the

---

[51] Tolstoy, "Sebastopol in May," 92.

[52] Tolstoy, "Sebastopol in May," 104.

[53] The irony of this approach (one perhaps not lost on the author) is that it also casts doubt on the very act of correctly re-telling a story. Since Tolstoy's own narration is so self-consciously biased, he may be commenting on the impossibility of relating a story, real or imagined, without somehow "fixing" it to fit in with an authorial design. The criticism of inaccuracies in Tolstoy's fictional representation of Napoleon sounds similar in many ways to Tolstoy's own narrative "corrections."

[parodied] targets often respond, but rather in 'too much' context—in a context the targets would have rather overlooked."[54] This technique is among the most effective of his satirical weapons, serving to expose vainglorious and self-important figures as little more than charlatans, and providing Tolstoy a negative model against which he can favorably compare those characters he believes to be more righteous, either in terms of a moral/religious sense or in the less clearly articulated ethical system of his own devising.

Once Hadji Murad actually arrives in Tiflis, Tolstoy becomes more lampooning and harsh in his satire, cutting a broad swath of semi-comic malediction across many segments of society:

> When Hadji Murad arrived at the prince's palace the next day, the waiting room was already full of people. Yesterday's general with the bristly moustaches was there in full uniform with all his decorations, having come to take leave. There was the commander of a regiment who was in danger of being court-martialled for misappropriating commissariat money, and there was a rich Armenian who wanted to obtain from the Government a renewal of his monopoly for the sale of vodka. There, dressed in black, was the widow of an officer who had been killed in action. She had come to ask for a pension, or for free education for her children. There was a ruined Georgian prince in magnificent Georgian costume who was trying to obtain for himself some confiscated church property. There was an official with a large roll of paper containing a new plan for subjugating the Caucasus. There was also a Khan who had come solely to be able to tell his people at home that he had called on the prince.[55]

Hadji Murad is then taken to the opera, to which he is described as "obviously indifferent" but sits through because of his "Oriental Mohammedan dignity."[56] This scene, and indeed Hadji Murad's entire interaction with the Russian *haute monde*, is similar to the episode in book 8, chapters 8–10 of *War and Peace* in which young Natasha is seduced, both by the social pageantry of her first opera-going experience

---

[54] Morson, *Boundaries of Genre*, 113.

[55] Tolstoy, *Hadji Murad*, 591.

[56] Tolstoy, *Hadji Murad*, 594.

and by the devious, somewhat predatory Anatole Kuragin. Hadji Murad is not as impressionable as Natasha is, but his perspective is similarly estranged from that of the Russians (removed to a Georgian setting in Tiflis) who are watching as "an Italian opera was performed at the new theater, which was decorated in Oriental style." The incongruous mélange of cultures represented by this scene furthers the comparison between the essential integrity (*chestnost'*) of Hadji Murad and the superficial banality of those around him. Morson specifically cites Tolstoy's description of opera (although without mentioning *Hadji Murad*) as part of a satirical gesture aimed toward not only characters but certain audiences as well:

> Parodies are usually described as being of (or "after") a particular author or work, but the parodist's principal target may, in fact, be a particular audience or class of readers. The etiology of utterance includes the pathology of reception.... Tolstoy's parodies of opera in *War and Peace* and *What is Art?*, for instance, are primarily concerned with why "rich, idle people" should enjoy such immoral artifice.[57]

By making opera ridiculous in the eyes of his hero, Tolstoy satirizes not only the members of Tiflis' *vysshii svet* but also anyone who sympathizes with them.

Tolstoy also combines his dislike of the foppishness of military officers and the strong criticism of sexuality that had so strongly marked the writings of his later career when he describes those who are present at "the usual evening party at the Vorontsovs'":

> Young women and women not very young wearing dresses that displayed their bare necks, arms, and breasts, turned round and round in the embrace of men in bright uniforms. At the buffet, footmen in red swallow-tail coats and wearing shoes and knee-breeches, poured out champagne and served sweetmeats to the ladies. The "Sirdar's" [Vorontsov's] wife also, in spite of her age, went about half-dressed among the visitors smiling affably, and through the interpreter said a few amiable words to Hadji Murad who glanced at the visitors with the same indifference he had

---

[57] Morson, *Boundaries of Genre*, 113.

shown yesterday in the theater. After the hostess, other half-naked women came up to him and all of them stood shamelessly before him and smilingly asked him the same question: How he liked what he saw? Vorontsov himself, wearing gold epaulets and gold shoulder-knots with his white cross and ribbon at his neck, came up and asked him the same question, evidently feeling sure, like all the others, that Hadji Murad could not help being pleased at what he saw.[58]

When contrasted with this *poshlost'*-filled rogues' gallery (reminiscent in many ways of the crowd gathered at the mayor's party in Gogol's *Dead Souls*) Hadji Murad becomes even more virtuous in the eyes of the reader, especially since it is the very characters whom Tolstoy satirizes that provide any criticism of Hadji Murad in Tiflis. These comments function in the story as slanders rather than believable observations, given the power of Tolstoy's corrective narrator. Hadji Murad's measured reaction (he responds to Vorontsov's above question "as he had replied to them all, that among his people nothing of the kind was done, without expressing an opinion as to whether it was good or bad that it was so"[59]) to the shallow carnival that he witnesses in Tiflis is enough to make the reader sympathize with him in regard to the probity of such matters, a viewpoint that the moralistic older Tolstoy would almost certainly share.

The characters who sympathize with Hadji Murad, other than his henchmen, are those who are either excluded from or choose to depart from the usual behavior of elite Russian society. For example, the servant woman Mar'ia Vasilievna is a positive Tolstoyan character type, reminiscent in many ways of Princess Mary or Anisia Fyodorovna from *War and Peace*. Similarly, Butler is first presented as a shallow young officer but gains greater insight through his direct interaction with Hadji Murad and his men. This process is similar to the growth that Pierre Bezukhov undergoes in *War and Peace*, especially his epiphany in the wake of meeting Platon Karataev. The younger Vorontsov also has some admiration for Hadji Murad, although his social/military rank, and the direct relation to the corrupted/corrupting society into which this

---

[58] Tolstoy, *Hadji Murad*, 594–95.
[59] Tolstoy, *Hadji Murad*, 595.

rank places him, makes him largely unable and unwilling to accept Hadji Murad fully. Understanding of and sympathy with Hadji Murad are the moral measures by which characters are judged in this story. The characters who are changed for the better (i.e., those who believe what they experience in his presence, rather than believing what they hear through the grapevine about him) by their exposure to Hadji Murad are the ones Tolstoy wishes to extol. Not only are they pardoned by Tolstoy, insomuch as they are mostly spared his satirical lacerations,[60] but they serve as the carriers of the ideals that he wishes to celebrate.

Hadji Murad, in the end, is not a saint either. He is violent and war-like (albeit not in the same self-aggrandizing way that Napoleon is), somewhat inconstant in his allegiances, and even stubborn at times. However, his unswerving devotion to his family, his relative equanimity and his strong sense of ethics (perhaps different from Tolstoy's, but based on a much more solid philosophical foundation than the fluid and capricious allegiances of the Petersburg-style social circles) are all qualities that make him far superior in Tolstoy's value system to the array of dissembling and opportunistic characters who surround him.

Satire remains an integral part of Tolstoy's methodology over the course of the more than fifty years of his writing career, both because it allows him to deride particular historical figures and because it gives him a means (via antithetical comparison) through which he can exalt characters who embody the virtues he believes to be commendable. His satire is not allegorical or fabulist in the manner of Gogol. Tolstoy usually fits satire into the form of realistic Russian prose, rather than transcending the form in the way that the more figurative *Dead Souls* does. However, his satirical voice can be every bit as damning as Gogol's, if not necessarily in its intensity, then in its consistency and its effectiveness. While he does not present the reader with as grotesque or pathos-inspiring a character as Gogol's Akakii Akakievich or Chichikov, Tolstoy does create characters who receive as clearly stated

---

[60] Butler is briefly satirized before he meets Hadji Murad, but in a very gently reproachful manner. Again, the similarity between Tolstoy's characterization of Butler and that of Pierre Bezukhov and Natasha Rostova in *War and Peace* is unmistakable. All three are criticized for their youthful inexperience, but not savaged because of it—perhaps since it is unavoidable. The fact that they are capable of change from their errant (to Tolstoy) ways once presented with alternate "truths" is what separates and elevates them in the author's eyes.

a satirical commentary, albeit in measured doses over the course of an entire novel, novella or short story. Tolstoy then moves a step further (at least in his later works) to present an alternative to the objects of his satire, being unwilling simply to deride without suggesting his own improvements.

Jerzy Kolodziej

Literary Parody as an Instrument of Political Satire: Zamyatin's *We*

> Old paint on canvas, as it ages, sometimes becomes transparent. When that happens, it is possible, in some pictures, to see the original lines…. That is called pentimento…; the old conception, replaced by a later choice, is a way of seeing and then seeing again.
>
> Lillian Hellman, from the introduction to *Pentimento*

This essay begins with the assumptions that a text of a given culture emanates from the traditions (literary and non-literary) of that culture and that it is addressed to readers who share the author's underlying experience about the culture, including the culture's memory of the past. There are many indications that after 1917 the new regime wanted both to cut itself off from the past and, in creating a new order, to obliterate society's memory of its past. Evgenii Zamyatin was one of a number of writers who used that very past as a way of commenting on what was taking place in the present and of pointing out implications for the future. These writers counted on their readers to understand their texts, in part, as subtexts referring to concerns found in the literature of the past, primarily in the literature of the nineteenth century.

It is the case that Zamyatin, in other works published during the period when he was working on *We* (1920–21), was critical of and satirized the revolution's dogmatic aspects and its tendency toward an enforced uniformity. This is especially evident from his play *The Fires of Saint Dominic*, from his *Fairy Tales for Adults*, and from his bold, passionate, and precisely crafted articles such as "Scythians," "Tomorrow," and "I Am Afraid," which ridicule the regime's uncompromising unconcern for individual freedoms. His short stories "Mamai" and "The Cave" debunk

Janet Tucker, ed. *Against the Grain: Parody, Satire and Intertextuality in Russian Literature.* Bloomington, IN: Slavica, 2002, 81–99.

any attempt at utopia-building by evoking in modern man the base instincts of his primitive past.

   While Zamyatin was blunt with his criticism of the regime in his articles, and while his satire was quite transparent in his fairy tales, his thrusts at the present were more modulated in his short stories and in *We*. In his novel, Zamyatin reached across the chasm that appeared to separate the past from the present and reconnected the realities of his day to those of the culture's past. *We* is rooted in Russia's cultural tradition: it pointedly employs that tradition and, in continuing and adding to the tradition, it becomes a satirical attack on the policies of the new regime. Zamyatin's principal satirical tools in *We* are literary quotation and parody of texts that had, in the past, dealt with the themes of the State and the individual, the rational and the irrational, conformity and rebellion, and utopia and dystopia. By his use of the past, Zamyatin was able to express his concern with the problems of his day and to directly address contemporaries. One may view his appropriation of the past as an attempt to demonstrate a continuity between the present and the past—an attempt to pick out of the revolution's rubble those remnants of traditional literary values that the revolution was demolishing so hastily and with such élan to make way for its new cultural edifice.

   Read from a cultural perspective, *We* is encoded with multiple subtexts. One subtext relies for meaning specifically upon the anti-utopian tradition of Dostoevsky and smuggles in the past's arguments that utopia is unattainable. Another subtext, not unrelated to the general theme of dystopia, relies for its meaning on the more specific anti-utopian Petersburg theme from Russian literature. It is on Zamyatin's use of the Petersburg theme that I will focus here. In his article "On Language," Zamyatin speaks of the device of "omitted associations," where the reader "fills in" the omitted central idea, which is only hinted at. The author creates "only the spirit of the idea without materializing it in words."[1] In "The Psychology of Creative Work," Zamyatin writes: "Art functions pyramidically: all new achievements are based on the utilization of everything that has been accumulated below, at the foundations of the pyramid."[2]

---

[1] Mirra Ginsburg, ed. and trans., *A Soviet Heretic: Essays by Evgeny Zamyatin* (Chicago: The University of Chicago Press, 1970), 188.

[2] Ginsburg, *A Soviet Heretic*, 160.

By redeploying the Petersburg theme in a new context—the context of the new—Zamyatin invites his readers to reconnect the present to the severed past. In the Petersburg theme, the city came to embody the myth of a nation about itself. Petersburg became a cityscape and a cosmos in which the dichotomies of nature and the principles of (Western) reason were locked in a struggle, where spontaneous man was pitted against an ordered State. The city came to symbolize its creator, perceived simultaneously as both autocrat and revolutionary. Writers like Radishchev, Pushkin, Gogol, Dostoevsky, Bely, and Blok perceived the city as a symbol of such dualities as iron will and rebellion, order and chaos, certainty and contingency, and reality and dream.[3] However diverse their responses to Petersburg as a reflection of Western culture might have been, Russian writers of the nineteenth and twentieth centuries were united in their perception of Petersburg as a city founded on utopian principles, and their treatment of the Petersburg theme assumed an anti-utopian character.

One of the first Soviet novels, *We* falls squarely within the Petersburg tradition and is one of the first to treat the Petersburg theme. I want to identify those physical features of the One State that are at least suggestive of Petersburg; I also want to identify the specific items that Zamyatin appropriated from other works in the Petersburg tradition and to locate those items as themes within the tradition. My purpose is to show that the ultimately unappetizing One State is Petersburg, that the future *We* describes represents a satire of Zamyatin's present, and that the necessary failure of the One State is Zamyatin's prediction for the new regime. Understandably, the implications of Zamyatin's message were not acceptable. Presuming to have overturned, even to have expunged, the old codes of behavior, the new regime viewed *We* either as a retrograde attempt to reinstate old values or as at least a rejection of the entirely new, ultimate *system* of values. The novel was published in Russia long after Zamyatin's predicted revolution had come to pass.

The city of the One State, if we were to locate it geographically, lies somewhere in the northern latitudes. The narrator, in his disquisition on

---

[3] For a discussion of the Petersburg theme, see Michael Holquist, "St. Petersburg: From Utopian City to Gnostic Universe," *The Virginia Quarterly Review* 48, no. 4 (Fall 1972): 537–57.

the circularity of history, refers to "the northern lights of the One State."[4] Earlier, he refers to "white nights."[5] There are many allusions to water in the novel, including to the waves of the sea, harnessed for energy.[6] By implication, there must be a river in the city because in the 21st Entry the narrator uses the simile of ice breaking up on a river, although he has never been beyond the Green Wall. In addition, the city is located on canals spanned by hump-backed bridges, as the following passage makes clear: "Instead of turning left, I turned right. The bridge offered its obedient, slavishly bent back to the three of us.... The brightly-lit buildings on the other side scattered lights into the water."[7]

One of the earliest and most famous literary images of Petersburg can be found in the "Prologue" to Pushkin's "Bronze Horseman":

> We have been destined by nature here
> To break a window through to Europe,
> And to gain a firm stance by the sea…
> A century passed, and the young city,
> Was ornament and wonder of the northern lands,
> In granite was the Neva clad;
> Bridges hung above her waters;
> With dark-green gardens
> Are her islands covered,
> One dawn yields to another
> It hies, giving night half an hour
> To the golden heavens….
> Or, breaking up her cobalt ice,
> The Neva bears it to the sea
> And, scenting spring days, exults.[8]

---

[4] Yevgeny Zamyatin, *We*, trans. Mirra Ginsburg (New York: Bantam Books, 1972), 20th Entry. All references will be to this edition.

[5] Zamyatin, *We*, 10th Entry.

[6] Zamyatin, *We*, 12th Entry.

[7] Zamyatin, *We*, 32nd Entry.

[8] All references to "The Bronze Horseman" will be to A. S. Pushkin, *Sobranie sochinenii v desiati tomakh* (Moscow: Khudozhestvennaia literatura, 1960), 3: 284–300. All translations are mine.

Here we have all the elements Zamyatin alludes to in *We*: Petersburg's northern location, White Nights, the sea, the river, bridges, and ice breaking up on the Neva in the spring.

The Green Wall that encircles the city is made of "impregnable, eternal glass," as are streets, pavement, and buildings. The narrator says of the Green Wall: "I cannot imagine a city that is not clad (*ne odetyi*) in a Green Wall." If one recalls Pushkin's line quoted above ("v granit odelasia Neva"—"in granite was the Neva clad"), one may suspect a connection between granite embankments of the Neva and the fittingly equivalent building material of the future utopia—eternal glass. The Green Wall, like the granite embankments restraining the unruly Neva, acts as a barrier against the irrational. That Zamyatin is, in fact, drawing such a parallel is supported by the water imagery used by the narrator to describe the elemental and irrational that lie beyond the Green Wall:

> From the illimitable green ocean behind the Wall rose a wild wave of roots, flowers, branches, leaves. It reared, and in a moment it would roll and break and overwhelm me—and instead of a man—the finest and most precise of instruments—I would be turned into…. But fortunately between me and the wild green ocean was the glass of the Wall. Oh, great, divinely bounding wisdom of walls and barriers! … The Green Wall … isolated our perfect mechanical world from the irrational….[9]

Elsewhere, Zamyatin quite clearly alludes to Pushkin's "The Bronze Horseman," which describes a catastrophic flood. Dimly suspecting the presence of the irrational within himself—an irrationality that might portend future calamities—the narrator states: "But this is absurd. This really should be stricken out: we have channeled all elemental forces [nami vvedeny v ruslo vse stikhii]—there can be no catastrophes."[10]

In "The Bronze Horseman" Pushkin writes:

Krasuisia, grad Petrov, i stoi
Nekolebimo, kak Rossiia,
Da umiritsia zhe s toboi
I pobezhdennaia stikhiia

---

[9] Zamyatin, *We*, 17th Entry.

[10] Zamyatin, *We*, 5th Entry.

Stand, city of Peter, in splendor
Unshakeable, like Russia,
And let the vanquished elements too
Make their peace with thee.

The "vanquished elements" have been interpreted by Russian literary
criticism as representing not only the untamed forces of nature but also
as symbolizing the human element, the revolutionaries who struggled
with tsarism.[11]

In *Petersburg*, written nearly one hundred years after "The Bronze
Horseman," Andrei Bely elaborates on the opposition of the rational
and the irrational, of culture and non-culture, and he gives the
"elements" a human aspect. On the one hand stands Peter the Great,
the city that he founded, and the Russian state—on the other, the Neva
and the unruly human element beyond it. The opposition is between the
institutional city proper as embodied in Apollon Apollonovich
Ableukhov's rational aspect and the islands across the Neva, from which
the revolutionary, Dudkin, emerges bearing a bomb.

Senator Ableukhov traces his lineage to Peter's passion for reason
and order that found its dogmatic expression in the latter part of the
nineteenth century in the rabidly nationalistic and rigidly bureaucratic
order of Pobedonostsev, the procurator of the Holy Synod, with whom
Ableukhov is associated in Bely's novel. As such, he represents what
Bely calls the "rectilineal principle." His vision is that

> ... the network of parallel prospects, intersected by a network of
> prospects, should expand into the abysses of the universe in
> planes of squares and cubes: one square per "solid citizen"....
> After the line, the figure which soothed him more than all other
> symmetries was the square. At times, for hours on end, he would
> lapse into an unthinking contemplation of pyramids, triangles,
> parallelepipeds, cubes and trapezoids.[12]

Ableukhov's vision is realized in the One State, which D-503 describes
as having "... straight, immutable streets, the glittering glass of the

---

[11] Ivanov-Razumnik, "Petersburg," *Vershiny* (Petrograd: Kolos, 1923), 167–68.

[12] Andrey Bely, *Petersburg*, trans. Robert A. Maguire and John E. Malmstad
(Bloomington: Indiana University Press, 1978), 11.

pavements, the divine parallelepipeds of the transparent houses, the square harmony of the gray-blue ranks."[13] And, in fact, just as the city of the One State is Petersburg projected into the future, so also the narrator is clearly a direct descendant of Ableukhov and his "rectilineal principle." He exclaims in a Euclidean frenzy: "Yes, to integrate the grandiose cosmic equation. Yes, to unbend the wild, primitive curve and straighten it to a tangent—an asymptote—a straight line. For the line of the One State is the straight line."[14] And later he speaks of "the beauty of the square, the cube, the straight line."[15]

But both Ableukhov and the narrator of *We* are carriers of a non-Euclidean dimension as well. For the Senator, it is "cerebral play"—images, that, once created, "become incarnate in this spectral world."[16] It is in this fourth dimension, in what Bely calls "yellowish spaces," that the irrational Mongolian blood lineage resides and where Russia's (Eastern) past is locked in a struggle with its (Western) future. The function of waking reason, of the passion for order, is merely to cover, to suppress the raging chaos underneath. Or, as the narrator in *We* puts it, using imagery appropriate to his station:

> ... all of us on earth walk constantly over a seething, scarlet sea of flame, hidden below, in the belly of the earth. We never think of it. But what if this thin crust under our feet should turn into glass and we should suddenly see....[17]

What he sees is the split inside himself: one half is the former "number D-503"; the other is the irrational square root of minus one and the hairy-pawed madman from Russia's past. Once unchained, like Ableukhov, he has access to the realm of cerebral play, and he "creates" the very embodiment of chaos and revolution, I-330. He becomes, like Ableukhov's son Nikolai—who also contains his father's duality—and like Pushkin's Evgenii, a potential parricide when he raises his hand against the authoritarian Benefactor. Like Dudkin and Nikolai, he is a reluctant, vacillating revolutionary who ultimately decides to destroy

---

[13] Zamyatin, *We*, 2nd Entry.

[14] Zamyatin, *We*, 1st Entry.

[15] Zamyatin, *We*, 4th Entry.

[16] Bely, *Petersburg*, 20.

[17] Zamyatin, *We*, 10th Entry.

the One State with the spaceship Integral. He is also a metaphoric time
bomb smuggled in from Bely's *Petersburg* as he hears himself "ticking
like a clock."[18] In a later Entry he states: "The pulse of my recent days
had grown ever drier, ever faster, ever more tense; the poles came ever
closer—a dry crackling—another millimeter: explosion, then—
silence."[19]

Apollon Apollonovich despises and fears the islands with their
"coarse human swarm" (*roi liudskoi*). His reincarnation, D-503, experiences similar feelings when he sees a beast or Mephi through the Green
Wall: "Through the glass the blunt snout of some beast stared dully,
mistily at me; yellow eyes, persistently repeating a single, incomprehensible thought."[20] In *Petersburg*, this swarm, "neither people nor shadows," has settled on the "boundaries of two worlds alien to one another." To Apollon Apollonovich (and to Bely in the first "Sirin" edition—1913–14) it appears that this "inhabitant of chaos is threatening
the capital of the Empire like the incoming clouds." Therefore, Apollon
Apollonovich would subject the islands to his "rectilinear principle":
"The islands must be crushed! Riveted with the iron of the enormous
bridge, skewered by the arrows of the prospects...."[21]

The characters of *Petersburg* have good reason to fear the irrational
because it is already there in the city and inside them. This is true not
only of Dudkin, who is being blown apart by it internally, and of the
anti-Kantian side of Nikolai Apollonovich, but also of Apollon
Apollonovich in the form of his "second space."[22] Indeed, how could the
irrational *not* already reside in them if it is one of the two aspects of
Peter himself—Peter as revolutionary—and if they are Peter's offspring:
"son" (synok), he calls Dudkin.

---

[18] Zamyatin, *We*, 19th Entry.

[19] Zamyatin, *We*, 20th Entry.

[20] Zamyatin, *We*, 17th Entry.

[21] Andrey Bely, *Petersburg* (Letchworth, England: Bradda Books reprint,
1967), 13–14. Further references to *Petersburg* will be to this (1916) edition,
which in unchanged form follows the 1913–14 "Sirin" text reviewed by
Zamyatin. Whenever there was an overlap of text, I used the excellent
Maguire/Malmstad translation, based on the altered Berlin edition of 1922.

[22] Bely, *Petersburg*, 149–54.

Zamyatin's integration into *We* of Bely's reworking of the Petersburg theme is of greater magnitude than his parody of other works dealing with the theme. This should not be surprising since Bely as novelist is Zamyatin's immediate predecessor and subsumes (potentially) within the scope of his novel any and all other works on this theme. In addition, unlike earlier writers, both Zamyatin and Bely deal explicitly with revolution; they extend the dimensions of the Petersburg theme in the realm of *active* revolt. Zamyatin specifically incorporates into his own work Bely's identification of the "islands" and, by extension, the rest of Russia as the element that threatens the stability of Peter's rationally conceived dream.

The Ancient House in *We*, preserved by the One State as a museum of nineteenth- and twentieth-century culture, is the most pervasive symbol of the past and plays a central role in the novel's plot—in both senses of the word: "The starting point of all the coordinates in this entire story is, of course, the Ancient House. It is the center of the axial lines of all the Xs, Ys, and Zs on which my whole world has been built of late."[23] It is here that D-503 experiences a personal liberation, and it is from here that plans are being made to overthrow the One State. Connecting the rational world of the State with the world of the Mephi (the remnants of the past), the function of the Ancient House is liminal. On a symbolic plane, it links the future with the reader's present. The Ancient House, with its "dark red walls," is located by the Green Wall and could represent one of the numerous palaces on the "Palace Embankment" facing on the Neva. But it refers, most probably, to the Winter Palace. Such a supposition is supported by the fact that the Winter Palace was, from at least 1905, painted a dark red color and remained so until at least 1928.[24] By a proclamation of the Soviet government in 1918, the Winter Palace and the whole complex of buildings including the Hermitage were declared a national museum. The Winter Palace was renamed the Palace of Art; one part was given over to the State Hermitage and the rest was occupied by the Museum of the Revolution. By a separate entrance, visitors were admitted to a part of the former Winter Palace which, like the Ancient House, was preserved

---

[23] Zamyatin, *We*, 17th Entry.

[24] Alexander Rado, *A Guide-Book to the Soviet Union* (New York: International Publishers Co., 1928), 231.

as an "historical memorial"[25] and contained the royal apartments of
Nicholas I, Alexander II, and Nicholas II.

A comparison of the royal apartments with the apartments of the
Ancient House reveals striking similarities. To reach the apartments in
the Ancient House, the narrator and I-330 ascend a "dark broad staircase" and cross room after room, the contents of which overwhelm D-
503 (much like I-330's music and the world of the Mcphi) by their wild
"riot of colors and forms." He describes them in part as follows:

> A white flat area above; dark blue walls; red, green and orange
> bindings of ancient books; yellow bronze chandeliers, a statue of
> Buddha; furniture built along lines convulsed in epilepsy…. Then
> more rooms, glimmering mirrors, somber wardrobes, intolerably
> gaudy sofas, a huge "fireplace," a large mahogany bed.[26]

There is, in addition, mention of a washstand, a bust of Pushkin "smiling
faintly," and a bronze, smiling statue of Buddha, which appears again in
a dream[27] with sap (later described as "golden-pink") flowing from its
eyes.

A guide-book from Zamyatin's day also gives a room-by-room description of the Tsar's and Tsarina's private living quarters. We find cat-
alogued here libraries, drawing rooms, bedrooms, and dressing rooms
appointed in rococo, baroque, and classical styles. There are chande-
liers, beds, wardrobes, and other furniture in the ornate Louis XV and
Louis XVI manner. In Alexander II's dressing room, there were
"bronze figures of Zhukovsky and Schiller." There was also a "beautiful
washing-basin" in Nicholas II's bathroom and, in his study, "[b]ehind
the sofa on a shelf, [stood] a ruby-eyed nephrite image of Buddha."[28]
We may be even more certain that Zamyatin specifically refers to the
discredited past and to the Winter Palace/Palace of Art from references
in the 6th Entry that explicitly point to the royalty of the personages
who had inhabited the apartments of the Ancient House. Thus, D-503
alludes to the grand piano as the "'royal' musical instrument"
(korolevskii) and, referring to the statue of Pushkin (and indirectly to

[25] Rado, *Guidebook*, 232.
[26] Zamyatin, *We*, 6th Entry.
[27] Zamyatin, *We*, 7th Entry.
[28] Rado, *Guidebook*, 233–34.

Nicholas I), I-330 states: "These poets were masters far more powerful than their crowned kings" ("posil'nee ikh koronovannykh").

Any discussion of Petersburg or the Petersburg theme would be incomplete without mention of the main avenue of the former capital, the famed Nevsky Prospect. To Petersburg, as Gogol notes in his story "Nevsky Prospect," "it is everything,"[29] and he proceeds to describe the frenzied activity and the precise choreography of the avenue—this main center of communication and microcosm of the society—from dusk until dawn. Gogol's *tour de force* describes the hustle and bustle of Nevsky— the rapidly passing phantasmagoria of color, the sheer variety of dress and people, their conversations, the slender and narrow waists of the women for whom, "upon meeting, you step aside so that you don't nudge them with a discourteous elbow," their smiles, which "can make you feel higher than the spire of the Admiralty," the "strange characters" and "inscrutable types" one may chance to meet and, of course, among other wares in this human display, "a lovely Grecian nose."[30] In the city of the One State, the main avenue, or Prospect as the narrator calls it, bears seemingly little resemblance to Nevsky Prospect:

> The numbers walked in even ranks, four abreast, ecstatically stepping in time to the music, hundreds, thousands of numbers, in pale blue unifs, ... Everything made of some single, radiant, smiling substance ... the straight, immutable streets, the glittering glass of the pavements, the divine parallelepipeds of the transparent houses, the square harmony of the blue ranks[31]

The contrast between Gogol's Nevsky and the narrator's description above is so stark that it evokes a comparison in contrasts from D-503. Reflecting on the harmony of the spectacle before him, D-503 feels himself to be its creator and a conqueror of the "old God and old life":

> I was like a tower, I dared not move an elbow lest walls, cupolas, machines tumble in fragments about me.... I remembered (evidently an association by contrast)—I suddenly remembered a

---

[29] Nikolai Gogol, "Nevskii Prospekt," *Sobranie sochinenii v semi tomakh* (Moscow: Khudozhestvennaia literatura, 1960), 3: 7. All references to Gogol will be to this volume.

[30] Gogol, "Nevskii Prospekt," 10–11.

[31] Zamyatin, *We*, 2nd Entry.

picture I had seen in a museum: one of their prospects, out of the twentieth century, dazzlingly motley, a teeming crush of people, wheels, animals, posters, trees, color.[32]

The narrator as a tower, not daring to move an elbow, alludes to Gogol's feminine "smiles" that "make you feel higher than the spire of the Admiralty."[33] It is also a sly reference to Zamyatin's own essay "Paradise," where he satirizes the tendency in post-revolutionary poetry to refer to heroes of the revolution as "Giants," "Titans," and "Colossi."[34]

D-503's thoughts about the "impassable abyss between the present and the past" produce his own laughter, which is suddenly echoed by the mocking laughter of I-330. This "strange" and "inscrutable" woman implants the worm of doubt into D-503's consciousness about the great contrasts with the past that he seems to perceive. Echoing his earlier thoughts about military parades, she tells him that a bridge can be thrown across the abyss of contrasts, between their present and the past—a past that also had its forms of regimentation in "drums, battalions, ranks." Her comments also make D-503 painfully aware of the great physical dissimilarities between the round O-90, the whip-like I-330, the grotesquely, Gogolesquely S-shaped S-4711, the atavistically shaggy hands of D-503 himself, and the suggestive (since the time of Gogol) differences in the shapes of noses.

Besides its sunny, diurnal aspect, Nevsky Prospect has its nocturnal manifestation as well when, as Gogol writes, "long shadows flicker on the walls and streets."[35] Gogol's "Nevsky Prospect" develops a central motif in the Petersburg theme: the dualities of appearance and reality—"the eternal strife between dream and substantiality":[36] "Oh, do not trust this Nevsky Prospect! ... All is delusion, all is a dream, not what it appears to be! It lies all the time, but most of all [at night] ... when the devil himself lights the street lamps for the sole purpose of showing ev-

---

[32] Zamyatin, *We*, 2nd Entry.

[33] Gogol, "Nevskii Prospekt," 11.

[34] Ginsburg, *A Soviet Heretic*, 61.

[35] Gogol, "Nevskii Prospekt," 13.

[36] Gogol, "Nevskii Prospekt," 28.

erything in its unnatural guise."[37] In works dealing with the Petersburg theme, the battleground of strife between dream and reality is the protagonist's mind. Most often it receives its written expression in the "most alienated form of discourse": a diary or notes.[38] Its physical manifestation is the frenzied, contradictory and self-canceling behavior of the protagonist or the narrator, and the consequences are almost always disastrous: madness, suicide, or death, physical or spiritual. The context in which strife between these two forces takes place are the streets of Petersburg, which are simultaneously a microcosm of Russia and a reflection of the protagonist's state of mind.

Often the catalyst for such mental peregrinations and sheer physical torture is a woman. But this woman is also a manifestation of Nevsky Prospect, and Gogol's admonition must be heeded: "But may God preserve you from peeping under the ladies' hats!"[39]—or from looking at their badges or engaging them in conversations about the length of noses, one might add. Certainly Gogol's exhortation applies to the "childish and simple-hearted."[40] Piskarev discovers that the angelic aspect of a woman "who, it seemed, flew down from heaven straight onto Nevsky Prospect,"[41] may perfidiously turn into the demonic: "Accompanied by loud laughter she was flung into the abyss by some terrifying will of a fiendish spirit thirsting to destroy the harmony of life."[42] Piskarev shares the fate of Evgenii from "The Bronze Horseman." He also sets the pattern for Gogol's mad diarist, for Dostoevsky's underground diarist, "doubles," and other characters who have difficulty reconciling reality with appearance, for Bely's Nikolai Apollonovich, Apollon Apollonovich, and Dudkin, and for Blok's protagonists—and possibly for Blok himself. The pattern is there as well in *We*.

---

[37] Gogol, "Nevskii Prospekt," 44.

[38] Michael Holquist, *Dostoevsky and the Novel* (Princeton: Princeton University Press, 1977; reprint Evanston, IL: Northwestern University Press, 1986), 26.

[39] Gogol, "Nevskii Prospekt," 44.

[40] Gogol, "Nevskii Prospekt," 31.

[41] Gogol, "Nevskii Prospekt," 14.

[42] Gogol, "Nevskii Prospekt," 20.

The outward manifestations of inner discord, of the impossibility of joining the object and its idea into a harmonious whole, produce the kind of response we observe in Piskarev after he meets his beauty on the Nevsky. Rejecting reality, he gives himself up to the world of dreams: "The annoying light with its dreary, unpleasant glow peered into his windows. His room was in such a gray, dull disorder.... Oh, how disgusting was reality. How could it even be compared to dreams."[43] Like his literary progeny, including D-503, Piskarev suffers in the world of tangible reality. His already fragile self is shattered when his "angel" from Nevsky mocks with demonic laughter his plan to provide her with respectability. The laughter also leads Piskarev into lunacy:

> Oh, this was simply too much! It was more than he could endure, and he rushed out of the room.... His mind clouded over. He wandered around all day stupidly and aimlessly: without seeing, without hearing, and without feeling anything.[44]

Like Evgenii, Piskarev loses his senses one by one. But Piskarev's fate was determined from the moment when the beauty from Nevsky smiled at him, and he followed her "without hearing, without seeing, without comprehending."[45] He ends his life by slashing his throat. Thus neither the world of waking reality nor the world of dreams provides harmony for the denizens of Nevsky. Both aspects are too extreme to submit to a bridging into a harmonious synthesis. They can only find the unity they seek, as their authors suspected all along, in "notime" and "nowhere"— only in uchronia or in utopia, only in death.

In contrast to Piskarev and other characters in Russian literature, D-503 has seemingly achieved perfect integration within himself and with his society. Unlike his predecessors, he has been able to do so in the beneficent milieu of a society that no longer poses the question of "dream or reality" (*son ili iav*). The narrator feels "fused into a single, million-handed body" and like a "hero of a mighty epic poem";[46] he is a "part of a great, powerful, single entity,"[47] even a creator. But the

---

[43] Gogol, "Nevskii Prospekt," 26.

[44] Gogol, "Nevskii Prospekt," 31.

[45] Gogol, "Nevskii Prospekt," 16–17.

[46] Zamyatin, *We*, 3rd Entry.

[47] Zamyatin, *We*, 7th Entry.

narrator's sense of integration is not to last. I-330's "demonic" laughter on the Nevsky Prospect of the One State violently jolts him out of his equilibrium. She destroys his "harmony of life" and consigns him to the hellish realm where reality and dreams lie intertwined—to the febrile night side of Petersburg. She reunites him with his lost past, the hovering presence of which had always disturbed him and which was symbolized by the square root of minus one. It is this repressed, irrational aspect of himself, once tapped or unleashed by a woman, that ultimately dooms him as it doomed Piskarev, Gogol's mad diarist, Dostoevsky's Underground Man, and Bely's Nikolai Apollonovich.

The effect that women, shadowy animas conducting the protagonist both to ecstasy and to the dark realms of the self, had on all such characters is similar. Piskarev, for example,

> ... held his breath and everything in him quivered, all of his feelings were ablaze and everything before him was covered by a mist; the pavement seemed to be heaving under him, carriages with trotting horses seemed to be immobile; the bridge became attenuated and was breaking in the arch, a house stood upside down, a sentry box reeled towards him, and the sentry's halberd, together with the gold letters of a signboard and the scissors painted on it, seemed to be flashing across the very lashes of his eyes.[48]

While they do not have the same psychedelic intensity as Gogol's description above, two descriptions of D-503's reaction to I-330 clearly recall Gogol's story:

> There were no longer any boundaries between sky and earth; everything was flying, melting, falling—nothing to get a hold of. No more houses ... the dark figures inside the houses were like particles suspended in a milky, nightmare solution....[49]
>
> In the smooth glass of the pavement, as in water, I see gleaming walls suspended upside down, and myself hung mockingly head down, feet up.[50]

---

[48] Gogol, "Nevskii Prospekt," 16.
[49] Zamyatin, *We*, 13th Entry.
[50] Zamyatin, *We*, 6th Entry.

Like Dostoevsky's Golyadkin, D-503 begins to doubt his real self and
concludes that there are two of him. From this point on, one part of the
narrator ceases to live in the "utopia" of the One State and begins a
separate existence in the "unreal city" of Petersburg.

Not only does Peter's city, constructed on an "idea," on Finnish mud
and water, have a questionable ontological status, but the shadowy existence or non-existence of Petersburg's denizens may depend on someone's dream, as Dostoevsky suggests in *The Raw Youth*: "They all rush
and dash about, and how can it be known that all this isn't someone's
dream and that not a single person or activity here is genuine and
real."[51] Bely extends this image in his *Petersburg*, where being or non-
being is dependent solely (solipsistically) on "unnecessary, idle, cerebral
play." Thus, Bely states, Apollon Apollonovich "creates" his house, his
son, and the stranger, Dudkin. But his consciousness also has a shadowy
existence because Apollon Apollonovich is, in turn, "the fruit of the
author's fantasy."[52] In *We*, once the narrator has registered the
Petersburg hero's essential complaint "I no longer knew what was
dream and what reality" ("chto son—chto iav'"),[53] as the author of a
"fantastic adventure novel" and by virtue of his "author's obligation,"[54]
he can also aspire to the role of a creator. However ephemerally, he can,
like Gogol's madman, Dostoevsky's Underground Man, and Bely as
author, attempt to regain control of his destiny and the destinies of
others through the re-creational medium of writing: "What if all of them
are only my shadows? Was it not I who populated with them all these
pages—just recently no more than white rectangular deserts? Without
me would they ever be seen by those whom I lead behind me along the
narrow paths of lines? Naturally I said nothing.... From my own
experience I know that the cruelest thing is to make a person doubt his
own reality...."[55]

Yet even this burst of creative ego cannot silence the emptiness and
sense of loss that, like Evgenii and his literary descendants, the narrator
feels in his separation from his beloved and from the State: "Numbers

---

[51] Cited in Ivanov-Razumnik, "Petersburg," 166.

[52] Bely, *Petersburg*, 35–36.

[53] Zamyatin, *We*, 18th Entry.

[54] Zamyatin, *We*, 18th Entry.

[55] Zamyatin, *We*, 21st Entry.

marched past me, row after row.... And only I was alone, cast out by a storm upon a desert island."[56] As happens with Evgenii and with Piskarev, who "wanders around all day stupidly and aimlessly," the narrator's sense of time has become monochronic, his perceptions monochromatic. While once he marched in time to the music of the One State, now, like his literary predecessors, he is out of step with time itself.

In his alienation from society, he has become literally disembodied—cut off from the body social. Like the Underground Man, he "lived apart from everyone, alone behind a soft wall that muted outside sounds."[57] He even takes on the proportions of Gogol's nose, which inexplicably disappeared from its owner's face and unnaturally assumed a separate identity on Petersburg's Nevsky Prospect: "I was alone.... It was essentially an unnatural sight: imagine a human finger cut off from the whole, from the hand—a separate human finger, running, stooped, and bobbing up and down along the glass pavement. I was that finger. And the strangest, the most unnatural thing of all was that the finger had no desire whatever to be on the hand, to be with others."[58] Ultimately D-503 falls into the final stages of the Petersburg hero's illness—the paranoid delusion that he is being followed: "And I run, I run faster and faster and feel with my back—my shadow runs faster behind me, and there is no escape, no escape anywhere."[59] Whereas Evgenii had the illusion that he was being pursued by the Bronze Horseman—that symbol of rectilineal, authoritarian Petersburg—D-503, like the characters in Bely's *Petersburg*, is followed by a shadow—metaphorically the shadow of his guilt, physically the real shadow of S-4711. The Guardian, S-4711, is a representative of the Benefactor-Lenin figure who, in turn, is the most recent and satirical manifestation of the authoritarian Peter Principle. The final irony is that, ultimately, the shadowy S-4711 represents the other aspect of Peter—that of a revolutionary.

---

[56] Zamyatin, *We*, 16th Entry.

[57] Zamyatin, *We*, 18th Entry.

[58] Zamyatin, *We*, 18th Entry.

[59] Zamyatin, *We*, 16th Entry.

In his 1921 article "Paradise," expressing his alarm at the "granite foundation of monophony" in Russian literature of the post-revolutionary period, Zamyatin wrote:

> In polyphony there is always the danger of cacophony.... There shall be no more polyphony or dissonances. There shall be only majestic, monumental, all-encompassing unanimity.... The cunning bringer of dissonance, the teacher of doubt, Satan, has been forever banished from the shining mansions. All we hear now are the voices of angels, and the rejoicing of kettledrums and bells, of hail and glory and hosanna.[60]

It is this cunning Satan, this necessary evil, that Zamyatin as Creator reintroduces from pre-revolutionary times into the shining mansions of the promised paradise in order to right the balance. His Satan reestablishes the dissonances of a dualistic universe and triumphantly unleashes the untamed elements of cacophony into the monism of the emerging State. D-503's spaceship, which was to transport his diary with its message of perfect happiness, reintersects instead the planes of the Earth and of Soviet Russia; and it repopulates the parallel streets of Petersburg with the usual suspects.

In Zamyatin's conception, history is cyclical. Ultimately, the society of the future duplicates the experience of the nineteenth- and early twentieth-century Petersburg types. We find in *We* the same sense of confusion between appearance and reality, the same fog and shadows, "doubles," government officials and spies, poets, parricides, and underground men, all longing for unity. In the end, the society of the future, having attempted to impose on its citizens happiness and equality—happiness as equality—and unable to resolve the contradictory pull of necessity and choice, just as its earlier manifestation did, turns to revolution.

By so insistently invoking both the physical features and literary tradition of Petersburg, Zamyatin provides a counterargument to the new regime's obsession with the material and rational, to its insistence on social leveling, to its arrogant exclusion of other points of view, and to its "scientific" claim to be the final social system. For Zamyatin, a fully and finally consensual society is not possible: there is no final revo-

---

[60] Ginsburg, *A Soviet Heretic*, 59.

lution. Zamyatin's recontextualization of the anti-utopian Petersburg theme argues once again that the irrational core in man will persist; the nocturnal guise of Petersburg will continue its underground existence whether it is faced with granite, is housed in a Crystal Palace, or finds itself isolated by a wall of eternal glass. In their eagerness to re-engineer social relations and their product, the human soul, the new regime's inventors were certainly not eager to hear this message; like his narrator, Zamyatin took pains to "carefully coat" his illicit message with the "thick syrup of adventure."[61]

---

[61] Zamyatin, *We*, 18th Entry.

Six

Janet Tucker

Skaz and Oral Usage as Satirical Devices
in Isaak Babel's *Red Cavalry**

Given the density and intricacy of his short-story collection *Red Cavalry*, justifiably regarded as one of the great prose works of twentieth-
century Russian literature, Isaak Babel is notoriously difficult to pin
down. Even the briefest of his tales masterfully develops the subject
central to all of them: the violence inherent in the October Revolution
and the Civil War that followed it. No writer explores this theme more
cogently than Babel. There is no single element in his stories that more
strikingly underscores the horror of this violence than Babel's use of
skaz and images from the folktale.

Babel's employment of *skaz*, coupled with his references to oral literature, reminds us that he is writing about semi- or illiterate people
who are still immersed in traditional culture. The very word *skaz*, from
skazat' ('to say' or 'to tell') suggests oral usage, which itself can variously encompass oral folk narrative (typically, in folktales, in prose) or
can appear as the speech of a semi- or uneducated narrator quoted by
the actual author.[1] Oral usage incorporates the epithets, turns of phrase,
and images typically encountered in Russian oral literature, whether
heroic tales or *skazki* (folktales or fairy tales); for reasons of space, only
skazki will be considered here. Since no discussion of *skazki* would be

---

* The present essay is based on a paper presented at a panel on satire and parody in Russian literature, at the annual meeting of the American Association
for the Advancement of Slavic Studies, Boca Raton, Florida, in September
1998. I would like to thank Professor Karen Ryan for graciously inviting me to
be on that panel. Dr. Joyce Story from Glendale Community College provided
many helpful comments. The insightful observations of Professor Anna
Brodsky of Washington and Lee University improved this essay immeasurably.
This essay appeared earlier in *Canadian-American Slavic Studies* 34, no. 2
(Summer 2000): 201–10, and is reproduced here with their gracious permission.

[1] Hugh McLean, "Skaz," in *Handbook of Russian Literature*, ed. Victor Terras
(New Haven: Yale University Press, 1985), 420.

Janet Tucker, ed. *Against the Grain: Parody, Satire and Intertextuality in Russian
Literature.* Bloomington, IN: Slavica, 2002, 101–12.

complete without consulting Vladimir Propp's *Morphology of the Folktale*, that work will also figure in my analysis. Propp considers the actions/functions of characters in the *skazki* to be the central element, the key to understanding these tales.[2] The purpose of this essay is to pinpoint examples of *skaz* and oral motifs in Babel, to attempt to discover his reasons for incorporating these motifs, and to discuss them as parodic/satirical devices.[3]

Skaz figures prominently in two *Red Cavalry* stories: "Pis'mo" ("The Letter") and "Sol'" ("Salt").[4] In the first, Babel's narrator Liutov reproduces for his readers a letter dictated by the youngest son of a family in which, in a microcosmic version of the Civil War, the father has killed one of three brothers and is in turned executed by another. Sub- or non-standard forms abound, emphasizing the oral or traditional orientation of this tale: *Ia est'* for 'I am', *zdesia* instead of *zdes'* for 'here', *prosiu* for *proshu* (I ask, request).[5] So does the traditional discourse associated with the *skazka*: "A takzhe nizhaiushche vam kla-niaius' ot bela litsa do syroi zemli…" (And likewise do I bow down low to you from my white face to the damp earth, with *mat' syra zemlia*— "Mother Damp Earth"—understood here; "Pis'mo," 12).

In "Sol'," the narrator Balmashev repeatedly says *Raseia* (Russia) instead of the standard literary form *Rossiia* ("Sol'," 97), *anteresnoe* (interesting, odd) rather than *interesnoe* ("Sol'," 97), *prosiut* for *prosiat* (to request, ask for) ("Sol'," 98). The *skazka* surfaces linguistically

---

[2] V. Ia. Propp, *Morfologiia skazki*, 2nd ed. (Moscow: Nauka, 1969), 24–28.

[3] Victor Erlich notes that Propp's *Morfologiia skazki* was originally published in Leningrad in 1928. Victor Erlich, *Russian Formalism: History – Doctrine*, 3rd ed. (New Haven: Yale University Press, 1981), 29 n. That publication of *Morfologiia skazki* postdated the appearance of Babel''s *Konarmiia* has no bearing on Babel''s own undoubted familiarity with the collection of A. N. Afanas'ev (1826–71). For information on Afanas'ev's career and publications, see Yu. M. Sokolov, *Russian Folklore*, trans. Catherine Ruth Smith (Hatboro, PA: Folklore Associates, 1966), 69, 70 n, 71–74, *passim*.

[4] There is even a story called "Salt" (#242) in Afanas'ev's collection. A. N. Afanas'ev, *Narodnye russkie skazki v trekh tomakh* (Moscow, Goslitizdat, 1938), 2: 341–44.

[5] "Pis'mo," Isaak Babel', *Konarmiia*, 3rd ed. (Moscow: Gosudarstvennoe izda-tel'stvo, 1928; reprint London: Flegon Press, n.d.), 12–13. Further references to Babel''s stories will be in the text.

rather than situationally in the introduction of Balmashev's letter to the "comrade editor": "za trideviat' zemel', v nekotorom gosudarstve, na nevedomom prostranstve" (beyond the thrice-ninth land, in a certain country, in an unknown place). ("Sol'," 94).[6] This pattern would be right at home in Afanas'ev's collection; in "Ivan Bykovich," the formula is: "V nekotorom tsarstve, v nekotorom gosudarstve, zhil-byl tsar' s tsaritseiu" (In a certain kingdom, in a certain country, there dwelled a tsar' with a tsaritsa).[7] Balmashev recites the story teller's typical formulaic hint at a reward for his/her efforts, but with a twist: in "ia tam byl, med pil, usy obmochil, v rot ne zaskochil" (I was there, drank mead, wet my mustache, didn't jump into my mouth), the mead becomes *samogonpivo* (home-brewed beer) ("Sol'," 94). Such banal transformational lowering of the original folk pattern reappears throughout the story.[8]

In each story, sub-standard locution and—even more strikingly—the language of the folktale are combined with the most appalling event of all: killing. Murder within the family context makes "The Letter" especially horrific. In "Salt," the "stain" that Balmashev wipes out is a woman smuggling salt, crucial in the smelting of steel and hence for the war effort ("Sol'," 98). Her salt disguised in swaddling clothes is, of course, no infant, but, because the reader sees her initially with a bundle disguised as a baby, she still bears the imprint of mother. She could be *any* mother, and mothers still command respect, which is why she has not been raped after a night of riding in a train car full of soldiers; hence, Balmashev seems to have committed matricide. The image of "mother," which links "The Letter" with "Salt," has folkloric as well as

---

[6] For an excellent examination of the Ukrainianisms, southern Russianisms, Oddessisms, and Yiddishisms in Babel, see Efraim Sicher, *Style and Structure in the Prose of Isaak Babel'* (Columbus, OH: Slavica Publishers, 1986), 72–79. Maurice Friedberg's "Yiddish Folklore Motifs in Isaak Babel's *Konarmija*" (in *Modern Critical Views*, ed. Harold Bloom [New York: Chelsea House Publishers, 1987], 191–98) contains a fine discussion of Babel''s treatment of the Hasidim.

[7] "Ivan Bykovich," A. N. Afanas'ev, *Narodnye russkie skazki v trekh tomakh* (Moscow: Gosudarstvennoe izdatel'stvo khudozhestvennoi literatury, 1957), 1: 278.

[8] Nor should we forget that the imperfective of *zaskochit'* (to jump) is *zaskakivat'*, related to *skakat'* (to gallop). Even where no horses appear *physically*, they are present *etymologically*.

societal and familial overtones. In "Vasilisa prekrasnaia" ("Vasilisa the Beautiful"), for example, Vasilisa's dying mother gives her a doll, a magical agent, that saves Vasilisa in her moments of greatest need and even seems, in dispensing wisdom to Vasilisa ("the morning is wiser than the evening"), to take her mother's place.[9]

What sort of impression does this nexus of the language of traditional culture plus savagery produce in Babel's reader? We know that these people have not lost all their values. In "The Letter," the young Kudriukov respectfully addresses his mother as Evdokiia Fedorovna and bows to the "damp earth" before her, conflating his own mother with the folk image of "Mother Damp Earth" (*mat' syra zemlia*). One assumes that he is not merely taking advantage of their relationship to get her to care for his horse Stepa, whom he genuinely loves and worries about ("Pis'mo," 13). Other familial relationships, after all, seem to count for very little in this story! In "Sol'," Balmashev still retains that regard for motherhood that is inherent in any culture. Yet something has clearly been lost, and that intangible "something" is the freshness, the innocence that the educated and jaded intellectual assumes should still exist in any traditional culture, especially *Russian* culture. If we consider the *narod*, the folk, in nineteenth-century works as disparate as Pushkin's *Eugene Onegin* and Tolstoy's *War and Peace*, we can hear their voices functioning as counterweights to the limitations and dubious worth of a culture modeled on that of the West. That sense of traditional values is ruined by the violence of a revolution and war that the *narod* but dimly understands.[10] *Skaz*, in which Babel's narrator Liutov stands to one side to let his readers hear the voice of the people directly, unadulterated by an outsider's views, underscores this loss.[11]

---

[9] A. N. Afanas'ev, *Narodnye russkie skazki* (Moscow: Akademiia, 1936), 1: 176–77, 179. In the *skazka* "Salt" from Afanas'ev's collection, Russian salt is a valuable commodity that makes a youngest son's fortune (as Joyce Story has reminded me). Significantly, the revolutionary train, with sometimes negative associations, is juxtaposed to the ship of the *skazka*.

[10] See, for instance, Babel''s "Moi pervyi gus'," from the same collection. Joyce Story has noted to me that, while the hero of the traditional tale is transformed (for the better), young Kudriukov from "The Letter" remains naive while, at the same time, causing his mother suffering with his letter.

[11] There is a precedent for the narrator as outsider among Cossacks in early nineteenth-century Russian literature. In "Kavalerist-devitsa," Nadezhda

Because Babel focuses on the cavalry from which the collection takes its name and on **Cossack** cavalry at that, the horse inevitably plays a central role. In all of these stories, the "heroes" have left home on horses (in Propp, the hero **abandons** home), and the narrator attempts to be a horseman like them, sometimes with disastrous results ("Argamak," 172–76).[12] Even where horses do not literally appear, as in the *skaz* masterpiece "The Letter," they intrude into the text. In "The Letter," young Kudriukov twice mentions his horse to his mother, thus underscoring the link between traditional family structure, oral usage, and the horse. That the soap for washing his horse is kept behind the icon elevates the horse still further, and the very act of washing here suggests baptism. Horses and riders form a nexus, with the Cossacks of the tales frequently exhibiting the swaggering bravado and confident nobility that links them with the "knights," or "heroes," of the heroic tales and *skazki* (folktales). *Skaz* and the horse operate in tandem as the "medium" and "message," respectively, of Babel's *Red Cavalry*. The *function* of the horse is what Babel stresses here; it serves as a reminder of the fact that Propp considered function to be the basic unit of the folktale.[13]

Durova rides with the cavalry disguised as a man, her deception echoed later in *Red Cavalry* as Babel's narrator Liutov attempts to merge with the Cossacks, overcoming two significant stigmas: being a Jew and being an intellectual in glasses. Horses, of course, play a significant role in Durova's work; see N. A. Durova, "Kavalerist-devitsa," in *Izbrannye sochineniia* (Moscow: Moskovskii rabochii, 1983), 31, 33, 46, 53, 55. Durova rides into battle with the Cossacks (46) and arouses the suspicions of a woman who sees through her disguise (48). Like Babel's descriptions of nature just over a century later, Durova's seem to mirror her narrator's mood: "Spring ... was ... sad, wet, cold, windy, dirty..." (147). The Cossack Platov, who resurfaces in Nikolai Leskov's short story "The Steel Flea," makes a cameo appearance in Durova's memoirs (47). I am grateful to Anna Brodsky for her valuable suggestion to consult Durova's "Kavalerist-devitsa."

[12] Propp, *Morfologiia skazki*, 40. For a discussion of the heroic in *Red Cavalry*, not only among the Cossacks but in the Jewish characters as well, see Judith Deutsch Kornblatt, *The Cossack Hero in Russian Literature: A Study in Cultural Mythology* (Madison: The University of Wisconsin Press, 1992), 113–14.

[13] Propp, *Morfologiia skazki*, 24–28; Erlich, *Russian Formalism*, 249–50.

Nowhere does the horse play a more dramatic role than in "Afon'ka Bida," about a bullying cossack whose horse is shot from beneath him by the Poles, and who goes on a mad rampage to avenge the death of his mount and acquire a new one. His abduction of a "replacement" mount serves as a reminder that the horse is part of his identity, not merely property or a means of transportation. Clearly, the horse functions here as a sort of magical agent indispensable for the Cossack.[14] Afon'ka Bida's later abduction of a replacement recalls the abductions perpetrated by villains—not heroes—in the *skazki*.[15] After Maslak has put Afon'ka's critically wounded horse out of his misery, a chorus of Cossacks comments on Afon'ka's loss.[16] "'He brought his horse [literally "steed"—*kon*] from home,' said the long-mustached Bitsenko." Note the word 'steed' (*kon*) hinting at the heroic tale. "'A steed—he's a friend [*drug*, suggesting 'other', 'bosom buddy'],' responded Orlov. 'A steed—he's a father,' sighed Bitsenko" ("Afon'ka Bida," 108), thus giving the horse the stature of an authority figure. As a mark of its great value, Afon'ka Bida pays for his new horse with his left eye (110). Clearly more than just a horse, it has acquired the characteristics of the talisman/magical agent noted by Propp.[17] Afon'ka's theft of the horse, combined with his rapacious plundering of the church and surrounding countryside ("Afon'ka Bida," 109–10) links him with the villains of the *skazka*[18] and blurs the line between Cossack heroism and Cossack villainy. (Magical agents in *Red Cavalry* are not necessarily restricted to horses; the Hasid Gedali's shop is full of "dead" ones, wondrous objects that have now lost their magical power; "Gedali," 36–37.)[19]

Nor are horses and other magical agents the only folkloric components of these stories; other folkloric elements, typically related to the functions of the characters, figure as well. One of the most significant of

---

[14] Propp, *Morfologiia skazki*, 40–41.

[15] Propp, *Morfologiia skazki*, 32–34.

[16] Interestingly this horse, like the one in "Pis'mo," is also named Stepan, although Babel' uses the full name here rather than the nickname.

[17] Propp, *Morfologiia skazki*, 43–44. Other stories with "magical" or special horses include "Istoriia odnoi loshadi," "Nachal'nik konzapasa," and "Zamost'e."

[18] See Propp, *Morfologiia skazki*, 34.

[19] Propp, *Morfologiia skazki*, 42.

these is the interdiction, sometimes in the form of the interdiction plus the proposal. In "My First Goose," Liutov's traditional Jewish interdiction against gratuitous slaughter collides with the traditional Cossack dictum that in wartime (the Cossack milieu) one **should** or **must** kill. It is only after having accepted the suggestion to "ruin" a lady, which he does circuitously by killing her goose (specifically, a gander) and using boorish language, that is, by accepting a cossack *proposal*, that Liutov is able to gain a degree of acceptance—at a price ("Moi pervyi gus'," 41–44).[20]

Interdiction and the difficult task are central to "The Rabbi" and especially to "The Rabbi's Son," where the last son of the "dynasty" foresakes his Hasidic heritage to serve the revolution. The young man desecrates the Sabbath by lighting a cigarette in "The Rabbi" ("Rabbi," 47), and the narrator encounters him in "The Rabbi's Son" near death, with his talismanic objects from the Jewish world and the world of the revolution clustered around him ("Syn rabbi," 169–70).[21]

Interdiction overlaps with the difficult task not only in "My First Goose," "The Rabbi," and "The Rabbi's Son" but in "The Death of Dolgushev" ("Smert' Dolgusheva," 58–60) as well, where Liutov, once again torn between Jewish and Cossack codes of behavior, turns down the dying Dolgushev's plea for a mercy killing and, almost shot by his friend Afon'ka Bida, suffers "banishment" (a traditional *skazka* form of punishment) as a consequence.[22] The request for mercy, a natural component of war stories, surfaces also in "Konkin" (86–89) and "The Ivans" (126–34).[23]

Babel's stories reveal *skazka* roots not only in their characters and the events in which these characters are involved, but also in their imagery. Nowhere is this particular link between the *skazka* and Babel's stories more pronounced than in "Salt," and even here we have the sug-

---

[20] On the deceitful proposal, see Propp, *Morfologiia skazki*, 32–33.

[21] In his incisive discussion of both stories, Friedberg reminds us that Spinoza, whom this youth resembles, was a rebel who was excommunicated and that Maimonides, whose portrait the rabbi's son carries along with that of Lenin, was forbidden fruit for the Hasidim who followed *Rebbe* Nahman of Braclav. Friedberg, "Yiddish Folklore Motifs," 195–96.

[22] Propp, *Morfologiia skazki*, 30–31, 38–39, 41, 56–57. Interdiction also figures in "Sashka Khristos'."

[23] Propp, *Morfologiia skazki*, 41.

gestion of horsemen, as can be seen below. The narrator/author has just
intruded into the *skaz* narrator Balmashev's letter with the lines: "And
the third bell having rung, the train started to move. And a glorious little night spread like a tent. And in that tent [note the repetition of
three] were star-lanterns." Then Balmashev resurfaces with the sentence: "After some time passed, when night changed its guard and the
little red drummers played reveille on their red drums, then the
Cossacks came over to me..." ("Sol'," 96). The red drummers not only
have the obvious political (Marxist) overtones but also echo figures
from the *skazka*.[24]

In the tale "Vasilisa the Beautiful," her cruel stepmother has sent
the heroine to the hut of the witch Baba Yaga ostensibly to get a light,
but actually to get her killed off. Aided by her magic doll (akin to the
salt bundle), the girl performs all the tasks assigned to her ("the difficult
task") and survives. As Vasilisa walks trembling to Baba Yaga's hut, she
encounters three horsemen: the first one gallops past, a white man
dressed in white, on a white horse with white reins, and it begins to get
light. Then the second one comes and flashes by; he himself is red,
wearing red and on a red horse, and the sun starts to rise. The third
horseman is black, is clad all in black, and gallops by on a black horse.
When he rides by, night falls. Babel's readers would surely have recalled
this tale from childhood and would remember the additional scary
details of the fence made of human bones, the skulls with eyes that light
up the night darkness, and the witch who is a cannibal.[25]

Babel has transformed the horsemen of the tale to drummers, perhaps because the noise of the train wheels over the sleepers is more akin
to the sound of a drum (these horsemen "ride" a train). The connection
with the sun, however, still holds, even though the white and black figures, part of the triad of riders, are missing from "Salt." In "Vasilisa the
Beautiful," we have a picture of innocent beauty, of goodness aided by
the magic helper (the doll her late mother has left her) and persecuted
by a cruel stepmother and stepsisters, maltreatment that becomes even
more severe during her father's long absence. The contrast of goodness

---

[24] The color red (*krasnyi*) here echoes the root for *prekrasnyi* (beautiful).

[25] Afanas'ev, *Narodnye russkie skazki*, 1: 178.

versus depravity climaxes when Vasilisa and Baba Yaga, eater of human flesh, are together.[26]

"Salt" contains a similar juxtaposition. When Balmashev notes the essential innocence of his young soldiers, their ruined lives, and the ruined lives of their wives and the girls they have raped (97), the reader who remembers the *skazka* can supply the missing component: like Baba Yaga, the war "eats" human flesh and human souls. As with Babel's use of *skaz*, traditional culture as embodied in the *skazki* encounters is ultimately corrupted by the forces of revolution and war. It is this very use of contrast, of the combination of opposites that runs through virtually all of his stories, the *Odessa Tales* as well as *Red Cavalry*, that may well be Babel's most striking and significant stylistic characteristic.[27] "The world of man," notes Karen Luplow in her essay on *Red Cavalry*, "consists of antithetical and irreconcilable ways of life based on conflicting, incompatible value systems."[28]

What effect does Babel's incorporation of *skaz* and of *skazka* motifs or situations have on *Red Cavalry*? On the most basic level, of course, the use of *skaz* directly relates the revolution and civil war to the immediate experience of the *narod* and demonstrates that on at least one level—the level of gratuitous violence—the revolution can be defined as "popular revolution." Revolution certainly is manifested most savagely in those tales of familial (and symbolically familial) violence, "The Letter" and "Salt," in which *skaz* is central. The use of *skaz* and of *skazka* motifs and images, combined with Babel's employment of striking color combinations, endows *Red Cavalry* with the sort of vitality identified with the world of Russian popular culture, so readily apparent in the painter Filipp Andreevich Maliavin's red-clad, exuberant, dancing peasant women.[29] This is the same sort of vigor that characterized the

---

[26] See Propp, *Morfologiia skazki*, 36. The villain of the folktale frequently threatens or even engages in cannibalism.

[27] Kornblatt discusses the combination of opposites as an aspect of Babelian myth. Kornblatt, *The Cossack Hero*, 118.

[28] Karen Luplow, "Paradox and the Search for Value in Babel's *Red Cavalry*," in *Red Cavalry: A Critical Companion*, ed. Charles Rougle (Evanston, IL: Northwestern University Press, 1996), 70.

[29] Babel' has been compared more than once with Chagall (see, for example, Victor Terras, "Line and Color: The Structure of I. Babel's Short Stories in *Red Cavalry*," in *Modern Critical Views: Isaac Babel*, ed. Harold Bloom (New York:

popular *Cossack* revolts that rocked Russia in the seventeenth and eighteenth centuries.[30]

The combination of the violence of revolution and war with the energy and innocence of traditional culture, when associated with an incomplete or unclear comprehension of the aims of that revolution for
those very men who are fighting for it (see "My First Goose," mentioned above), creates the impression of a cause that somehow, for all
the dynamism of its appeal, has gone horribly wrong. The brutality of
the civil war shreds families ("The Letter") or surrogate families
("Salt"), turns a "hero" into a villain ("Afon'ka Bida"), and defiles
magical objects ("Gedali") and "magic people" ("The Rabbi," "The
Rabbi's Son"). Violation of the interdiction and acceptance of the proposal lead to loss instead of the expected redemption, as in the last sentence of "My First Goose" when the narrator, having killed the goose,
records how his "heart ... crimsoned with murdered, creaked and
flowed out" (like the brains of the murdered goose, 44). An attempt to
fulfill the difficult task, which typically leads to success in the *skazki*—
marrying a princess, acquiring wealth, merely staying alive[31]—leads instead to failure and death ("The Rabbi's Son"). The narrator's inability
to accept the plea of a dying man, an acceptance which typically results
in some sort of reward for the hero of the *skazka*, instead nearly causes
Liutov's death at the hands of Afon'ka Bida ("The Death of
Dolgushev"). The traditional values of the *skazki* are violated countless
times in *Red Cavalry* and, always, the revolution and civil war are depicted as the cause.

Chelsea House Publishers, 1987), 108; Toby W. Clyman, "Babel' as Colorist,"
Slavic and East European Journal 21 (Fall 1977), 333; Rochelle H. Ross, "The
Unity of Babel's *Konarmija*," *South Central Bulletin* 41, no. 4 (Winter 1981),
116 (this last item cited in Kornblatt, *The Cossack Hero*, 202 n. 22). Clyman not
only mentions Chagall (333–34) but also observes that "Babel' was aware of
Kandinsky's theoretical stance" on color. Clyman, 337–39.

[30] The horses' names Stepa (from "The Letter") and Stepan (from "Afon'ka
Bida") recall Stepan Razin, leader of a great Cossack revolt in the seventeenth
century. Nicholas V. Riasanovsky discusses Cossack revolts of the seventeenth
and eighteenth centuries in *A History of Russia*, 4th ed. (Oxford and New
York: Oxford University Press, 1984), 175–82, 260–64.

[31] Propp, *Morfologiia*, 58–60.

How do *skaz* and elements of the *skazka*, which enable Babel to analyze and castigate the revolution and the civil war that followed in its wake, function as satirical devices? Satire is a mode rather than a genre, a means of making a form of art out of the examination and criticism of, to cite Karen Ryan, "the social, political or moral life of the culture it treats." She comments further that the parody of genre conventions is a significant component of contemporary Russian satire.[32] There is also a precedent for such parody in nineteenth-century Russian literature, as in Dostoevsky's parodies of Gogol, described by the Formalist critic Iurii Tynianov.[33]

Babel provides a prime example of such parody during the 1920s, but are *skaz* narrators parodies of the traditional story tellers and his stories, in turn, mere parodies of the *skazka*? Since, as Karen Ryan notes, satire attacks such external targets as politics, societal codes of behavior, and "cultural institutions,"[34] Babel's *Red Cavalry* tales manage at once to function as both parody and satire.

First of all, Babel uses *skaz* to mock the figure of the narrator himself. If the conventional narrator of the *skazka* recounts his/her tales to uphold the traditional values of the Russian oral tradition, then Babel's *skaz* narrators instead find themselves in the midst of a bewildering world in which these traditional values are perilously close to being lost forever. Nor are narrators always reliable in *Red Cavalry*; even the non-*skaz* "frame" narrator of "The Letter," who swears that he is recounting young Kudriukov's message to his mother in its entirety, makes a parenthetical aside to the reader about leaving out the young man's enumeration of his various relations and godparents (12) and, hence, undermines his own position. Most significantly for our purposes, *skaz*, which typically functions as a droll mode of discourse (as in the stories of Nikolai Leskov or Mikhail Zoshchenko), is completely stripped of any humorous aspects in the grim world of *Red Cavalry*. *Skazki* that figure in Babel's stories are similarly undermined and lampooned (although,

---

[32] Karen Ryan-Hayes, *Contemporary Russian Satire: A Genre Study* (Cambridge: Cambridge University Press, 1995), 3–4.

[33] Iurii Tynianov, "Dostoevskii i Gogol' (k teorii parodii)," in Iu. N. Tynianov, *Poetika, istoriia literatury, kino* (Moscow: Nauka, 1977), 293.

[34] Ryan-Hayes, *Contemporary Russian Satire*, 4.

once again, without any humorous overtones), devoid of the ingenuous charm that distinguished the original models of Afanas'ev's collection.

If satire can be understood as a means of exposing societal shortcomings or flaws, then the tales of *Red Cavalry* certainly qualify as satirical. Unlike Mikhail Zoshchenko, who satirized a more settled Soviet community of the NEP period of the 1920s, Babel instead assailed a society that was undergoing the painful, horrific transition of revolution and civil war, a world in which the accepted norms were in the process of being turned upside down or even destroyed. Hence, a Jew could ride with the Cossacks, nay, almost *become* a Cossack (as in "Argamak"). A family could devour itself, divided between the two sides in the revolution ("The Letter"). Most significantly, the common, traditional values of an entire civilization, as epitomized by the oral culture of its folk, its *narod*, could be fatally compromised by revolutionary upheaval, in which the civil war functions as a violent component. Babel parodies the traditional teller of tales and the tales themselves in order to comment satirically on the wasteful violence of revolution and the civil war. As in Olesha's 1927 novel *Envy*, Babel employs imagery, motifs and narrators to express his doubts about the efficacy and legitimacy of the Soviet revolution.[35] It was a revolution that, however lofty its design, nonetheless managed to discredit its goals in the course of a violent genesis.

---

[35] See Janet Tucker, *Revolution Betrayed: Jurij Oleša's Envy* (Columbus, OH: Slavica Publishers, 1996).

Seven

Janet Tucker

The Visual Battleground of Iurii Olesha's *Envy*

"There are novels," notes Edward J. Brown, "which catch and concentrate the essence of a particular historical moment. Such was Olesha's *Envy*."[1] Poised Janus-like between the aesthetic experimentation of Russian Modernism and the wasteland of the nineteen-thirties, the age of Five-Year Plans and socialist realism, Olesha's visual images capture Russia at the juncture of these two eras. Twin sets of warring characters—Nikolai Kavalerov and Ivan Babichev versus Andrei Babichev and Volodia Makarov—embody the antithetical world-views of the novel. While Kavalerov and Ivan Babichev represent the imaginative experimentation reflecting the initial revolutionary impulse, Volodia and Ivan's younger brother Andrei personify the Soviet regime, with its marked insensitivity to aesthetic values. These four major characters embody the "opposition between the useful and the 'useless,' the engineer and the artist, science and art," central to *Envy*.[2] While all the characters suffer from greater or lesser degrees of exaggeration or distortion,[3] Olesha *does* take sides, his preferences expressed through the visual images that symbolize the underlying struggle inherent in this novel and period.

What role does the ability to create striking visual images, make them palpable, and let them loose in the world play here? Given that

---

[1] Edward J. Brown, *Russian Literature since the Revolution*, revised and enlarged edition (Cambridge: Harvard University Press, 1982), 64. *Envy* was published in 1927. See Marietta Chudakova, *Masterstvo Iuriia Oleshi* (Moscow: Nauka, 1972), 7–8.

[2] This character doubling is the engine driving the novel and, as Ingdahl notes, there are elements of satire—incorporating satirical doubling—even in an early draft of *Envy*. Kazimiera Ingdahl, *The Artist and the Creative Act: A Study of Jurij Oleša's Novel "Zavist'"* (Stockholm: Minab/Gotab, 1984), 124–25.

[3] Neil Cornwell, "The Principle of Distortion in Olesha's *Envy*," *Essays in Poetics* 5, no. 1 (1980): 27–28. See also D. G. B. Piper, "Yuriy Olesha's *Zavist'* [Envy]: An Interpretation," *Slavonic and East European Review* 48 (1970): 31.

Janet Tucker, ed. *Against the Grain: Parody, Satire and Intertextuality in Russian Literature*. Bloomington, IN: Slavica, 2002, 113–29.

Olesha was not the only contemporary writer to divide characters between the impotent but gifted and empowered but obtuse (Isaak Babel',
Veniamin Kaverin, and Evgenii Zamyatin are but three analogous figures who come to mind here), this theme could be considered a dominant one of the nineteen-twenties.[4] The present essay focuses on these
very issues, central to the structure of the novel and one of its overriding
themes: political control and related cultural dominance on the threshold of Stalinism, as embodied in the visual image. One need only consider the proliferation of film and propaganda posters after October to
see that mastery over the visual image translates into political authority.

Russian writers, who traditionally used the invisible world of the
imagination as a counterweight to political power, have always played a
major role as social and/or political critics. Olesha is no exception.
Embodied in its visual images, the parodic message he delivers in *Envy*
is double-edged, incorporating the writer's/artist's response not only to
encroaching authority, but also against his own (earlier) incarnation as
revolutionary experimenter. Olesha's characters waltz together in an intricately choreographed dance: linguistic visionaries (Kavalerov and
Ivan) incapable of sustained action and actors (Andrei and Volodia)
grounded in the physical world yet devoid of vision.[5]

Why does the visual image carry so much weight throughout *Envy*?
The answer may well lie in Russian history. From the Orthodox icon to
the Stalinist icon (including Andrei's *Chetvertak*) and at points in between (the *Peredvizhniki* [Wanderers] come to mind here), the visual
image in Russian culture embodies societal values or reaction against
them. *Envy* incorporates both of these aspects of the visual image, the
"orthodox" and the reactive.

The very title, *Zavist'* (*Envy*), recalls the related verb *zavidovat'* ("to
envy") and stresses the overriding significance of the visual image (as in

---

[4] And continuing beyond, if we take into account such works as Boris
Pasternak's *Doctor Zhivago* and Veniamin Erofeev's *Moskva–Petushki*.

[5] One is reminded here of Camille Paglia's binary in *Sexual Personae: Art and
Decadence From Nefertiti to Emily Dickinson* (New York: Vintage, 1991), 17;
cited in David Bethea, *Realizing Metaphors: Alexander Pushkin and the Life of
the Poet* (Madison: University of Wisconsin Press, 1998), 47. "[C]an the divine,"
asks Bethea, "be 'finger-fashioned,' ... or does the crafting begin with the invisible—the relationship between words on Moses' tablets?" Bethea, *Realizing
Metaphors*, 47.

videt', "to see") throughout. The "double-voiced" intimation of two speakers—to draw on Bakhtin—is basic to the very concept of envy, with its inherent bivalent structure embodied in the four major characters of Olesha's novel.[6] Language molds perception, and Olesha's visually astute artists/writers attempt to prevail through the imagination and language, the word made palpable. "To a modern sensibility," notes David Bethea, "rods don't actually turn into serpents, and so the text can't *mean what it says*. Instead what we must be talking about is language's ability to transform itself, to make metaphors."[7] That Ivan and Kavalerov can literally transform their world through language symbolizes the power of language, now exploited by the Soviet system. Why cannot a character incorporate vision as well as power? Perhaps empowered visionaries were far too dangerous in the newly-established regime, especially once they had outlived their usefulness. And the state seems perfectly capable of getting along without them, and does so by the end of the novel.

Andrei's visual limitations are systematic and systemic, denoting the blindness of Soviet society.[8] As seen from Kavalerov's point of view, he is "eyeless," his obtuseness marked by a literal inability to see and symbolized by a sausage-like physicality.

He [Andrei] flashed by once: his torso went past…. It disappeared… And once again it appeared overhead…. In a wild foreshortening I caught sight of his figure, flying in immobility—I didn't see a face, only nostrils did I see: two holes, as though I were looking at a monument from below.[9]

A later scene at the airfield further underscores Andrei's blindness: "Babichev's face turned to me. For one-tenth of a second it directed its

---

[6] See Gary Saul Morson, *The Boundaries of Genre: Dostoevsky's "Diary of a Writer" and the Traditions of Literary Utopia* (Austin: University of Texas Press, 1981), 108, for comments on the bivalent structure of parody.

[7] Bethea, *Realizing Metaphors*, 46; emphasis in original.

[8] "Readers surmised," observes Belinkov, "that Babichev [Andrei] was supposed to be their ideal, but at the same time it was obvious that this ideal seemed a nonentity to the author." Arkadii Belinkov, *Sdacha i gibel' sovetskogo intelligenta: Iurii Olesha* (Madrid: Ediciones Castilla, 1976), 209.

[9] Iurii Olesha, *Zavist', Povesti i rasskazy* (Moscow: Khudozhestvennaia literatura, 1965), 44, 48.

attention at me. *There were no eyes.* There were two mercurially shining plates of a *pince-nez*,"[10] an image at once recalling Rodchenko's photograph of Osip Brik on the cover of *Lef* (*Left Front of the Arts*) and condemning the aesthetic revolutionaries who prostituted their "vision" for the state. Andrei's *pince-nez* (ridiculous and pretentious on a Soviet official) simultaneously spoofs Rodchenko's image—synonymous with artistic experimentation—and undercuts the supposed proletarian bias of the new workers' paradise. Olesha's irony is particularly apt, given that the dialectic underlying Soviet Marxism "foresees" a predictable future.

His back turned, Andrei becomes faceless, eyeless, dehumanized. As Kavalerov, the narrator of part 1, comments: "I saw this back, this corpulent torso from the back, in sunlight, and almost cried out. His back gave everything away, with the fat of his body glowing tenderly yellow,"[11] like his sausage:

> Imagine an ordinary cooked snack sausage: fat, an absolutely round beam, cut off from the start of a big, heavy-weight hunk. At its *blind end* (*v slepom kontse*), from its wrinkled skin tied in a knot, a little string tail hangs down.... A sweaty surface, *yellow bubbles of subcutaneous fat.* At the cut place, that same fat resembles white spots... The sausage dangled like something alive from Babichev's pink official's palm.[12]

Light glinting off lenses and fat echoes the mirrors that play such an important role in the novel, with powerful characters taking refuge behind shiny surfaces. Reflections from buttons and suspenders intensify the impact of the *pince-nez*: the sun "is concentrated (*kontsentriruetsia*) in two burning rays in the metal clips of Andrei's suspenders."[13] Buttons have an analogous function, representing "Kavalerov's first exploitation of a reflecting surface in the form of mirrors, panes of glass, lenses, and other objects,"[14] his first attempt to wrest control from Andrei. The

---

[10] Olesha, *Zavist'*, 46; emphasis added.

[11] Olesha, *Zavist'*, 26.

[12] Olesha, *Zavist'*, 39; emphasis added.

[13] Olesha, *Zavist'*, 21.

[14] Janet Tucker, *Revolution Betrayed: Jurij Oleša's "Envy"* (Columbus, OH: Slavica Publishers, 1996), 118.

mother-of-pearl button on Andrei's drawers reflects the "azure and rose world of the room."[15] When he washes himself at the beginning, he is as noisy as "a boy ... [he] pipes, hops, snorts, utters loud cries."[16] And, Kavalerov implies, he splashes water, fragmenting the reflective surface in the basin that he would otherwise be looking into.

Nor is Andrei the only representative of the new regime associated with limited vision or hiding behind a mirrored surface. Volodia's dream of looking through a telescope with Valia links Soviet Marxist hype, in Olesha's striking image, with rodents. As they gaze at the moon together, he tells her: "Over there, below, is the Sea of Crises (*More krizisov*)." She mishears him and responds, in a parodic pun: "The Sea of Rats? (*More krys*)."[17]

The reader first encounters Volodia behind the shiny glass of a picture frame: "'Andrei Petrovich ... who's this, in the frame?' [asks Kavalerov]. There's the photograph of a swarthy youth standing on his table."[18] When Kavalerov encounters him in the flesh, Volodia flashes a "Japanese smile," displaying shiny, mirror-like teeth. Just as Andrei's blank *pince-nez* parodies two icons of the avant-garde, Osip Brik and Aleksandr Rodchenko, Volodia's photograph undermines the integrity of that most sacred of Russian effigies, the icon. Volodia emerges as a worldly saint of Soviet Marxism, his exemplary life a parody of a *zhitie* (saint's life):

> Long ago, on a dark night ... two people were running away: a commissar and a boy. The boy saved the commissar.... The boy lived with the giant [Andrei].... His [the boy's] comrades came to love him, grownups came to love him.... His presence inspired his comrades to emulate him.[19]

The purpose of a "Life" is to instruct not only a particular saint's fellow-countrymen, but all Christians. In this context, "Christians" denote "true believers,"[20] read, Soviet Marxists. Functioning as a verbal

---

[15] Olesha, *Zavist'*, 19–20.

[16] Olesha, *Zavist'*, 20.

[17] Olesha, *Zavist'*, 90.

[18] Olesha, *Zavist'*, 29–30.

[19] Olesha, *Zavist'*, 89.

[20] Dmitrij Čiževskij, *History of Russian Literature from the Eleventh Century to the End of the Baroque* ('s-Gravenhage: Mouton, 1962), 42.

equivalent of the icon, this "saint's life" is tied in with the visual images that dominate in this novel.

Kavalerov's and Ivan's magical ability to create a palpable world from visual images contrasts starkly to Andrei's and Volodia's—Soviet Marxist—limitations. Kavalerov transforms a rainy Moscow into a mirror late in part 1,[21] an image at once recalling the mirrored surfaces that recur throughout and capturing the stereoscopy and depth central to the visual imagery of *Envy*. Reflections figure so pervasively that the two parts of the novel reflect each other, like mirrors, "with the street mirror … at the end of Part One … signal[ing] the approaching shift in point of view and radiat[ing] its distorted reflections backwards and forwards through both halves of the text."[22] Imaginatively-gifted children and writers use reflections to transform the world, but political muscle hovers in the background behind these mirrors, manipulating what it cannot create. Standing in a window, a boy catches the sun in a piece of mirror,[23] creating striking visual images.[24] Olesha realizes this metaphor more fully in part 2 with the ultimate outsider, a Gypsy, using the sun as a mirror:

> The day was closing shop. A Gypsy … was carrying … a copper basin. Day was moving away on the Gypsy's shoulder. The disk of the basin was bright and blinding. The Gypsy was walking slowly, the basin oscillated slowly, and day was swinging within the disk. The wayfarers [Ivan, Kavalerov] looked after it. And the disk set, like the sun. The day was over.[25]

Olesha combines inventiveness with rebellion, as when Kavalerov tries to dominate by using a street mirror. As Wayne Wilson observes:

> [H]e seeks final refuge in a street mirror… Kavalerov clearly attempts to reassert himself here; his face dominates the center of the mirror, and everything else falls away, becoming almost un-

---

[21] Olesha, *Zavist'*, 62–63.

[22] Cornwell, "The Principle of Distortion," 26–27.

[23] Olesha, *Zavist'*, 62–63.

[24] The child and the poet see the world in similar ways, linked with *ostranenie* ("making strange"). See Chudakova's *Masterstvo Iuriia Oleshi*, 24.

[25] Olesha, *Zavist'*, 182.

recognizable. This convex mirror is the optical correlative of Kavalerov's egocentric point of view; it is the most powerful weapon in his optical arsenal...[26]

But, even here, Kavalerov's efforts fall short. Always perceived in duplicate, mirror images echo the doubling inherent in parody and introduce a note of uncertainty.

> You can never say for sure (as long as you don't turn away from the mirror) which direction a pedestrian you've observed in the mirror is going ... a pedestrian [Ivan] was walking toward the mirror, having appeared somewhere off to the side.[27]

As their images compete in a street mirror, Kavalerov and Ivan replicate and parody the greater conflict between the political haves and have-nots of the novel:

> A pedestrian was walking toward the mirror, having appeared to the side. *I disturbed his reflection....* I continued to think about optical illusions, about the mirror's tricks and then I asked.... "Which side did you come up from? ..." "Where'd I appear from? ... I invented myself."[28]

Synonymous with self-visualization and self-invention, reflection is especially apt in Ivan's case. But mirrors can be dangerous. "In Anechka Prokopovich's room there stood a remarkable bed made of expensive wood, covered with dark-cherry lacquer, with mirror arcs inset inside its ends."[29] Identified with her widowhood, which is synonymous here with final defeat and death, this "terrifying bed" engulfs Kavalerov (and Ivan) at the end.[30] Artists, too, can be swallowed up by their own creations, as in the case of Ivan later in the novel.

Never empowered when recording his visual impressions, Kavalerov observes while lying down or from a distance. Like Turgenev's narrator

---

[26] Wayne P. Wilson, "The Objective of Jurij Oleša's *Envy*," *Slavic and East European Journal* 18, no. 1 (Spring 1974): 34–35.

[27] Olesha, *Zavist'*, 64.

[28] Olesha, *Zavist'*, 64–65; emphasis added.

[29] Olesha, *Zavist'*, 91.

[30] Olesha, *Zavist'*, 33, 115–16, 120.

in *A Sportsman's Sketches*, Kavalerov tries to stay invisible. He escapes initially by "hiding," as when he feigns sleep while watching Andrei:

> When he goes past me in the morning from the bedroom (*I'm pretending to be asleep*), my imagination follows him. I hear his commotion in his little booth of a bathroom, where it's too cramped for his large body.... An oval frosted glass is inset in the door. He flips the switch, the oval is illuminated from within and becomes a beautiful, opal-colored egg. With a mental gaze I see this egg hanging in the darkness of the hallway.[31]

Along with Kavalerov, we see Andrei *behind* a piece of glass—here, the oval of the bathroom door—not in front of it. The image of Andrei behind glass presents a striking parallel with Volodia's photograph. Not hemmed in by visual limitations, Andrei's immensity denotes authority, compensation enough for a power broker. Kavalerov sarcastically invites a Soviet Tiepolo to paint the Feast of the Sausage, celebrating Andrei's power by parodying the patron-artist relationship of the West and hinting at the state-writer connection inherent in the new Soviet order. Kavalerov's mental image commemorates Andrei's new wurst, just approved by sausage expert Solomon Shapiro:

> New Tiepolo! Hie over here! Here are some feasting personages for you.... They're sitting under a brilliant hundred-candle lamp around a table and engaged in lively discourse. Paint them, new Tiepolo, paint the "Feast at the Captain of Industry's Place."[32]

Tiepolo's ceiling paintings seen from below reverse Kavalerov's observations from above, as in the following scene, where the threatening presence of the Kremlin looms in the background *behind* him.[33] Although Kavalerov attempts to ignore this symbol of authority, the reader is well aware of it:

> The Palace of Labor was on my left, *behind me was the Kremlin*. There were boats and swimmers on the river. A launch slid swiftly by beneath my bird's-eye view (*pod moi ptichii polet*).

---

[31] Olesha, *Zavist'*, 19–20; emphasis added.

[32] Olesha, *Zavist'*, 43.

[33] This image is later replicated in Venedikt Erofeev's novel *Moskva Petushki*.

From *my height* what I saw instead of a launch resembled a gigantic almond that had been cut in two lengthwise ... near the smoke-stack [of the launch] I saw two men eating borsch from a pot.[34]

Kavalerov magically alters the mundane objects he spies from his vantage point high above the river,[35] his creative powers transforming the launch into an almond. But because he can only change the world theoretically, never in actuality, his abilities ultimately fail him.

His frustrations inevitably lead to verbal aggression, a feeble substitute for physical action. No single image more aptly captures Kavalerov's weakness than his complaint early on about a world out to get him:

Things don't like me.... If some rubbish—a coin or stud—falls off the table, then it usually rolls under some piece of furniture that's hard to move out. I crawl on the floor and, raising my head, see the buffet laughing at me.[36]

The perpetual clash between verbal images and the world of objects recalls the double edge of parody central to *Envy*. To the bungler Kavalerov, Olesha juxtaposes Andrei, "ruler" of the material world ("Things like him"[37]) with Andrei's striking corpulence underscoring his love affair with things.

Kavalerov attempts to seize control by transforming Andrei's *pince-nez* into a bicycle and achieves a temporary enormity by shrinking the objects around him, but he can never attain any real stature in the novel:

I amuse myself with observations. Have you ever paid attention to the fact that salt falls off the tip of a knife without leaving the slightest trace ... that a *pince-nez* crosses the bridge of your nose like a bicycle, that a person is surrounded by little inscriptions: on forks, spoons, plates, on the rim of a *pince-nez*.... No one notices them. They are carrying on a struggle for existence. They pass

---

[34] Olesha, *Zavist'*, 42; emphasis added.

[35] As Chudakova points out, Kavalerov was *an observer from above*. See *Masterstvo Iuriia Oleshi*, 23; emphasis in original.

[36] Olesha, *Zavist'*, 20.

[37] Olesha, *Zavist'*, 20–21.

from species to species, right up to enormous sign-board letters!
They rise up, class against class: street sign letters battle with the
letters on posters.[38]

In a later scene at the airfield, he stays at the periphery, too far away to
control or even participate in the action. Now inaudible as well as invisible, and stung when Andrei fails to notice him, to see him, Kavalerov
explodes:

> "Sausage man": "Comrade Babichev" … he heard me calling
> him…. I was about to cry…. I got up on tiptoe … and into that
> *unattainable place* (*storona*) sent a resounding howl: "Sausage
> Man!" And once more: "Sausage Man!" … "Sausage Man!"…. [39]

When Kavalerov bemoans the transformation of Lilienthal's light flying
machine, a mechanical bird, into a heavy fish,[40] the soldier on duty ignores him. Kavalerov's observations, however cogent, are outside the
novel's visible power spectrum:

> I rushed toward the gate, toward the exit onto the field. But I was
> detained. A soldier said "Not allowed" and laid his hand on the
> edge of the gate…. "Let me pass, comrade!" I repeated, touched
> the soldier on the sleeve, and in answer I heard: "I'll remove you
> from the airfield." "But I've already been there…. Comrade, I'm
> not just a simple citizen…. I'm from there." "You're not from
> there," smiled the soldier.[41]

Any challenge to authority "is always fraught with risk."[42] One need
only recall Oedipus or Niobe, Don Juan, Evgenii's defiance in "The
Bronze Horseman."

A similar transformation takes place when Andrei drags Kavalerov
to the workers' kitchen. Kavalerov's imagined *verbal* response acquires
intense visual coloration, underscored in the original Russian by alliter-
ation. The instrumental case (in italics) functions here as a marker of his

[38] Olesha, *Zavist'*, 22.

[39] Olesha, *Zavist'*, 45–46; emphasis added.

[40] Olesha, *Zavist'*, 45–46.

[41] Olesha, *Zavist'*, 45–46.

[42] Bethea, *Realizing Metaphors*, 49.

aptitude for altering the world through language. Andrei has already made a total hash of things, including breaking a glass (especially important in *Envy* because of the connection with mirrors). This, muses Kavalerov, is how he would have stepped up to the plate (complete with his typical, requisite reflective imagery), had he only been empowered to do so:

> Women! We'll blow the soot off you, clean the smoke out of your nostrils, the din out of your ears…. We'll turn your little puddles of soup into *sparkling seas*, we'll ladle out cabbage soup like an *ocean*, we'll pour out buckwheat groats by the burial mound (literally, mounds—*kashu nasyplem kurganami*)…. a tile floor will be *flooded with sunshine*…. [43]

Mirrored surfaces, be they water or sunlit tile floors, are components of the reflective images Kavalerov attempts to control. The burial mounds (here, the typical traditional Russian dish of buckwheat groats), suggest perceptible layers of material emphasizing the visual impact of this miniature drama. That Kavalerov is never sufficiently empowered to articulate his eloquent speech recalls the basic fault line dividing the visually-gifted but impotent from the visually-impaired but powerful. And, because he is merely an inept phrase-monger who can envision change but not control it, Kavalerov loses Valia. She represents the single most valuable entity in the novel, her beauty reducing even him to virtual speechlessness. He can only gasp out one phrase, overwhelming in its visual and aural intensity: "You rustled noisily past me like a branch full of flowers and leaves."[44] He and Valia never actually connect: she is on the point of asking him something, but he interrupts her with his magical compliment. Divorced from any real control over his fate, Kavalerov's aptitude for transforming reality through the visual image fails to gain him his desired reward and deprives him of his beautiful dream. The "fork" on her chest echoes the branch and flower imagery generally associated with this character.[45]

---

[43] Olesha, *Zavist'*, 23; emphasis added.

[44] Olesha, *Zavist'*, 38.

[45] Her lightness recalls Gogol's "virginal" characters, specifically the governor's daughter from *Dead Souls* and the young girl in Our Lady of Kazan' Cathedral from "The Nose."

[S]he was lighter than a shadow, the lightest of shadows could have envied her—the shadow of falling snow ... she didn't listen to me with her ear, but with her temple, bending her head slightly; yes, her face looked like a nut ... on her chest I caught sight of the sky-blue fork (*rogatka*) of a vein.[46]

Then Kavalerov tries to describe her in Andrei's language, as a chess piece (with overtones of a contest or duel between kings). But he fails. Andrei emerges the winner here, as he does in the earlier scene when Kavalerov prostitutes his verbal aptitude to proofread Andrei's memo (recalling in the process Akakii Akakievich's copying from Gogol's "The Overcoat" and Tiepolo's dependence on a patron):

Thus, the blood collected during slaughter can be processed either into food, for the preparation of *sausages*, or for the manufacture of light and dark albumin, glue, *buttons*, paints, fertilizers and feed for cattle, fowl, and fish.... The heads and hooves of sheep with the aid of electric drills, automatically operating cleaning machines and gas-operated lathes can be processed as food products, industrial bone oil, the cleaned hair and bones for various articles.... [47]

Buttons serve as a reminder that Andrei prevails over the very object Kavalerov transformed poetically early on in the novel. The sausage recalls Andrei himself, his presence intruding here not only linguistically, but also as a totem object. Nor should Olesha's/Kavalerov's earlier allusion to Harun al-Rashid, sultan from *The Thousand and One Nights*, be overlooked. The inherent tension between ruler (Harun al-Rashid, Andrei) and artist (Scheherazade, Tiepolo, Kavalerov) encapsulates the basic dichotomy inherent in parody and in the power struggle that drives this novel.[48]

Ivan fails to do any better than Kavalerov. While Ivan can invent and assert himself within a circumscribed milieu, he eventually fails in

---

[46] Olesha, *Zavist'*, 53.

[47] Olesha, *Zavist'*, 38; emphasis added. Karl Marx took a satirical swipe at sausage makers and button manufacturers. Rufus Mathewson, *The Positive Hero in Russian Literature* (Stanford: Stanford University Press, 1975), 139–40.

[48] See Tucker, *Revolution Betrayed*, 81–82, for a discussion of the significance of Scheherazade in *Zavist'*.

spite of his special gifts. His "inventions" (*vydumki*) start with the "dream machine" of childhood and recall Olesha's link between children and visual inventiveness.[49] Even at this early point in Ivan's life, his ability to breathe life into imagined visual images pits him against authority, here, Father's. Father's exploitation of Ivan's gift foreshadows and parallels Andrei's later abuse of Kavalerov.

> From his childhood on, Ivan amazed his family and acquaintances. As a twelve-year-old boy, he demonstrated—within his family circle—a strange kind of device that somewhat resembled a lampshade with a fringe of bells and assured them that with the help of his device they could summon up any dream—to order. "Fine," said his father, the director of a gymnasium and a Latinist. "I believe you. I want a dream from Roman history." "What exactly?" asked the boy efficiently. "Anything. The Battle of Pharsalus. But if it doesn't work, I'll skin you alive."[50]

That the Battle of Pharsalus was a Roman revolt should not be overlooked in the larger context of the novel, with its overriding theme of art/vision pitted against authority[51] and in the parodic dichotomy of art/vision versus the state.

Ivan's next invention is a soap bubble balloon (comparable to Lilienthal's flying machine). Flight echoes the height and distance associated earlier with Kavalerov looking at the launch. At this point, Ivan is still empowered:

> It seems that he invented a special soap compound and special little pipe, by means of which one could put out an enormous soap bubble. This bubble would enlarge in flight, achieving in turn the dimensions of a Christmas tree ornament, of a ball, then of a ball the size of a dacha flower-bed, and on and on, right up to

---

[49] For an excellent discussion of the child and the visual image, see Richard Borden's "The Magic and the Politics of Childhood: The Childhood Theme in the Works of Iurii Olesha, Valentin Kataev and Vladimir Nabokov" (Ph.D. diss., Columbia University, 1987), esp. 74.

[50] Olesha, *Zavist'*, 68.

[51] See Tucker, *Revolution Betrayed*, esp. chap. 1.

the size of an aerostat,—and then it would burst, pouring a short golden rain over the city.[52]

Golden rain recalls Danaë (a reference Ivan's classicist father would have been aware of) and underscores the intense rivalry between vision and authority central to *Envy*. While Kavalerov creates beautiful pictures and reaches the simmering point only later, in adulthood, Ivan's rebellious streak surfaces early on.

In a parodic echo of Valia as a flowering branch, Ivan conjures up a flower from an aunt's wart.[53] This time, Ivan expands his horizons by tackling an unrelated authority figure, the aunt of a friend's would-be girlfriend. Auntie has just sent Lilechka, object of the student Shemiot's affection, off to Kherson for the summer. Shemiot enlists Ivan's help. Plotting revenge, Ivan puts his skills to work: "Auntie had a big wart.... My friends, the student was avenged. From auntie's wart a flower grew, a modest field bluebell. It quivered gently from aunt's breathing. Disgrace descended on her head."[54] So did a bee, fitting punishment for a martinet.

This aggressive progession of realized visions finally culminates in the robot Ophelia, now considerably more threatening than any earlier invention. Like Andrei's *Chetvertak*, Ophelia replicates Russian Constructivist art, particularly Tatlin's unrealized *Monument to the Third International*.[55] Olesha kicks Constructivism and Suprematism out of their empowered position associated with the initial revolutionary impulse and the mastery of space (read, the world).[56] Lilienthal's plane/fish, encountered at the airfield, anticipates and symbolizes this surrender of the avant-garde, and Ophelia's aggressive attack foreshadows the fate of an entire generation of artists consumed by their own revolution. She is a self-contained parodic device here, combining art and rebellious power in an untenable combination. "And," Ivan wistfully remarks, "I gave her the name of a girl who went out of her mind

[52] Olesha, *Zavist'*, 69.

[53] Olesha, *Zavist'*, 38.

[54] Olesha, *Zavist'*, 72.

[55] Tucker, *Revolution Betrayed*, 126, 144–48.

[56] See Janet Tucker, "A Re-examination of Jurij Oleša's *Envy*," *Slavic and East European Journal* 26, no. 1 (Spring 1982): 56–62. This same competition for the mastery of space is central to Zamyatin's *We*.

from love and despair—the name of Ophelia ... the most human, the most touching."[57] But Ivan's Ophelia is hardly touching, and machine and destruction are synonymous here:

> The terrible iron thing was slowly moving across the grass in [Ivan's] direction. From that part of it that could be called a head, a shining needle noiselessly materialized. Ivan ... sat down, pressing his back to the wall, covering his face with his hands. The machine moved toward him, tearing up dandelions in its path.... Ivan quietly bent forward, turning around the terrible axis.[58]

With her terrifying presence suggesting revolutionary violence, Ophelia threatens her creator Ivan with a deadly needle. She foreshadows Mukhina's statue of the worker and peasant holding their hammer and sickle, a parodic figure of revolution gone awry. All of his inventions (Ophelia, the dream machine with the Battle of Pharsalus, the flowering wart, the golden rain suggestive of Zeus and Danaë and her son's inevitable murder of her father) parody revolt.

Roaming through nocturnal Moscow, Ivan leaves rumors in his wake. He inspires beer-hall legends that circulate by way of Moscow's *chërnye lestnitsy* (back stairs, but *chërnyi* also means black),[59] tales that parody Christ's miracles.[60] As an uninvited guest at a wedding, Ivan parodies and reverses the miracle at the Wedding at Cana, where Christ changed water into wine. That Christ ushered in a new world order underscores Ivan's frustrated attempts to control events and his inability to create a new society himself through his *vydumki* (inventions):[61]

---

[57] Olesha, *Zavist'*, 95.

[58] Olesha, *Zavist'*, 118.

[59] Olesha, *Zavist'*, 68–77.

[60] Olesha, *Zavist'*, 96–97.

[61] An argument can also be made for considering the three Babichev brothers in the context of near-contemporary Russian and Soviet history. Reinhard Lauer links the three Babichev brothers (including the oldest, the executed Roman) with the three Ulyanovs, of whom Vladimir Il'ich Lenin was the middle brother. Lauer, "Zur Gestalt Ivan Babičevs in Olesha's 'Zavist'," *Die Welt der Slaven* 7, no. 1 (June 1962): 46–48. See also Leonore Scheffler, "Jurij Olešas Roman *Zavist'*—ein Kommentar zur Zeit," *Zeitschrift für slavische Philologie* 36, no. 2 (1972): 287–90; and Anthony Vanchu, "Jurij Oleša's Artistic Prose and

> A story was composed about how an unknown citizen went to a
> wedding at the tax-collector's ... (shabby, a suspicious looking
> man—none other than he—Babichev, Ivan) and ... demanded
> attention, with the object of giving a speech ... to the newlyweds
> ... the guest left, mortified ... the wine in all the bottles ... had
> turned to water.[62]

Ivan's brilliantly visualized adventure encapsulates, reverses and parodies the original Gospel scene. That the tax-collector functions as an
arm of the state in the Gospels as well as in contemporary Soviet society
should not be overlooked.

The account of Ivan's arrest and his interrogation at the GPU recall
Pontius Pilate's inquisition of Christ. "Do you call yourself a king?" asks
the interrogator. Ivan responds: "Yes, king of the vulgar.... Good-bye
..." he tells Kavalerov. "They are taking me to Golgotha."[63] Yet Ivan's
subsequent betrayal of Kavalerov not only parodies Christ, but identifies Ivan as a negative Christ (the Anti-Christ?) or, as Andrew Barratt
suggests, links him with Judas, himself a parodic version of Christ.[64]
Like Volodia, Ivan parodies and undermines an image central to
Christianity and, significantly, to traditional Russian culture.

Similarly, Ivan's and Kavalerov's linguistic inventiveness recalls the
Word: Logos, the Word made Flesh, made *visible*, the second incarnation of the Deity, Christ. Given the pictorial quality of much of Ivan's
and Kavalerov's language, the Word should have palpable weight, a
physicality linking it with the icon, its pictorial equivalent. But Ivan's
and Kavalerov's words are stripped of all power. As a skewed version of
Christ, Ivan goes down to defeat along with Kavalerov. Nothing stresses
this loss more cogently than their exile to the periphery of society, like

---

Utopian Mythologies of the 1920s" (Ph.D. diss., University of California, 1990),
92–94. Vanchu presents Ivan as a travesty of Leninist hagiography, 97–100.

[62] Olesha, *Zavist'*, 77. Olesha gives the official designation as in a police report,
drawing a parallel here between Judea under the Romans and the new Soviet
order.

[63] Olesha, *Zavist'*, 77, 87–88.

[64] Barratt also notes Ivan's pseudo-Biblical diction in the middle of a prosaic
passage. Andrew Barratt, *Yurii Olesha's "Envy,"* (Birmingham, England:
Birmingham Slavonic Monographs, 1981), 29, 30.

the miniature letters on the *edges* of things that Kavalerov comments on early in the novel.[65]

Linguistic defeat translates into literal failure. While Andrei and Volodia dominate center stage—the airfield, the future *Chetvertak*, Valia, the soccer field—Ivan and Kavalerov must content themselves with the wings in the form of the tavern, the vacant lot, a widow's bed. Ivan animates his early visions triumphantly but eventually retreats, skewered by his own inventiveness in the form of Ophelia. His "word made flesh" evolves into a monster with trappings of the new order. Nor does Kavalerov fare any better, forced at the end to sleep with a parodic echo of his ideal woman and share her favors with Ivan.[66] However compelling Kavalerov's visual images and Ivan's animated visions, both must eventually yield to the blind political force that defines Soviet Marxist society and eventually prevails. Subordinated to the triumphant yet perverse iconography of the state, where the obtuse are empowered and the artists impotent, Olesha's visionaries are forced "underground" by the end of the novel, no longer viable or necessary.

Their surrender echoes the operation to excise the imagination that concludes Evgenii Zamyatin's *We* and records the precipitous decline of the initial revolutionary impulse into bureaucratic entropy. The struggle to control the visual images in *Envy* replicates the conflict in the larger society between imaginative revolutionaries and their visually-limited heirs. Ultimately Olesha condemns both sides in an outcome with no clear-cut victors.

---

[65] Olesha, *Zavist'*, 22.

[66] Valia herself seems to parody the contemporary Soviet ideal of youth.

Eight

Julie A. Cassiday

Flash Floods, Bedbugs, and Saunas: Social Hygiene in Mayakovsky's Theatrical Satires of the 1920s*

Satire has enjoyed a long and distinguished history on the Russian stage: since the eighteenth century, playwrights such as Denis Fonvizin, Aleksandr Griboedov, Nikolai Gogol, Aleksandr Ostrovsky, Aleksandr Sukhovo-Kobylin, and Anton Chekhov created a classical repertoire for the Russian theatre comprised primarily of satires. Vladimir Maya-kovsky's dramatic work continued this rich tradition of satire in the Russian theatre and applied its techniques to the creation of propaganda on politically aligned stages after 1917. Much like his eighteenth- and nineteenth-century predecessors, Mayakovsky ridiculed contemporary foibles, blended and bent traditional literary and theatrical genres, drew upon topical material, and chastised society in the hopes of reforming it.[1] His three plays from the 1920s—*Misteriia-buff* (*Mystery-Bouffe*, 1918 and 1921), *Klop* (*The Bedbug*, 1928), and *Bania* (*The Bathhouse*, 1929)—helped to bring Revolutionary satire out of the cabarets of Moscow and Petrograd and into the repertoires of the Moscow Art Theatre and the Meyerhold State Theatre among others. By incorporating modernist scenic innovations and his own raw verbal energy into these plays, Mayakovsky adapted the tried and true formula for satirical success on the stage to the demands of the post-Revolutionary theatre of the 1920s.

Although he followed the pattern of the most admired works in the Russian theatrical repertoire, Mayakovsky's plays met stiff critical opposition in the Soviet cultural establishment of the decade. The play-

---

* This essay has been reprinted with the gracious permission of *The Slavonic and East European Review* 76, no. 4 (October 1998): 643–57.

[1] For the broadest contours of the satirical mode in literature, see Brian A. Connery and Kirk Combe, "Theorizing Satire: A Retrospective and Introduction," in *Theorizing Satire: Essays in Literary Criticism*, ed. Brian A. Connery and Kirk Combe (New York: St. Martin's Press, 1995), 1–15, esp. 4–9.

Janet Tucker, ed. *Against the Grain: Parody, Satire and Intertextuality in Russian Literature.* Bloomington, IN: Slavica, 2002, 131–48.

wright composed all three of his plays for the era's most visible and controversial director, Vsevolod Meyerhold, and worked in close contact
with Meyerhold to create each play's *mise-en-scène*. As a result of this
collaboration, the premiere of each of Mayakovsky's plays inspired the
same impassioned debate that characterized Meyerhold's other productions during the decade, for example, his controversial stagings of
Gogol's *Revizor* (*The Inspector General*) in 1926 and of Griboedov's
Gore ot uma (*Woe from Wit*) as *Gore umu* (*Woe to Wit*) in 1928.
Regardless of Mayakovsky's and Meyerhold's proclaimed political correctness and the relative popular success of these productions, *Misteriia-
buff*, *Klop*, and *Bania* caused critics to challenge the political orthodoxy
of each play's satirical message at a time when the viability of satire in
Soviet literature and theatre had fallen into question.[2] The critics' increasingly skeptical and eventually hostile attitude toward
Mayakovsky's plays indicated the unacceptability of the satirical tradition in the Russian theatre by the end of the decade.

Soviet critics' discomfort with the defiantly chaotic and hybrid nature of satire is entirely understandable in the context of dramatic art
devoted to Revolutionary propaganda. Politically aligned theatres of the
time, both amateur and professional, wished to convey a clear message
to their audiences; they sought to advance palpably the construction of
socialist society by depicting revolutionary transformation and progress
on the stage. On the one hand, according to the first Commissar of
Enlightenment Anatolii Lunacharsky, other theatrical genres such as
melodrama offered the clearest means for reaching peasant and proletarian spectators with this message.[3] On the other hand, satire, by its
very definition, resists the teleology and closure inherent in melodrama

[2] J. A. E. Curtis, "Down with the Foxtrot! Concepts of Satire in the Soviet
Theatre of the 1920s," in *Russian Theatre in the Age of Modernism*, ed. Robert
Russell and Andrew Barratt (New York: St. Martin's Press, 1990), 219–35, esp.
225–28. See also Konstantin Rudnitsky, *Russian and Soviet Theatre: Tradition
and the Avant-Garde*, trans. Roxane Permar, ed. Lesley Milne (London:
Abrams, 1988), 205–07.
[3] Anatolii Lunacharskii, "Kakaia nam nuzhna melodrama?" in *Sobranie sochinenii* (Moscow: Khudozhestvennaia literatura, 1963–67), 2: 212–15. See also
Daniel Gerould and Julia Przybos, "Melodrama in the Soviet Theater 1917–
1928: An Annotated Chronology," in *Melodrama*, eds. Daniel Gerould and
Jeanine Parisier Plottel (New York: Literary Forum, 1980), 75–92, esp. 75–77.

and demanded by the revolutionary theatre. In place of the well-or-
dered and formulaic representation of melodrama, satire offers carnivalization of both content and form: the satirical play borrows its characters from the reality beyond the footlights and appropriates a melange
of literary and scenic forms for their depiction. The dual mockery of
form and content produces a distinctive friction between stage and life
that gives theatrical satire its didactic edge.[4] In the Soviet Union of the
1920s, playwrights such as Mayakovsky, Nikolai Erdman, and Mikhail
Bulgakov pushed the theatre toward ever greater satiric carnivalization
while political demands and artistic strictures pulled it in the opposite
direction.[5] By 1930 this conflict came to a head and satire found itself
exiled from the very social order it had once sought to chasten.
Mayakovsky managed to use satirical carnivalization successfully in the
1921 production of *Misteriia-buff*; however, by the end of the decade,
Klop and *Bania* not only undid the playwright's intended political message but also undid themselves as stage satires, signaling the end of
satire's productive life in the early Soviet theatre.

The rising carnivalization that transformed Mayakovsky's political
correctness into heresy is clearly visible in tropes for personal and social
hygiene in his plays. At first glance, the appearance in all three plays of
metaphors of cleanliness seems coincidental, but closer examination reveals that hygiene played a central role in the era's conception of satire,
not only from the playwright's point of view, but also from that of the
cultural establishment as a whole. The ongoing debate over satire's viability in Soviet culture focused on its social function, on its usefulness as
a tool "to cleanse" (*raschishchat'*) the consciousness in order to prepare
it for a reconstruction unexampled in the whole world."[6] The vocabu-
lary of the time shows that the concept of cleansing entailed a wealth of
related terms tied to cleanliness on both the personal and the social
level. The verb *chistit'* (to clean) and its related noun *chistka* (cleaning

---

[4] Connery and Combe, *Theorizing Satire*, 5.

[5] Gay Sibley, "*Satura* from Quintilian to Joe Bob Briggs: A New Look at an
Old Word," in *Theorizing Satire*, 66–67.

[6] "O putiakh sovetskoi satiry," *Literaturnaia gazeta*, no. 13 (15 July 1929): 1.
For Mayakovsky's contribution to the public debate on the viability of satire,
see "Vystuplenie na dispute 'Nuzhna li nam satira?'" in *Polnoe sobranie sochinenii* (Moscow: Khudozhestvennaia literatura, 1959), 12: 512. All translations
are the author's own unless otherwise noted.

or purging) referred not only to polishing shoes and scrubbing kitchen floors, but also to purging unwanted elements from the Communist Party and socialist society. All that was socially undesirable and merited such cleansing fell under the rubric of *meshchanstvo* (petty bourgeoisie or philistinism) and could be removed from the individual and society through the process of *samokritika* (self-criticism). Proponents of satire claimed that *samokritika* was an efficient and effective means for cleansing society of its philistine elements.[7]

As a revolutionary artist, Mayakovsky employed the terminology of social cleansing both in his plays and in debates defending satire as a mode of dramatic expression. Unlike other playwrights of the era, Mayakovsky embraced this associative cluster with unusual enthusiasm, most probably due to his own obsession with personal hygiene. According to one contemporary, Mayakovsky "was a maniac for cleanliness and felt an almost pathological fear of infection. He washed his hands an unusual number of times a day, and whenever he was away from home, he used the soap he carried in his [own] soap holder."[8] It comes as no surprise that someone who displayed what psychologists now label obsessive-compulsive behavior would adopt and expand the metaphors of social hygiene in his writing. For example, in a 1923 article titled "Mozhno li stat' satirikom?" ("Is it Possible to Become a Satirist?"), the playwright answered this question in the affirmative and encouraged aspiring satirical writers to realize "the possibility to clean [*pochistit'*] the Soviet interior" more seriously in their writing.[9] In his own plays, Mayakovsky took this advice to heart and actualized the implications of the hygiene metaphor that initially promised to clean the dirt but ultimately purged such satires from Soviet society of the time.

As Mayakovsky's first play written in service of the Revolution, *Misteriia-buff* established what one critic called "the style of new the-

[7] For this defense of satire, see G. Iakubovskii, "O satire nashikh dnei," *Literaturnaia gazeta*, no. 11 (8 July 1929): 3; "O putiakh": 1; and M. Rogi, "Puti sovetskoi satiry," *Literaturnaia gazeta*, no. 14 (22 July 1929): 3. These three articles were written in response to V. Blium's attack upon satire in "Vozroditsia li satira?" *Literaturnaia gazeta*, no. 6 (27 May 1929): 2. For further discussion of the satire debate, see Curtis, "Down with the Foxtrot!" 227.

[8] Wiktor Woroszylski, *The Life of Mayakovsky*, trans. Boleslaw Taborski (New York: Orion Press, 1970), 331. See also 224, 459, 469.

[9] Mayakovsky, "Mozhno li stat' satirikom?," in *PSS*, 12: 30.

atrical writing, the rhythm of the new theatrical Revolution."[10] Much of the play's success arose from Mayakovsky's skillful use of the satirist's traditional tools: he mixed the genres of medieval mystery and opera-bouffe, as the play's title indicates; he incorporated topical material that would, according to his own instructions, be changed in subsequent productions; and he lampooned the bourgeois and imperialist West in figures such as French Premier Georges Clemenceau and British Prime Minister David Lloyd George.[11] But a large part of the play's success as a satire came from the fact that Mayakovsky not only conceived of *Misteriia-buff* as a satirical cleansing of post-Revolutionary society but also portrayed this cleansing in the very action of the play.

The plot of *Misteriia-buff* is extremely simple: a flood, symbolic of world-wide Revolution, swallows up the earth, and all that remains of humankind are seven pairs of the bourgeois Clean and seven pairs of the proletariat Unclean. Mayakovsky puts the hygiene metaphor at the very heart of his drama by reworking the Biblical story of the flood into a modern-day mystery of Every Proletariat.[12] In the 1913 play *Vladimir Maiakovskii: Tragediia* (*Vladimir Mayakovsky: A Tragedy*) and the 1923 poem *Pro eto* (*About That*), images of floods had intensely personal significance, originating in the poet's tears which flowed into rivers that became oceans engulfing the earth. While *Misteriia-buff* shares this imagery of an elemental and uncontrollable force, the flood in the play is taken out of the subjective realm of the playwright's grief over lost love and given distinctly political significance. Like a planetary tidal wave, the flood of Revolution surges from country to country, east and west, north and south, until it encompasses the world-wide prole-tariat. The deluge washes away the bourgeoisie and all its evils to leave the world cleansed of capitalism and purified for the building of com-munism. In order to survive the flash flood, the Unclean build an ark and overthrow the oppressive rule of the Clean on their way to the promised land.

---

[10] Samuil Margolin, "Vesna teatral'noi chrezmernosti," *Vestnik rabotnikov*, nos. 10–11 (1921): 122.

[11] Mayakovsky, *Misteriia-buff*, in *PSS*, 2: 243–46.

[12] For a discussion of the significance of water and flood symbolism in Mayakovsky's poetry, see Edward J. Brown, *Mayakovsky: A Poet in Revolution* (Princeton: Princeton University Press, 1975), 133, 200.

Mayakovsky's names for the two choruses in the play, the Clean and the Unclean, extend the social hygiene metaphor. At first, it seems that Mayakovsky confuses his labels and contradicts the expected aftermath of the Revolutionary flood. If the deluge cleanses the world and purifies humanity, why do only those labeled dirty, impure, and Unclean survive its bath? However, Mayakovsky uses the apparent contradiction to create a word-play based on both meanings of *chistyi* as physically clean and spiritually pure. The chorus of the Unclean has the grimy fingernails and thick calluses of the working class and, hence, is unwashed in the literal sense of the word. Despite the actual dirt that covers them, the hearts and minds of the Unclean are immaculate. Conversely, the chorus of the Clean is comprised of well-groomed, fashionably-dressed, and delicately-perfumed ladies and gentlemen, whose souls capitalism has fouled and dirtied. The external cleanliness of the Clean superficially covers their spiritual filth. Mayakovsky has chosen his labels for the Clean and the Unclean not only out of a love of irony but also to describe the inverse relationship between the characters' external and internal purity in the play.

Although the Unclean are actually far cleaner than their Clean counterparts, they nonetheless undertake a journey to purify themselves further. The Unclean pass through hell and heaven and into a *chistil-ishche* (purgatory) that they themselves must tidy up to become the masters of earth and the builders of a worldly paradise. The *dénouement* of *Misteriia-buff* takes place as the Unclean collectively labor to restore order in *Razrukha* (the Land of Ruin) and construct paradise on this earth by the sweat of their own brows. Interestingly enough, Mayakovsky includes a laundress and chimney sweep among the Unclean to illustrate their role as the janitors of the planet. When the Unclean enter the Land of Ruin, one of their number explains this duty: "What should we do? We need to clean up [*raschistit*]."[13] Although the flood of Revolution swept over them uncontrollably at the play's beginning, the Unclean now sanitize the earth and make "The path even, smooth, and clean [*chist*]."[14] Mayakovsky emphasizes the agency of the Unclean in constructing the earthy paradise, clearly contrasting them with the passive and freeloading Clean.

---

[13] Mayakovsky, *Misteriia*, 331.

[14] Mayakovsky, *Misteriia*, 340.

Mayakovsky's use of the terminology for personal and domestic hygiene in *Misteriia-buff* suggests another closely related metaphor of the time, that of parasites sucking the life blood of the working class. In an article previewing the 1918 production of the play, first Commissar of Enlightenment Anatolii Lunacharsky provides the label to which Mayakovsky merely alludes by describing *Misteriia-buff* as "a cheerful, symbolic voyage of the working class which gradually frees itself from its parasites after the revolutionary flood."[15] As Mayakovsky's subsequent plays would prove, parasites became increasingly difficult to exterminate and germs ever harder to disinfect as the 1920s progressed. Nonetheless, during the era of *Misteriia-buff*, eliminating the enemies of the Revolution seemed as simple, inevitable, and permanent as the flood imagery in the play implied. By realizing the very metaphor for satire in the action of *Misteriia-buff*, Mayakovsky created a play whose Revolutionary form, content, and function were unambiguous and received the applause of critics and audience members alike.

Unlike *Misteriia-buff*, *Klop* offered a markedly more ambiguous satire of the *nouveaux riches* that profited from the capitalist retrenchments of the New Economic Policy (NEP). Although the action of *Klop* duplicated the division between chaotic present and utopian future as in *Misteriia-buff*, the later play extended the trope of cleanliness to a degree that undermined its intended social satire. As a result, critics treated *Klop* skeptically, but audiences applauded Mayakovsky's hilarious verses and Meyerhold's playful *mise-en-scène* which provided a breath of fresh, comic air in the theatre at the end of the decade. The increased irony and ambiguity of *Klop* arose from Mayakovsky's development of the metaphors of germ and parasite which the trope of cleanliness had only implied in *Misteriia-buff*.

Critics and spectators immediately recognized the hero of *Klop*, Ivan Prisypkin, as the quintessence of the petty bourgeoisie, as "a character who has been petty-embourgeoisified to the point of complete bestiality."[16] More rightfully called the play's anti-hero, Prisypkin appears in the cast of characters as "a former worker, a former Party member, currently a fiancé," and he is anything but the model Soviet

[15] Lunacharskii, "Kommunisticheskii spektakl'," in *SS*, 3: 40.

[16] Mayakovsky, "'Klop.' Novaia p'esa Vl. Maiakovskogo," *Vecherniaia Moskva* 1 (1513) (2 January 1929): 3.

citizen.[17] As the playwright's designation suggests, Prisypkin represents an unusually pestiferous class of *byvshie liudi* (former people): renegade proletarians who joined the Communist Party as part of the Lenin enrollment but subsequently abandoned the working class for the petty bourgeoisie. Prisypkin hopes to profit from his impeccable proletarian lineage and his newly acquired Party membership by arranging a marriage with the daughter of a prosperous Nepman, the curvaceous and alluring beautician Elzevira Davidovna Renaissance. Prisypkin epitomizes the petty bourgeoisie that was subjected to *samokritika* and *chistka* throughout the 1920s.

The first half of *Klop*, set in 1929, develops the character of Prisypkin by correlating his superficial personal hygiene with deeply embedded moral filth, as Mayakovsky had done earlier in *Misteriia-buff*. As his very name indicates, Prisypkin is a *syp'* (rash or eruption) on the skin of Soviet society that requires *prisypka* (dusting powder) to alleviate the itch. Regardless of his brand-new lacquered shoes, his freshly sprouted sideburns, his ability to fox-trot, and his new, kitschy surname "Skripkin" (from *skripka*, violin), Prisypkin will always be associated with itchy maladies of the skin that discomfort the Soviet body politic. Just like the Clean in *Misteriia-buff*, Prisypkin's personal hygiene is only skin-deep, as his former working-class mates point out. Prisypkin dresses and carries himself like a gentleman, but "He's got sideburns like a dog's tail, and he doesn't even wash—he's afraid to muss them."[18] Prisypkin betrays this personal filth by scratching the vermin infesting his person while he practices the latest dances in preparation for his upcoming wedding. Prisypkin's marriage to the Renaissance family reinforces the superficiality of his cleanliness. Prisypkin has thrown over his working-class fiancée Zoia Berezkina to wed the daughter of a stereotypically avaricious family of Jewish Nepmen. Interestingly enough, every member of the Renaissance family works in the personal hygiene trade in the family barber shop and beauty salon. Mr. and Mrs. Renaissance shave and coif customers while their daughter Elzevira provides manicures. Prisypkin has abandoned his proletarian heritage of dirty calluses earned by manual labor to join a family with carefully filed fingernails and intricately styled hair. It scarcely comes as a surprise

[17] Mayakovsky, *Klop*, in *PSS*, 11: 220.
[18] Mayakovsky, *Klop*, 229.

when the wedding of "unknown but great labor with prostrate but charming capital" turns into a drunken brawl as the guests at the wedding show their true, dirty colors.[19] The wedding party grows ever more inebriated, until the uncultured and unclean nature of Prisypkin and his in-laws agitates and literally ignites the marriage celebration, which is consumed in the ensuing flames.

In the second half of *Klop*, set in 1979, Mayakovsky extends the hygiene metaphor to include the parasites, vermin, and germs referred to by the play's title. As Prisypkin's itching in the first half of the play indicated, he has carried a tiny insect-passenger on his person into the world of the future, which resurrects both of them after fifty years of frozen sleep in the burned-out basement of the wedding party. Prisypkin's thin layer of grooming no longer hides his petty-bourgeois filth from the world of 1979, whose standards of cleanliness are much higher than those of fifty years ago. The present world in the first half merely criticized Prisypkin's betrayal of class, country, and Revolution, but the world of the future correctly labels him the true parasite in the play: Prisypkin is a leech sucking the blood of socialist society, a virtual Typhoid Mary spreading a host of social ills.

The audience first glimpses the future as two custodians tidy up a room designed to house a complex voting apparatus that relieves the citizens of the future from voting in person and risking the spread of harmful microbes. As the elder of the two janitors reminisces about the long-lost era of his childhood, the spectators listen to him describing the stark contrast between the smelly and grimy auditorium in which they sit and the disinfected and gleaming vision on stage. When representatives from all regions of the earth discuss resurrecting the frozen Prisypkin via teleconference, the threat of bacteria and infection from the past immediately enters the debate. If the future decides to resuscitate the petty-bourgeois Prisypkin, it will have to worry about "the danger of spreading the bacteria of brown-nosing and conceit … about the possibility of introducing an epidemic of brown-nosing!"[20] In actual fact, as soon as Prisypkin comes back to life, the diseases of love, profanity, smoking, and drinking appear in society for the first time in fifty years.

---

[19] Mayakovsky, *Klop*, 238.

[20] Mayakovsky, *Klop*, 247, 249.

Prisypkin's *antisanitarnye obychai* (unsanitary customs) prove to be dangerously contagious in the sterile environment of the future.[21]

Ironically, the scientists of the future show more interest in the rare insect Prisypkin has brought into their midst than they do in its smelly and infectious host. Only by offering himself as a source of food for the bedbug and as a rare specimen of wildlife in his own right does Prisypkin find a home for himself in the zoo of the future. The zoo's director explains the complex relationship between the human parasite Prisypkin and the insect he feeds:

> ... I have just become convinced, by means of interrogation and comparative beastiology, that we are dealing with a terrifying, anthropomorphic impostor, and that it is the most startling and parasitic of parasites... They are two, differing in size but the same in essence: they are the famous *Bedbugus normalis* and ... and the *Philistinus vulgaris*. Both are found in the musty mattresses of time. *Bedbugus normalis*, when it has grown fat and drunk on the body of a single human, falls under the bed. *Philistinus vulgaris*, when it has grown fat and drunk on the body of all humankind, falls on top of the bed. That's the only difference![22]

In fact, Prisypkin poses a much greater threat to the society of the future than the common bedbug, as the play's action proves.

With great curiosity, the future world labels Prisypkin a parasite and ultimately, determines that he is less than human. The same quasi-scientific, quasi-medical, and ultra-hygienic terminology that emerged in conjunction with show trials of the enemies of the people during the 1920s had made its way into the popular imagination and dramatic representation by 1928. Only a few months before Mayakovsky composed *Klop* in the autumn of 1928, the first Stalinist show trial, the so-called Shakhty Affair, had condensed these associative clusters into a single term *vreditel'* (wrecker or saboteur), which described a new hybrid of man and insect strikingly similar to Prisypkin:

> Wrecker, this is a new word in the Soviet vocabulary. Before, this word and such a term didn't exist. Rather, this term was used only for insects and birds who damaged crops and destroyed

---

[21] Mayakovsky, *Klop*, 255.
[22] Mayakovsky, *Klop*, 271–72.

wooden buildings. Wrecker, this was some kind of little beetle or grasshopper undermining young stems. Wrecker, this is some kind of worm eating away the beams of buildings, an aphid damaging vineyards. Until this time, there hasn't been such a profession among people... There were human vices, and there were no virtuous insects, beetles or worms... People-wreckers never existed before. This breed of human-insect was created by capitalists in their struggle against communism. Only hatred for socialist construction and only a consciousness that this construction is possible could cause a man to turn into a louse.[23]

Mayakovsky transposes this damning description into a satirical register in order to dehumanize Prisypkin in *Klop*. As the play comes to its close, Prisypkin is more and more frequently compared to vermin, to bacteria, and even once to a mastodon. Finally, through the use of the neuter pronoun *ono* (it), the zoo director demotes Prisypkin permanently to the status of an insect or animal. In spite of countless attempts to raise Prisypkin "up to human level," he remains a dangerous source of what one critic called "the bacilli of love and drunkenness."[24] As a social parasite, Prisypkin must be quarantined and kept behind a series of filters that eliminate the threat of an epidemic of petty-bourgeois backsliding—called *tarakanovshchina* (cockroachitis)—among the citizens of the future.[25]

---

[23] L. Zaslavskii, "Vrediteli," *Pravda* 115 (3947) (19 May 1928): 3. Lenin used similar terminology as early as 1917 when he called for mass participation in "the reckoning and control of the rich, the swindlers, the spongers, the hooligans [which] will defeat these remnants of accursed capitalist society, this refuse of humanity, these hopelessly rotten and deadened limbs, this infection, plague, curse, inherited by socialism from capitalism ... the cleansing of the Russian land from all dangerous insects, from the flea-swindlers, from the bedbug-rich, and so on." "Kak organizovat' sorevnovanie?" *Polnoe sobranie sochinenii*, 5th ed. (Moscow: Izdatel'stvo politicheskoi literatury, 1975–78), 35: 200, 204. For other examples of such terminology from the 1920s, see Anatolii Lunacharskii, *Byvshie liudi: Ocherk istorii partii es-erov* (Moscow: Gosudarstvennoe izdatel'stvo, 1922), 79; and A. Agranovskii, Iu. Alevich, and G. Ryklin, *Liudi-vrediteli: Shakhtinskoe delo* (Moscow and Leningrad, 1928).
[24] Mayakovsky, *Klop*, 263. B. Alpers, "'Klop' v Teatre imeni Vs. Meierkhol'da," in *Teatral'nye ocherki v dvukh tomakh* (Moscow: Iskusstvo, 1977), 2: 130.
[25] D. Tal'nikov, "Novye postanovki: 1. 'Klop,'" *Zhizn' iskusstva*, no. 11 (10 March 1929): 10.

In Meyerhold's words, Prisypkin's fate illustrates graphically that "The petty-bourgeois element is sucking us dry, a nirvana of Oblomovitis, nothing brings us out of the state of indifference."[26] In spite of this politically attuned message, as a piece of satirical propaganda *Klop* displayed several shortcomings that critics quickly noticed and questioned. Prisypkin never realizes the superficiality of his personal hygiene, never grooms his soul as he does his body, and never joins the sterile society that cages him in the zoo. He is not only incapable of doing this, but also unwilling. The unregenerate petty bourgeois longs for the small creature comforts (and discomforts) that gave his life meaning fifty years in the past and keep him in a state of primitive filth in the future. Prisypkin never finds sufficient reason to join the society of 1979 and, consequently, he never cleans up his act so that he can become part of the future.

In spite of the fact that he represents all the ills of the petty bourgeoisie, Prisypkin elicits the spectator's sympathy with his sentimental poeticizing, earthy *joie de vivre*, and his final appeal to his contemporaries in the audience at the play's end. Prisypkin's dislike of the sterile world of the future makes it less appealing to the audience watching the play. The reaction of this dirty and drunk degenerate alone, however, cannot turn the utopia portrayed by Mayakovsky in the second half of *Klop* into a dystopia. But when taken with the curious response of the citizens of the future to the infectious Prisypkin, spectators must wonder how desirable this utopia is. While most of the citizenry of the future runs in fear from Prisypkin, a small portion finds itself inexorably drawn toward the symptoms of the diseases he carries, so much so that some even volunteer as candidates for infection. The germs of petty-bourgeois degeneracy are highly virulent and, indeed, they cross lines between species to infect dogs in the play. As the scientifically designed air-conditioner separating Prisypkin from his keepers and visitors in the zoo shows, even momentary contact with a carrier results in infection in the form of fox-trotting, beer-drinking, and love-making. The sterile society of the future cannot control the spread of Prisypkin's diseases and finds that "The epidemic is spreading... The epidemic is becoming an ocean"

---

[26] V. E. Meierkhol'd, "Vystuplenie v Tsentral'nom dome VLKSM Krasnoi Presni, 12 ianvaria 1929 goda," in *Stat'i, pis'ma, rechi, besedy* (Moscow: Iskusstvo, 1968), 2: 177.

that threatens to undo the Revolutionary flood depicted in *Misteriia-buff*."[27] The social ills Prisypkin brings with him from the past find a surprisingly quick and firm foothold in the future, and, as a result, Prisypkin's dislike of the new social order acquires a dangerous veracity.

The very possibility of eliminating the petty-bourgeois diseases at issue comes into question by the end of *Klop*. When taken together with the attraction of these ills and the almost palpable fondness for the lost past that emerges in the second half of the play, the need for such a sterile future devoid of dirt, feeling, and romance becomes highly equivocal. The critic Boris Alpers sensed this equivocation in the play and criticized *Klop* for not taking its satire far enough. According to Alpers, Mayakovsky's script focuses on an insignificant part of the petty-bourgeoisie and as a result paints the object of its satire in only the most general of contours.[28] Yet exactly the opposite is true: the playwright accurately reveals a dangerous element lurking in Soviet society and depicts Prisypkin's crimes in living colors. However, Mayakovsky extended the satirical cleansing metaphor to its logical but paradoxical end. In spite of the playwright's intent to cleanse society in *Klop*, his satire no longer contained the simple propaganda message that the theatre of 1928 demanded, and, instead, his play questioned the very social order it meant to defend.

In *Bania*, Mayakovsky repeated many of the dramatic techniques found in *Klop* and *Misteriia-buff*, such as splitting the play's action between the present day and a utopian future and dividing its *dramatis personae* into friends and foes. Mayakovsky aimed his satire in *Bania* at the leviathan Soviet bureaucracy. In addition to railing against Russian red tape, Mayakovsky included a small play within a play that chastised the contemporary theatre for uninspired and incomprehensible Revolutionary propaganda. The metatheatrical third act of *Bania* created understandable tension between Mayakovsky and his critics; nonetheless, *Bania* as a whole provided much clearer and less problematic satire than *Klop*. In place of Prisypkin, who receives the audience's simultaneous scorn and sympathy, Mayakovsky placed an undeniably anti-Soviet enemy who bears the full brunt of spectators' condemnation.[29]

---

[27] Mayakovsky, *Klop*, 258–59.

[28] Alpers, "'Klop' v Teatre," 130–32.

[29] During the rehearsal of *Bania*, Mayakovsky wrote additional material that was performed in Meyerhold's theatre. Unfortunately, these additions have not

For his paragon of bureaucracy, Mayakovsky created a speaking name that decides his anti-hero's fate at the end of *Bania.* "The super-bureaucrat and superidiot Pobedonosikov" bears a farcical name whose multiple connotations point to the character's enemy status and intimate that he will be purged from the idyllic future described in the play.[30] First, the name Pobedonosikov refers to the ideologue of tsarist reaction under Alexander III and Nicholas II, Konstantin Pobedonostsev, whose name came to signify reaction itself at the beginning of the twentieth century. Second, Pobedonosikov is a variation of the epithet *pobedonosets* (bearer of victory), which typically followed the names of saintly princes who sacrificed their lives in holy battle to defend Russia's honor. Mayakovsky ironically styles Pobedonosikov as a bearer of victory on the bureaucratic front of Soviet society. However, inserting the diminishing syllable "ik" turns the lofty epithet into an insulting tag: no longer does the character's surname refer to bearing victory in adminis-trative battle but instead to someone who has a *nosik* (little nose) for bureaucratic victory, a nose for sniffing out a comfy post and a poten-tially lucrative position. Third, Mayakovsky's abbreviation for Pobedo-nosikov's official post, *glavnachpups*, reinforces the impression of Pobedonosikov's self-serving nature. By carefully selecting the syllables that constitute the abbreviation, Mayakovsky suggests that Pobedono-sikov is more the boss of his own *pup* (navel) and self-gratification than he is of any bureau or ministry. In confirmation of these negative insin-uations, the other characters in the play quickly discover that Pobedo-nosikov's political pedigree reflects an overriding concern for personal profit and welfare. On questionnaires that require an explanation of the *glavnachpups*'s activities before 1917, Pobedonosikov ambiguously an-swers "Was in the Party," without specifying exactly which political party he has in mind.[31] As the critic Ermilov pointed out, Pobedono-sikov epitomizes the problem of Party degeneracy at its very worst.[32]

---

been preserved. My discussion of the play is therefore based on the surviving script as published in Mayakovsky's complete collected works. See Mayakovsky, *PSS*, 11: 674.

[30] N. Goncharova, "'Bania' V. Maiakovskogo," *Rabochaia gazeta* 65 (2414) (21 March 1930): 7.

[31] Mayakovsky, *Bania*, in *PSS*, 11: 288.

[32] V. Ermilov, "O trëkh oshibkakh Meierkhol'da," *Vecherniaia Moskva* 63 (1876) (17 March 1930): 3.

Such self-absorption and dubious political ties mark Pobedinosikov clearly as the enemy in *Bania* and lead predictably to his exclusion from the time machine driven by the Phosphorescent Woman to bring exemplary workers to the society of the future.

Mayakovsky's play legitimated the purging of this new species of Bolshevik, the bureaucratic boss. Critics recognized Pobedonosikov's emblematic character in the play and coined the word *pobedonosikovshchina* (Pobedonosikovitis) to describe not only what plagued the world of *Bania* but also the real-life red tape on which the play was based.[33] Only with extreme irony does Mayakovsky place accusations of being a member of "the petty-bourgeoisie … a remnant of the past, chains of the old way of life" in Pobedonosikov's mouth since he himself is their clearest illustration.[34] Although the *glavnachpups* uses contemporary political phraseology to rid himself of people who put obstacles in his hedonistic path (in this case, his own wife, whom he encourages to commit suicide), he presents the most conspicuous example of what the Phosphorescent Woman calls the "parasites and enslavers" infesting Soviet society.[35] To add to this irony, references to *chistka* and *samokritika* also fall from the lips of Pobedonosikov, who himself is purged and forced into self-criticism by the time the curtain falls in the last act. While *Bania* depicts the necessity of cleansing the Soviet state of bureaucracy, the play also contains a thinly veiled warning as to the potential abuses of the terminology for social hygiene by enemies such as Pobedonosikov lurking in the state bureaucracy.

Pobedinosikov's fall from power and exclusion from the future paint a convincing picture of the need to scrub the bureaucratic dirt out of the Soviet state and to sweep the artistic dross out of the theatre. Mayakovsky all but eliminates the vermin and germ metaphors from the dramatic action of *Bania*; nonetheless, the trope of cleansing effectively explains the satirical function of his play. By the time Mayakovsky composed *Bania*, the terminology of wreckers, purging, and self-criticism had been fully articulated, and, instead of elaborating the hygiene metaphor in the action of the play, Mayakovsky reserved it for his title.

---

[33] V. Ermilov, "O nastroeniiakh melkoburzhuaznoi 'levizny' v khudozhestvennoi literatury," *Pravda* 67 (4512) (9 March 1930): 4.

[34] Mayakovsky, *Bania*, 318–19.

[35] Mayakovsky, *Bania*, 325.

But what relationship does the title of *Bania* bear to its satirical, anti-bureaucratic message? In jest, Mayakovsky claimed that he named his play *Bania* "Because it's the one thing that isn't there."[36] All jesting aside, Mayakovsky's title refers to no action within the play itself, but to the play's didactic function as a work of satire that strove *ustroit' baniu* (to make/organize a bathhouse), that is, to carry out a purge.[37] In an article introducing a published excerpt from act 6 of the play, Maya-kovsky explained, "What is *Bania*? Whom does it wash [*moet*]?" *Bania* is a "drama in six acts with a circus and fireworks. *Bania* washes [*moet*] (it simply launders) bureaucrats. *Bania* is a piece of publicistic jour-nalism."[38] In a slightly later article of the same type, Mayakovsky repeated the idea that "*Bania* cleans and washes [*chistit i moet*]. *Bania* defends horizons, inventiveness, enthusiasm."[39] Mayakovsky also in-corporated the cleansing metaphor in the slogans which he composed to hang on the walls of Meyerhold's theatre during performances of the play. For example, "We can't clean the swarm of bureaucrats right away / And there are neither enough bathhouses nor enough soap for us."[40] On another poster, Mayakovsky wrote, "Clean and purge [*vypar' i prochist'*] every bureaucrat— / with the worker's broom and art's brush."[41] In his title and commentary on the satiric function of *Bania*, Mayakovsky repeated the cleansing and social hygiene tropes that lay at the base of his earlier plays.

While examining Mayakovsky's choice of title, we cannot forget that much of his defense of "horizons, inventiveness, [and] enthusiasm" had profoundly personal as well as broader social application. At the time, Mayakovsky was embroiled in long-term politico-literary hostilities, not the least of which revolved around *Bania* itself.[42] The argument over his

---

[36] Mayakovsky, "Vystupleniia na zasedanii khudozhestvenno-politicheskogo soveta Gos. teatra imeni Vs. Meierkhol'da (Na chtenii i obsuzhdenii 'Bania'), 23 sentiabria 1929 goda," in *PSS*, 12: 379.

[37] Professor Gregory Freidin of Stanford University provided this popular metaphor of the period for purging.

[38] Mayakovsky, "Chto takoe 'Bania'? Kogo ona moet?" in *PSS*, 12: 200.

[39] Mayakovsky, "V chem delo?" in *PSS*, 12: 202.

[40] Mayakovsky, "(Lozungi dlia spektaklia 'Bania')," in *PSS*, 11: 350.

[41] Mayakovsky, "Lozungi," 351.

[42] Brown, *Mayakovsky*, 336–51.

rights, duties, and affiliations as a satirical playwright threatened his artistic horizons, questioned his inventiveness, and certainly diminished his own enthusiasm. When taken with the play within a play in act 3 of *Bania*, the threat to Mayakovsky's artistic freedom provides one more answer to the question, "whom does *Bania* wash?" Maiakovsky wanted his comedy to launder the Soviet state of its bureaucracy and simultaneously to cleanse the contemporary theatre of productions that he jokingly named "*The Squaring of the Cherry ... Uncle of the Turbins.*"[43]

Unfortunately, the reasoning of those who called the theatre "Back to the classics!" in act 3 of *Bania* reflected a good deal of the controversy surrounding the playwright and his play.[44] The jabs made at *Glavrepertkom* (the Main Committee on Repertoire which functioned as the primary theatrical censor) and Mayakovsky's critics reflect the real-life struggle to pass *Bania* through the censorship, as well as the genuine bitterness with which critics reacted to the play and in which Mayakovsky's struggle with critics and censors ended. Lunacharsky's famous catch-phrase, "Back to the classics!" is soundly condemned within *Bania*, but, outside the play, Mayakovsky represented a dwindling minority that had not yet taken this slogan to heart. As a result, *Bania* simultaneously satirized the stagnation of Soviet bureaucracy and questioned the viability of such theatrical satire in the Soviet Union of 1930. Mayakovsky attempted to maintain his charismatic power as a writer of theatrical satire and to preserve satire's social function, which other institutions in Soviet society had long since usurped. However, the satire in *Bania* decreased neither the bureaucracy of the Soviet state nor the artistic stagnation in the Soviet theatre, but it did make the playwright highly suspect and susceptible to the very cleansing and purging that he elaborated in all three of his major plays of the decade.

Mayakovsky contributed to the popularity and development of satire in the Soviet theatre and literature during the 1920s.[45] Yet he discovered that the satirical techniques he had developed in *Misteriia-*

---

[43] Mayakovsky, *Bania*, 317.

[44] Mayakovsky, *Bania*, 310.

[45] For a discussion of Mayakovsky's role in the development of prose satire during the 1920s, see Richard L. Chapple, *Soviet Satire of the Twenties* (Gainesville, FL: University Press of Florida, 1980); and Karen L. Ryan-Hayes, *Contemporary Russian Satire: A Genre Study* (Cambridge: Cambridge University Press, 1995), 1–4.

buff and *Klop* were distressingly out of place and time in 1930. In *Bania*, the satire of Soviet bureaucracy as represented by Pobedonosikov proved so general that it was, in effect, a critique of the entire Soviet state. In the aftermath of *Bania*, the playwright found himself accused of ideological as well as artistic counter-Revolution.[46] The trials and tribulations of bringing *Bania* to the stage left the playwright so bitter that he made a final jab at his most prominent critic, V. Ermilov, who charged Mayakovsky with petty-bourgeois leftishness, in the note explaining his tragic suicide only a month after the play's premiere.[47] Ironically, Mayakovsky had helped develop the very metaphors of cleansing that would purge him, his theatrical works, and theatrical satire as a whole from the Soviet stage of the next decade. By employing "satire's parasitic appropriation of other forms," Mayakovsky's plays of the 1920s effectively exterminated themselves from the active theatrical repertoire of the time.[48]

---

[46] The critic S. Mokul'skii accused Mayakovsky of describing the world of the future in *Bania* with an anti-Soviet tinge, "Eshche o 'Klope,'" *Zhizn' iskusstva* 13 (24 January 1929): 10. Other critics of *Bania* also pointed out Mayakovsky's insulting portrayal of Soviet reality and his apparent lack of faith in the very regime he claimed to support in the play. For an example, see "'Bania,'" 7.

[47] The critic Ermilov, who initiated the bitterest of the exchanges around the play, attacked Mayakovsky's slogan quoted above, precipitating its removal from the play's staging. In his suicide note, Mayakovsky writes, "Tell Ermilov that it's a pity the slogan was removed; we should have fought it out." For the slogan satirizing Ermilov, see "Lozungi," 350; for the suicide note, see Mayakovsky, "Pis'mo 168," in *PSS*, 13: 138.

[48] Connery and Combe, *Theorizing Satire*, 5.

Nine

Alexander Prokhorov and Helena Goscilo

Absurdity Normalized: Irony in Dovlatov's *Ours*

> All of Dolmatov's [sic] characters, includ-
> ing the narrator himself, are depicted
> from a rather comic point of view.
>
> V. Kuritsyn

> The aesthetic ideal is *our* life.
>
> V. Ermilov

Sergei Dovlatov is the Gentle Giant of Stagnation prose, a bogatyr'
manque whose larger-than-life size, appetites, and temperament peculiarly positioned him, it seems, to perceive and respond to the colossal
discrepancies of existence with the benign irony of tolerant bemusement. Since bifocalism is the essence of irony, Dovlatov's narrative
mode invariably proceeds via a dialogized perspective that spotlights the
irrationality of human behavior and its incommensurability with life.

Dovlatov's credo may be summarized by the refrain "Our world is
absurd," iterated by the main narrator in the fourth of Dovlatov's autobiographical fictionalized memoirs, *Ours* (*Nashi*, 1983). As though in
polemical reaction to this existentialist perspective, the relatives com-
prising the work's cast of characters attempt to justify their entry into,
and role in, this world. Their self-assessments, in turn, are subjected to
the skepticism of the narrator, whose irony not only throws all such
subjective readings into question, but also functions as an (admittedly
imperfect) defense against the inescapable absurdity of human
existence.

As the humorous perception of inconsistency, in which an ostensibly
straightforward statement or event is undermined by a context that
gives it a different, often antithetical, significance, irony in *Ours* is not
merely a trope, but a vision of the world. This vision richly informs the
narrator's group portrait of his expanded family. Anne Frydman's Eng-

Janet Tucker, ed. *Against the Grain: Parody, Satire and Intertextuality in Russian
Literature*. Bloomington, IN: Slavica, 2002, 149–66.

lish translation of the title, *Ours: A Russian Family Album*, makes
explicit the verbal portrait's implication in a visual genre: a collection of
snapshots that expose the inherent incompatibilities and aporias not
only of a biologically-linked family, but also of the traditional Russian
"collective" (*nashi*), ruled during the Soviet period by successive
Fathers of All Peoples. Both families metonymize humanity at large and
evoke Walter Benjamin's dictum about a family photograph as the last
locus of aura value in art: "It is no accident that the portrait was the fo-
cal point of early photography. The cult of remembrance of loved ones,
absent or dead, offers a last refuge for the cult value of the picture. For
the last time the aura emanates from the early photographs in the fleeting expression of a human face."[1]

Dovlatov's philosophical irony operates in three related spheres: in
the interaction between characters and the narrator; within the narrator's bifurcated voice, in the irony and self-irony of both intra- and
extra-diegetic narrators;[2] and in the discursive play that feeds many of
the text's comic devices.

All in the Family: Relative Life and Its Narrator

Dovlatov structures each chapter of *Ours* around a set of
"characterizing" episodes from the life of one of the narrator's relatives.
The tone of each section depends on the degree of the narrator's affinity
for the given character and on the potential accommodation of that life
to a readymade cultural genre. Wherever a life lends itself to an established form of literarization, the narrator destabilizes that identification
through ironic comments, which undermine the conventional associations of that narrative paradigm.

Critics have observed that the first generation of "ours" possesses
epic features: gigantic size, monumental deeds, and epic heroes' names.[3]

---

[1] Walter Benjamin, "The Work of Art in the Age of Mechanical
Reproduction," in *Film Theory and Criticism*, 5th ed., ed. Leo Braudy and
Marshall Cohen (New York: Oxford University Press, 1999), 738.

[2] Karen Ryan-Hayes, "Narrative Strategies in the Works of Sergei Dovlatov,"
Russian Language Journal 45, no. 153 (1992): 160; Shlomith Rimmon-Kennan,
Narrative Fiction: Contemporary Poetics (London: Methuen, 1983), 175.

[3] Il'ia Serman, "Teatr Sergeia Dovlatova," *Grani* 140 (1985): 140; Igor' Sukhikh,
Sergei Dovlatov: Vremia, mesto, sud'ba (St. Petersburg: Kul'tInformPress,
1996), 178–80.

Accordingly, the first chapter of *Ours* opens with a Biblical name and possessive adjective ("our great grandfather Moses"), signaling the epic dimensions of the story of origins that follows. Almost immediately, however, the narrator subverts the epic beginning by invoking popular Russian stereotypes and the ending of Nikolai Gogol's absurdist story "The Nose":

> The fact is, to be both a Jew and a peasant was rather rare, but it sometimes happened in the Far East... His son Isaak moved to the city, which is to say, he got things back to normal.[4]

> Say what you like, but such things do happen—not often, but they do happen.[5]

In addition to establishing Dovlatov's narrative mode, the first two paragraphs of *Ours* raise the work's central question of the balance between normal and absurd in human life. "Everything's normal/as usual" ("Vse normal'no"), a standard Soviet response to the query "How are you?", suggests what Dovlatov's family album collectively illustrates: the acceptance of lunacy itself as normal.

Having sounded the work's major thematic motif, the narrator continues the saga of his grandfather, constantly oscillating between epic narrative devices and ironic observations that deflate them. Like Il'ia Muromets or Peter the Great, Grandpa Isaak is of mythic proportions, with the hyperbolic appearance of a warrior: "Grandpa was almost seven feet tall. He could put an entire apple in his mouth. His mustache drooped to his rifle sling."[6] Isaak performs superhuman deeds in battle and in events on which the fate of the nation hinges.

> He was assigned to an artillery battery. If a horse gave out from exhaustion, Grandpa would drag the cannon through the swamp. Once, the battery took part in a battle. Grandpa was in the front line of the attack. An armed detachment was supposed to cover the front-line soldiers, but most of the guns were silent. My

---

[4] Sergei Dovlatov, *Ours: A Russian Family Album*, trans. Anne Frydman (New York: Weidenfeld and Nicolson, 1989), 3.

[5] Nikolai Gogol, "The Nose," in *The Overcoat and Other Tales of Good and Evil*, trans. David Magarshack (New York: W. W. Norton & Co., 1965), 232.

[6] Dovlatov, *Ours*, 4.

grandfather's back, it turned out, was blocking their view of the enemy.[7]

> He held a negative view of the Revolution, more than that, he even slowed its progress a little.... At the outbreak of the Revolution, masses of people ... began rushing towards the center of the city. Grandpa decided it was a pogrom against Jews. He got out his rifle and ... when the crowds drew near, he began firing into the air... Nevertheless, the Revolution won. The great mass of people made it to the center of town by the alleyways.[8]

Although the second passage begins as a clichéd Soviet revolutionary epic ("masses of people," "rushing towards the center of the city"), its elevated tone is immediately undercut, first by Isaak's mundane, knee-jerk misapprehension of events ("Grandpa decided it was a pogrom"[9]), then by the narrator's ironic explanation of how the revolution came to Vladivostok ("by the alleyways"). And at chapter's end, the epic tenor of Isaak's life undergoes further debasement by comic analogy with the narrator. Dovlatov reduces their impressive Rabelaisian appetite and physical magnitude to the practical, and socially embarrassing, quandary of filling their stomachs:

> Grandpa Isaak ate a great deal.... When he and Grandma Raya were invited out to dinner, Grandma was always blushing on account of him.... I often think of my grandfather... For instance.... my wife may say to me: "Tonight we're going to the Dombrovskys for supper. We should get you something to eat beforehand."[10]

Isaak's life therefore cannot be comfortably pigeonholed according to the "norms" of any single genre, for the narrator's sardonic perspective prevents such a straightforward, unambiguous reading. Viewed from diverse angles, that life resists finalization. Such a dialogized treatment, with constant shifts between the narrator's sardonic commentary and the characters' one-dimensional self-definitions, also dominates the

---

[7] Dovlatov, *Ours*, 4.

[8] Dovlatov, *Ours*, 5.

[9] Dovlatov, *Ours*, 51.

[10] Dovlatov, *Ours*, 6, 8.

chapters devoted to Uncles Roman and Leopold, Aunt Mara, and the narrator's father.

Uncle Roman believes that his life enacts the Roman maxim *Mens sana in corpore sano* (in Russian, *V zdorovom tele—sootvetstvuiushchii dukh[11]*), a formula enthusiastically embraced by the Soviet regime, as evidenced by A. Deineka's numerous paintings of energetic, beaming athletes. The semantic emptiness of the word *sootvetstvuiushchii*, however, allows the narrator to unveil the tragic irony of his uncle's borrowed motto: the sportsman extraordinaire succumbs to insanity. A maniac stabs his wife, the dog he buys for protection attacks her, and Uncle Roman mentally unravels. Committed to a psychiatric hospital, he purportedly recovers:

> A month later, he was well... He would talk about jogging the whole way around the Forestry Institute each day. About how he felt healthier and fitter than ever before. ... I imagined my uncle jogging early in the morning by the fence of the Forestry Institute. Whither, O Lord?[12]

The Gogolian rhetorical question that concludes the chapter points to men's delusional attachment to optimistic homilies in the teeth of lived experience. Uncle Roman's daily circular motion around the campus becomes an ironic symbol of the "normal" human condition. The narrator's alternative reading of Roman's life—as a series of absurd, horrifying episodes à la Daniil Kharms—provides an ironizing counter-perspective to that irrationally proclaimed norm. A parallel treatment partially debunks Uncle Aron's genre-specific life, which "zigzags like the history of the Soviet Union itself,"[13] and Uncle Leopold's, which resembles an adventure novel ("his escapades took their place among the adventures of James Fenimore Cooper and Mayne Reid heroes").[14]

Dovlatov juxtaposes the individuals who insist on a fixed monological life-narrative to those who rebel against their "destiny." Since the latter ruffle the calm surface of their own life-flow by challenging its

---

[11] Sergei Dovlatov, *Nashi*, in *Sobranie prozy v trekh tomakh* (St. Petersburg: Limbus Press, 1993), 2: 164.

[12] Dovlatov, *Ours*, 21.

[13] Dovlatov, *Ours*, 45.

[14] Dovlatov, *Ours*, 26.

course, they liberate the narrator from that task, leaving him merely to recount the incidents that most vividly exemplify their struggle against their fate. The chapter on the narrator's second grandfather, Stepan, typifies this mode of enabling interaction between the narrator and his relatives. Grandpa Stepan's story focuses on his two duels with God; the first ends in a draw, the second in tragedy for Stepan, some of whose concerns coincide with the narrator's.

> Perhaps the universe, such as it was, did not suit him. I wonder, did it not suit him in its entirety, or just in certain details? Was it the changing of the seasons? The indestructible order of life and death? ... I don't know.[15]

While the narrator downplays his customary irony in this chapter, Stepan's carnivalized skirmishes with his creator compensate for that loss. Grandpa's weapon in his verbal battle with God is the magic word "Kakem! ... I crap on you!"[16] This carnival image challenges—more-over, in a visually stunning spatial reversal—the hierarchy of a supreme divinity and the human created in His image. When Stepan dies, his posthumous voice (in a parodic vulgarization of deism) sounds irrep-ressibly in the gurgling of a stream: "only then ... through the unceasing noise of the stream skirting the gloomy boulders, could they hear, con-temptuous and menacing: 'Ka-a-kem!'."[17]

The characters who interrogate or protest against a monological reading of their lives—whether imposed or self-posited—are sufficiently close to the narrator's own perspectival stance to escape his ironic treatment. The dramatic irony that inheres in the internal conflict be-tween their fate and their resistance to it suffices to maintain the ironic ambivalence and ambiguities indispensable for Dovlatov's narrative manner. Indeed, the narrator's sympathy towards such relatives verges on the sentimental, reintroducing the outdated cult value of the work of art. A prime instance of such a (con)fusion of character zones occurs in the chapter on his cousin Boris, who, as the illegitimate son of a high-ranking party official in Leningrad, seems preordained to the role of a successful Party functionary.

---

[15] Dovlatov, *Ours*, 12.
[16] Dovlatov, *Ours*, 10.
[17] Dovlatov, *Ours*, 13.

In unfolding the criminal saga of Boris's life, the narrator directs his irony not at his relatives, but at the Soviet system, whose iron laws Boris manipulates and fights with ingenious but ultimately unavailing skill. From the outset Dovlatov mordantly formulates Boris's moral dilemma as a career choice between the lesser evil of violating the law and the greater one of Partying: "Life turned my cousin into a criminal. It seems to me he was lucky. Otherwise, he would inevitably have become a high-ranking Party functionary."[18] To preserve self-respect, Boris, "a natural-born existentialist,"[19] must become a criminal. In a sense, Boris is the antithesis of Uncle Roman: the latter blindly adheres to an unexamined platitude that screens off and reduces the complexities of life, whereas Boris can engage only those complexities. Hence his periodic invasion of the narrator's zone (a narrator who similarly drinks, philosophizes, and weighs options, hesitating "between Paris and prison"[20] and "prison and America.")[21]

The most intimate mode of interaction between Dovlatov's narrator and his relatives, however, is reserved for the women in *Ours*: his mother, wife, daughter, and bitch Glasha. They all function as mirrors for the narrator's self, and he recounts their stories primarily in the first-person singular or plural. This technique periodically relegates these characters to the background, while foregrounding the narrator. The most representative chapter in this respect is the one about his mother, which opens, tellingly, with information about the narrator: "From early childhood my upbringing was politically tendentious.... I myself knew.... I knew.... That does not mean that I was a ... reflective boy. It was simply that I was told these things by ... my mother."[22] Shifting to a first-person plural narrative voice, the narrator moves from a description of the communal apartment he shared with his mother after his parents divorced to a rapid survey of the disasters and misfortunes that dominate his life and *therefore* profoundly affect his mother (whom, in a revealing displacement, he "kept threatening with marriage").[23]

---

[18] Dovlatov, *Ours*, 75.
[19] Dovlatov, *Ours*, 96.
[20] Dovlatov, *Ours*, 73.
[21] Dovlatov, *Ours*, 108.
[22] Dovlatov, *Ours*, 53–54.
[23] Dovlatov, *Ours*, 60.

Acknowledging his role as "a constant source of grief" for her, the narrator laces his self-irony with sentiment. In fact, this chapter gradually metamorphoses into a love story—a tale of elective affinities and kindred souls that remain united, even when confronted with the trauma of emigration:

> I didn't even ask my mother if she was ready to make the journey out with me. I was amazed to learn that there were families who took months to make up their minds... Now we live in New York, and we'll never part. Just as we never parted before.... [24]

Whereas absence of conversation with his wife symptomatizes their lack of communication, silences with his mother reflect their mutual comprehension, which requires no words.

The "female-centered" chapters in *Ours* emphasize the indestructible absurdity above all of the narrator's own existence. His inability to make sense of his own life provides a powerful source of self-irony and a prophylactic against finalizing others. As a result, Dovlatov's narrator appears endearingly unjudgmental and porous, open to radically diverse experiences and individuals. Indeed, the creature with whom he feels the most empathetic bond is the remotest one biologically, his fox terrier Glasha, whom the narrator maximally humanizes: "We have a lot in common. We're both not young, easily irritable foreigners with complexes ... we both like to steal sausage out of the fridge."[25] The English version of *Ours* replaces this ironic closure with Glasha's death in New York and the family's acquisition of the "Americanized" dachshund Yashka (a canine clone of Arnold Schwarzenegger ["has no neuroses ... always in a good mood"],[26] named in honor of *Novoe russkoe slovo*'s editor, Andrei Sedykh).[27] In this affectionate chapter, the humor automatically built into the device of anthropomorphizing animals saves Dovlatov's narrator from bathos.

If Glasha duplicates, and his mother overlaps with, the narrator, his wife defines him through contrast. The hilarious chapter titled "The Colonel Says I Love You" spotlights the narrator's bafflement in the

---

[24] Dovlatov, *Ours*, 64.

[25] Dovlatov, *Nashi*, 115.

[26] Dovlatov, *Ours*, 110.

[27] Aleksandr Genis, *Dovlatov i okrestnosti* (Moscow: Vagrius, 1999), 188.

midst of romance parodying Turgenev's tales of superfluous men and strong women. His future wife, Lena, embodies the active principle, her energy mobilizing his entropic habits: the decisions to move in with him, to divorce him, to emigrate, and to live with him again in the United States belong to her alone. Just as Glasha's suitors prove absurdly ineffectual, so does the largely passive narrator vis-à-vis Lena. Accordingly, in a quintessentially ludicrous displacement, not he, but a KGB colonel declares the narrator's love for his wife and daughter: "It was in this way that my love for my wife ... became a fact. And the person who stood witness to it turned out to be a KGB colonel."[28] Little wonder, then, that the narrator characterizes his marital situation as "normalized lunacy": "Our madness took everyday, commonplace forms."[29] An analogous self-irony dictates his summary of relations with his daughter: "My daughter treated me well. A bit of compassion, a bit of contempt."[30] Of the four females sharing his domicile, the narrator's hierarchy of affection places Glasha and mother above spouse and daughter. Dovlatov's language recreates the normalized lunacy of all in the family via a paradoxical misalliance of distancing irony and intimate, sentimental reminiscences.

Fragmented "Facts" and Discursive Dementia

Like his relatives, the narrator has a multiple identity or narrating persona: as intra-diegetic narrator he participates in the events of the stories he tells, whereas as extra-diegetic narrator he stands outside those stories and tends to ruminate on the meaning of lives he sketches in for the reader.[31] Both narrators confine themselves to fragmented episodes from their relatives' biographies or, in the words of one critic, to "microabsurdities,"[32] i.e., selective miniatures in which personae, setting, plot, and especially language fracture conventional logic.

Joseph Brodsky maintains, with some validity, that the narrator's language is the cardinal element in Dovlatov's writing: "Plot ... is just an

---

[28] Dovlatov, *Ours*, 123.

[29] Dovlatov, *Ours*, 118, 117.

[30] Dovlatov, *Ours*, 131.

[31] Ryan-Hayes, "Narrative Strategies," 160.

[32] Viktor Toporov, "Dom, kotoryi postroil Dzhek: O proze Dovlatova," *Zvezda* 3 (1994): 175.

excuse for the discourse itself."[33] In fact, the irony of microabsurdities in *Ours* pivots on a combination of "normalized" illogicalities with comic rhetorical devices. The most frequent among the former is the neutralizing of absurdity, whereby an absurd statement remains unchallenged, rendered commonplace by elaboration or multiple repetitions. For example, "Like all discharged lieutenant colonels, he [Uncle Roman] was put in charge of security technology at his place of work... (Full colonels are assigned to head personnel departments)."[34] The ironic effect here derives from the utter untenability of a universal equation between the rank of discharged officers and their area of responsibility in civilian life, an illogicality compounded by the parenthetical afterthought, which suggests an entire system of illogicalities that operate as a "norm." A kindred "everyday insanity" rules conduct in the chapter on cousin Boris: "My aunt already knew everything [her son had killed a man]. She made telephone calls to writers who had connections with the militia. To Yuri Gherman, to Metter, Saparov... As a result, my cousin was left in peace until the trial."[35] Here the irony stems partially from the discrepancy between the tone of the narrator and the expectations of the implied reader. The narrator matter-of-factly presents as "normal" his aunt's appeal for aid to those writer-friends who have written about the Soviet militia. For the implied Russian reader who understands the Soviet network of influence (*blat*), it is a foregone conclusion, albeit a wildly irrational one, that authors of fiction about the militia will actually have an impact on real-life militia investigating a bona fide crime. The narrator ironizes the Soviet version of modernism: art transforming life, writers helping to manipulate the legal process. And, for the Western reader, that ridiculous state of affairs is itself criminal.

The ploy of deceived expectations, likewise founded on arbitrariness, is another of Dovlatov's favorite ironic devices. The narrator or a character violates shared cultural stereotypes by replacing the second part of a proposition with a semantically possible but culturally non-idiomatic statement: "People like him [Uncle Roman] are valued in

---

[33] Iosif Brodskii, "O Serezhe Dovlatove," *Petropol': Pamiati Sergeia Dovlatova* 5 (1994): 169.

[34] Dovlatov, *Ours*, 16.

[35] Dovlatov, *Ours*, 89.

wartime. Even in peacetime he loved to raise hell."[36] Instead of the anticipated hero whose bravery and endurance qualify him for the epic deeds of war, the narrator offers the reader a local hoodlum, simultaneously reducing war to the level of neighborhood scandal. In a passage that echoes the memorable opening of Joseph Heller's *Catch-22*, Dovlatov uses the device, in a slightly different key, to characterize Uncle Aron: "He fell in love with ... Sakharov ... mainly because he had helped invent the hydrogen bomb in the Soviet Union and then hadn't become a drunk but fought for the truth."[37] Uncle Aron's life becomes a series of amorous infatuations with public figures ranging from Lenin, Stalin, Malenkov, and Khrushchev to Sakharov and Solzhenitsyn.

Thwarted expectations are not the exclusive property of the extra-diagetic narrator. The intra-diagetic narrator also deploys this stratagem for ironic effect ("We touched on a rather narrow range of themes: lynching, the decline of morals, the Vietnam epic.... "),[38] as do the work's characters. At the jubilee celebrations of the Georgian Republic's seventh anniversary, the first phrase of Aunt Aniela's speech is completed in absurdly anomalous fashion by her brother, Uncle Roman: "'It has already been seven years,' she began ... and then ... my uncle's voice rang out: 'It's already been seven years and no one's married Aniela.'"[39] The device works most powerfully when logical expectation becomes not only frustrated, but turned on its head: "I've seen good reviews of the plays he [the narrator's father] directed. Of course, at that time, there were plenty of bad reviews of the great Meyerhold's productions."[40] The first sentence could provide a perfect closure to a paragraph assessing his father's modest talent. Yet the second sentence neatly reverses the gist of the preceding one, for through eloquent juxtaposition, negative critiques of "the great Meyerhold's" productions discredit the authenticity of the positive reviews received by the narrator's father.

---

[36] Dovlatov, *Ours*, 16.

[37] Dovlatov, *Ours*, 47.

[38] Dovlatov, *Ours*, 47.

[39] Dovlatov, *Ours*, 15.

[40] Dovlatov, *Ours*, 66.

A device closely related to that of unrealized expectations is ironic specification, whereby an ostensibly precise qualification actually generates a discrepancy between what is said and what is meant: "The Colonel was glad that Mama had at last found personal happiness, and what was even better, with a politically mature comrade."[41] Double-voiced discourse creates the irony here, for the colonel's "naive" voice is filtered through the "distanced" discourse of the extra-diagetic narrator. Elsewhere Dovlatov enhances a parallel instance of ironic specification by the ambiguity of the key word "appointment" (in Russian, *svidanie*): "And I had an appointment at five-thirty. To make matters worse, it was not with a woman, but with Brodsky."[42] Besides the expectation-thwarting illogicality of the specification "to make matters worse," irony surrounds the ambiguous meaning of the Russian word *svidanie* for meeting, which is closer to the English "date" or "rendezvous." That instability of meaning reinforces the narrator's self-irony at a key juncture in his negotiations with his future wife.

Many of Dovlatov's ironic microabsurdities rely on paronomasia, and the significance of word play as ironic device in *Ours* cannot be overestimated. Paronomasia represents moments of verbal chaos, slippage, a gap in the chain of signifiers. Moreover, it affords maximum possibilities for irony, for miscommunication, and for discrepancies in meaning.

> For days on end she [mother] would fight agonizing battles for quiet. Once ... she hung a ... sign on her doors: "A half-corpse [*polutrup*] is resting inside. Silence please!" And suddenly it became ... quiet in the apartment... Tikhomirov ... kept grabbing everyone by the arm and hissing, "Quiet! A political instructor (*politruk*) is spending a night in Dovlatova's room."[43]

What accentuates the irony here is the not unpersuasive argument that, morally speaking, a political instructor *is* a semi-corpse.

Newspaper typos similarly offer opportunities for word play. As the narrator notes, "For example, take a headline like 'An order from the Commander in Chief.' 'Commander in Chief (*glavnokomanduiushchii*)

[41] Dovlatov, *Ours*, 56.
[42] Dovlatov, *Ours*, 114.
[43] Dovlatov, *Ours*, 55–56.

is such a long word, all you had to do was drop the letter 'l' in Russian and you got the equivalent of 'Commander in Shit'."[44] The narrator concludes his list of microabsurdities on newspaper typos with a Lacanian insight, "As everyone knows, the only truth in *our* papers is the misprints."[45] The numerous oxymorons in *Ours* lay bare the same incompatibility and instability of meanings: "He wrote that the *camp* was a *good* one, and the *camp administration* fairly *humane*."[46] Dovlatov's good camps and humane camp administrations satirically anticipate Vladimir Sorokin's vacations in Dachau.

The ironic devices of deceived expectations, non-logical specification, word play, and oxymoron shape a set of implicit norms that find their narrative expression in microabsurdities. These microabsurdities dialogize the structure of chapters in *Ours*, providing its dehierarchized discourse. "The mixture of the everyday and the absurd"[47] antecedes the sense, the logic that the heroes of *Ours* project onto the world as a defense against its enigmatic absurdity. Whenever a character tries to impose a coherent teleology on his life story, Dovlatov ensures that a series of ironic discrepancies emerge between the unifying unilinearity of that design and the narrator's microabsurdities. Uncle Aron, for example, adopts love of his motherland as his ruling algorithm; the principle of microabsurdities, however, transforms him into the fickle whore of grotesque ideological romance: his worship of one Soviet political leader after another ends only with the unrequited lover's death.[48]

Although both intra- and extra-diegetic narrators are present in all chapters of *Ours*, the relative distribution of the two narrative modes in the book is uneven. Whereas the extra-diegetic narrator dominates the first eight chapters of the book, in the last five he cedes to the intra-diegetic one. This switch brings the implied reader closer to *Ours*' implied author, a maneuver used earlier in *Zona*: "With this shift to the first person, we gain a more intimate, more visceral knowledge of the experiences that underlie the implied author's attitudes and opinions."[49]

---

[44] Dovlatov, *Ours*, 55.

[45] Dovlatov, *Ours*, 55, emphasis added.

[46] Dovlatov, *Ours*, 92, emphasis added.

[47] Dovlatov, *Ours*, 114.

[48] Dovlatov, *Ours*, 46–48.

[49] Ryan-Hayes, "Narrative Strategies," 160–61.

This technique of increasing proximity acquires particular importance when the narrator addresses the most volatile issue of the entire book: the loss of one's cultural and national identity for a newly adopted one—in other words, the meaning of the title *Ours*. Although Dovlatov can hardly be said to treat this problem exhaustively, his narrator voices several opinions that appear controversial, especially in the context of Russian tradition. Foremost is the notion, so blasphemous within Russian cultural mythology, that a change of citizenship and cultural environment (i.e., the "loss of 'Russianness'")[50] may be traumatic, but disqualifies as tragedy. The Russian edition of *Ours* ends not with a nostalgic sob, but on a note of bemusement implicitly projected into the future of a new beginning: "On December 23, 1981 in New York, my little son was born…. He's an American, a citizen of the U.S. His name is, can you imagine, Nicholas Dowley. That's what my family and motherland have come to."[51]

A key question related to the phenomenon of identity is what makes people close.[52] Throughout the volume, the narrator demonstrates that blood ties, common language, and shared experiences cannot account for human intimacy and understanding. The seemingly arbitrary and unpredictable occurrence of empathy elicits the narrator's favorite explanation for things inexplicable: "Life is absurd! It has to be absurd if I can feel closer to a German than to my own uncle [Leopold]."[53]

Both narrators not only alternate in the course of the book, but also interact with each other. When the intra-diegetic gravitates toward a finalized cultural model, the extra-diegetic narrator subverts his authority through ironic remarks. For example, in the chapter about Uncle Leopold, the intra-diegetic narrator tends to occupy the position of a detached onlooker above the story's events, who concurs with his German friend's sweeping generalization that "inactivity is the only moral condition known to man. All waking activity finishes in corruption."[54] This vantage point of philosophical wisdom is dialogized by the tongue-in-cheek pseudo-naiveté of the extra-diegetic narrator's confes-

---

[50] Ryan-Hayes, "Narrative Strategies," 167.

[51] Dovlatov, *Nashi*, 244.

[52] Also noted by Ryan-Hayes in "Narrative Strategies," 167–68.

[53] Dovlatov, *Ours*, 37.

[54] Dovlatov, *Ours*, 37.

sion that follows: "To tell the truth, I don't know how he [the German] got into the story. I was talking about an entirely different person, my uncle Leopold."[55]

The voice of the extra-diegetic narrator who wields irony to dialogize all potentially authoritative discourse in the text has a complex structure. For his microabsurdities and commentary on them, he resorts to two types of double-voicing: anticipatory discourse and stylization. The first anticipates the word of various characters or the implied reader. While noting his Aunt Mara's excellence as an editor, for example, he poses a rhetorical question that has no ultimate answer:

> I think my aunt was a good editor. That's what I've been told by the writers she edited.... Nevertheless, I still believe a writer does not need an editor. ... Why didn't Dostoyevski want to eliminate a glaring error?[56]

The narrator's proleptic word creates an irony of expediency; after conceding the high quality of this or that profession (or someone's performance), he proceeds to question the necessity of its existence at all. Elsewhere the narrator adopts a calculatedly ingenuous stance when asking rhetorical but morally loaded questions intended to explode the veracity of self-serving disclaimers: "There's one thing I don't understand. How come my ordinary parents knew everything [about Stalin's murderous activities], while Ilya Ehrenburg didn't?"[57]

The anticipation of the other's word also finds expression in ironic apostrophes that invite the reader to believe in the most paradoxical or outlandish suppositions. For example, in a passage omitted from the English version, the narrator implicates the reader is a wholly fantastic theory of a connection between people's names and fates:

> Agree that a person's name to a significant extent defines his character and even his biography. Anatoly is almost always pushy and a bully... Zoya—a single mother... The name Mikhail is a

[55] Dovlatov, *Ours*, 37.
[56] Dovlatov, *Ours*, 40–41.
[57] Dovlatov, *Ours*, 54; Ryan-Hayes, "Narrative Strategies," 168.

hollow omen of an early death. (Recall Lermontov, Kol'tsov, Bulgakov...).[58]

Dovlatov ignores, of course, the notorious counter example of Mikhail Sholokhov, whose style he explicitly derides in a subsequent passage.

Stylization constitutes another aspect of the narrator's double-voiced discourse, thereby contributing to the illusion of a conversation among competing views. Among the forms and authors engaged through stylization are the fairy tale exposition ("My Jewish grandfather ... had three sons, just as in fairy tales"),[59] Nekrasov's idealistic paeans to peasant children (only in the Russian text),[60] and, by negation, the flash and dash of Sholokhov's Cossack tales. Repudiating in advance any chance similarity between an episode in his narrative and Sholokhov's, the narrator obviates the danger of Sholokhovism through omission: "And it even came about that I stood guard over my cousin... I don't really want to write about it. Otherwise everything would come out sounding overliterary, like Mikhail Sholokhov's *Tales from the Don*."[61]

Although the narrator's rewriting of others' stories multiplies voices, it ultimately emphasizes the unchangeable, ubiquitous nature of "normalized lunacy."[62] The consciousness of regularized madness is reiterated in the voice of both narrators, but with the aid of different strategies. The intra-diegetic narrator opts for framing, whereas his extra-diegetic counterpart favors the device of catalogue. An example of the former occurs in the chapter about his wife, where a newspaper serves as the element linking two moments that capture the unremitting absurdity of their marital relations. When he meets his future wife in Russia, "'Look the other way,' Lena said. I covered my face with a newspaper."[63] That scene is replayed in America, where, after their divorce, the narrator joins his wife: "Then Lena said, 'Look the other

---

[58] Dovlatov, *Nashi*, 26.

[59] Dovlatov, *Ours*, 22.

[60] Dovlatov, *Nashi*, 101.

[61] Dovlatov, *Ours*, 83.

[62] Dovlatov, *Ours*, 118.

[63] Dovlatov, *Ours*, 113.

way.' I covered my face with an American newspaper."[64] The extra-diegetic narrator conveys the same notion of fundamental, unabating irrationality through a list:

> When the police took away … Liabin, the choirmaster … my father reminded everyone that Liabin was an anti-Semite. When they arrested the philologist Roginski, it was revealed that Roginski drank. … And Shapiro, the cinematographer, conducted himself with amazing assurance for a Jew.[65]

The monotonous repetition, iconicized in the catalogue, makes murder a "justifiable" everyday event. Onlookers discover "rational" explanations for these arrests, according to the law articulated by the narrator's father: "Each flaw was punished."[66] Embedded as they are in the discourse of the main narrator, and immediately preceding the information that Grandpa Isaak, a "manifestly good man," also disappeared, the father's words acquire an ironic cast. That irony exposes men's habit of manufacturing reasonable causes for the basic insanity that underlies the human condition.

The ratio of normal to insane in our lives makes up the paradoxical identity of *Ours*. It supplies a structure of sorts to the narrative, and nowhere more tellingly than in the volume's sequence of chapters. Indeed, the concluding chapter questions the entire project and (in the English translation) ends with an ironic paradox: "He [the narrator's American son] will have his own history, but it will be the history of another, American family. With Kolya, this book is done. I hope that it has been clear to everyone that it has been his story."[67]

An ideal narrative mode for registering discrepancy, irony in *Ours* attains the stature of a worldview. Dovlatov's profound awareness of life's absurdities and inconsistencies rejects the summative stability of finalization; hence not only the indeterminate genre of *Ours* (and of his other quasi-"memoirs"), but also the divergence in viewpoints within the work and the disparities between the Russian and English versions of the text. It is, surely, Dovlatov's capacity for disengagement—for

---

[64] Dovlatov, *Ours*, 126.
[65] Dovlatov, *Ours*, 67.
[66] Dovlatov, *Ours*, 67.
[67] Dovlatov, *Ours*, 133.

perceiving all phenomena ironically—that made him the quintessential outsider in any milieu, while simultaneously enabling his literary exploitation of that status in a humorously philosophical key. In *The Invisible Book* Dovlatov's narrator maintains that irony directed at oneself is "always a sure sign of intelligence."[68] By that measure, Dovlatov may best be remembered as one of the most intelligent, as well as most human, prosaists of Russia's Stagnation Era.

---

[68] Dovlatov, *Ours*, 32.

Ten

Caryl Emerson

Sinyavsky's Rozanov, Tertz's Pushkin, and Literary Criticism as Creative Parody

> Of course, Abram Tertz is a mask, but a mask that is tightly fitted to my soul…. First I invented Tertz and then fantastic realism.
>
> Andrei Sinyavsky, during an interview in Arlington, Virginia, January 1, 1990[1]

> Had the connection remained undiscovered, … the two would probably have continued to coexist peacefully, "the impudent, fantastic 'Abram Tertz' alongside Andrei Sinyavsky, the honest intellectual, inclined to compromises and to an isolated and contemplative life."
>
> Donald Fanger discussing the author and his alter ego, quoting from Tertz's *Goodnight!*[2]

In the late 1960s, Andrei Sinyavsky, serving his term in Dubrovlag in Soviet Mordovia, clandestinely transmitted to the outside world portions of his *Progulki s Pushkinym* (*Strolls with Pushkin*) in the form of letters to his wife. Three decades later, after the second wave of scandals had already broken over that marvelous text, Sinyavsky was asked during an interview what authority he claimed for his notorious book.

---

[1] Catharine Theimer Nepomnyashchy, "An Interview with Andrei Sinyavsky," (Arlington, Virginia, January, 1990), *Formations* 6, no. 1 (Spring 1991): 6–23, esp. 6 and 8.

[2] Donald Fanger, "Conflicting Imperatives in the Model of the Russian Writer: The Case of Tertz/Sinyavsky," in *Literature and History: Theoretical Problems and Russian Case Studies*, ed. Gary Saul Morson (Stanford: Stanford University Press, 1986), 111–24, esp. 115.

Janet Tucker, ed. *Against the Grain: Parody, Satire and Intertextuality in Russian Literature.* Bloomington, IN: Slavica, 2002, 167–84.

For it had agitated and offended readers across a wide critical spectrum. In it, Pushkin appears not as the somber icon of Russian genius but as a fidgety, polymorphously erotic, generous, profoundly tolerant figure, a poet whose godterm was *pustota* (emptiness) and whose worldview was "lightness in relation to life."[3] Sinyavsky replied that *Strolls* was not literary criticism but "*fantasticheskoe literaturovedenie*" (fantastic literary scholarship). In this genre, he assured his interviewer, the critic "emphasizes some things, exaggerates others," even consciously "does things wrong"; in any event, he insisted, *Strolls* was never intended as a "textbook for the study of Pushkin."[4]

Strolls with Pushkin was later joined by a second, similarly eccentric work of literary criticism, *V teni Gogolia* (*In the Shadow of Gogol*). If the earlier book had portrayed Pushkin's life—so strewn with genuine risk and crisis—as vibrant, even inexhaustible, then Nikolai Gogol (whose biography, we learn, was "poor in events and awesomely full of material benefits and good fortune") is depicted as a man "in the process of dying his whole life long"; the book opens on its own epilogue.[5] Both these "fantastical," speculative works were signed "Abram Tertz." The other critical works of Sinyavsky's Parisian emigration—*Ivan-Durak* on Russian folk belief, a series of Sorbonne lectures on Soviet civilization, and a monograph on Vasilii Rozanov—were published under "Andrei Sinyavsky." We might assume, therefore, that this second group of academic exercises were not exaggerations; that on their pages things were consciously done right, and that they were reliable enough to serve, at least to some extent, as "textbooks."

This essay examines the distinction between Andrei Sinyavsky and Abram Tertz as literary critics. Considerable scholarly attention has been devoted to the relationship between the real-life author and his pseudonym (for Sinyavsky did not abandon "Tertz" after the political necessity for that persona had passed); that work will not be repeated here. My task is narrower: to consider the Sinyavsky–Tertz relationship

---

[3] Abram Tertz [Andrei Sinyavsky], *Strolls with Pushkin*, trans. Catharine Theimer Nepomnyashchy and Slava I. Yastremski (New Haven: Yale University Press, 1993), 50.

[4] Nepomnyashchy, "An Interview with Andrei Sinyavsky," 10.

[5] Abram Terts [Andrei Sinyavsky], *V teni Gogolia*, in *Sobranie sochinenii v dvukh tomakh* (Moscow: Start, 1992), 2: 6, 7.

as a sort of parody. I invoke the term not as a synonym for ridicule or satire, however, nor do I assume its dynamics to be necessarily binary (that is, parody as the subversion or negation of an original, singular authority). Rather I have in mind parody as it originated in classical drama—where the burlesque vigor, the irreverence and comic inventiveness bestowed upon a variant set of scenes enacted during or after the performance of a tragedy was intended to celebrate the perpetual human appetite for alternatives *other than what you see*, for possible parallel unfoldings of the main plot. Mikhail Bakhtin relies on just such a concept of parody in his discussion of the "fourth drama" and "comic Hercules"/"comic Odysseus"—popular travestying images that introduced "the corrective of laughter [and] the corrective of reality" into the higher, more serious, canonically fixed genres.[6] Thus my use of the term resembles what Gary Saul Morson recently has called "sideshadowing," his term for a narrative strategy that unsettles our sense of inevitability and linear sequence by restoring a "field of possibilities" (that is, a sense of the "reality of unactualized possibilities") to the present moment.[7] To the extent that parody succeeds in satisfying this "basic impulse for emotional counterpoint to tragic themes,"[8] it can be said to model not only the creative process but perhaps even the psychic contours of hope itself, ever being renewed out of inert materials and latent potentials. This capacious definition of parody seems appropriate for *Strolls with Pushkin*—that naughty, non-canonical portrait of a constantly harassed and yet bouyantly free poet, composed by an inmate in a Soviet prison camp to be sent out into an unsure political twilight.

Sinyavsky has confirmed that he signs his straight academic articles and books with his own name. The alternative "Abram Tertz" is used whenever a spirit of transgression is dominant; for Tertz, Sinyavsky explains, is less a persona than a "stylistic definition" compounded of the

---

[6] Mikhail Bakhtin, "From the Prehistory of Novelistic Discourse" (1940), in *The Dialogic Imagination: Four Essays by M.M. Bakhtin*, trans. Caryl Emerson and Michael Holquist (Austin: University of Texas Press, 1981), 54–56.

[7] Gary Saul Morson, *Narrative and Freedom: The Shadows of Time* (New Haven: Yale University Press, 1994), esp. chap. 4, "Sideshadowing."

[8] From the entry on "Parody" in *Princeton Encyclopedia of Poetry and Poetics*, ed. Alex Preminger (Princeton: Princeton University Press, 1974), 600.

"grotesque" and of "hyperbole, irony."[9] I would go further, however, and suggest that in the straight "Sinyavskian" genre, the more crooked and complex the figure or topic, the more straightforward is the treatment. My case in point—exemplary because so extreme—will be Sinyavsky's monograph on the most deliberately contradictory and crooked work written by Vasilii Rozanov, the two aphoristic, chaotic volumes of *Fallen Leaves*. This sober monograph will be contrasted with *Strolls*: for, unlike his progenitor Sinyavsky, Tertz practices creative parody. He does so, I suggest, not only to enable him to approach the personality and works of a primary creator with the perogatives of a special, more liberated sort of literary critic. Such a stance also enables him and his readers to taste, in the brilliant instance of Aleksandr Pushkin, the energy that drives literary creativity itself.

To begin with the more famous book. Two waves of scandal were set off by *Strolls with Pushkin*. The first simmered among emigrés in the mid-1970s; the second, in the late 1980s, exploded on home ground. Both stirred many famous minds to memorable invective about patriotism, pluralism, and the sanctity of the Russian classics. During these bitter, often *ad hominem* debates, however, only the most irregular attention was paid to formal questions of *genre*.[10] In fact, both the scandals and the rehabilitation were highly curious.

In its October 1990 issue, the literary journal *Voprosy literatury* (*Questions of Literature*) published a forum on critical reactions to the offending book.[11] In his entry, the critic and senior Pushkinist Sergei

---

[9] Nepomnyashchy, "An Interview with Andrei Sinyavsky," 6.

[10] For more detail, see Catharine Theimer Nepomnyashchy, "Notes on the Context of Siniavskii's Reception in Gorbachev's Russia," *Russian Studies in Literature* 28, no. 1 (Winter 1991–92): 3–11; and also Catharine Theimer Nepomnyashchy, *The Poetics of Crime: An Approach to the Writings of Abram Tertz* (New Haven: Yale University Press, 1995), chap. 1, "The Trials of Abram Tertz."

[11] For this forum in full, see "Obsuzhdenie knigi Abrama Tertsa 'Progulki s Pushkinym'," in *Voprosy literatury* (October 1990): 77–153; for a translation of an abbreviated selection (roughly one-third the entries, including Valentin Nepomnashchy, Sergei Bocharov, Alla Marchenko, Petr Vail, Aleksandr Genis, and Dmitrii Urnov), see "A Discussion of Abram Tertz's book *Strolls with Pushkin*," in *Russian Studies in Literature* 28, no. 1 (Winter 1991–92): 63–88.

Bocharov acknowledged that *Strolls* did not necessarily slander Pushkin, that in fact it paid him high tribute. And yet Bocharov attributed the book's tone, form, and (as he put it) its "desperate aestheticism" largely to external factors, to the grim conditions of Dubrovlag, and to the consequent need of its imprisoned author to posit, by means of a "Tertzized" Pushkin, the ideal of "pure art."[12] In a kindred, similarly evasive maneuver, the postmodernists Petr Vail and Aleksandr Genis insisted that Sinyavsky was opposed to *all* ideology, cliché and conventionalized genres—and that *Strolls* was not literary criticism at all but its own special genre, "fictional literature about fictional literature," a "fascinating realistic novel about the ideal poet."[13] Even to this sophisticated forum, then, the most sensitive issue remained the right of a critic to try out such an "intimate" approach on Russia's greatest poet (a right that Sinyavsky's fellow critics were most reluctant to bestow), rather than any special insight into Pushkin's creativity that this approach might open up. In his closing words to the forum (regrettably not included in the truncated English version), Valentin Nepomnyashchy lamented the fact that none of his fellow scholars called Sinyavsky to account for his *larger* irresponsibility, which the critic saw as two-pronged. First there was Sinyavsky's desire to "struggle against the deification and idolatry of Pushkin"—in itself, a worthy struggle—while at the same time despising those who loved that idol and drew sustenance from it (Nepomnyashchy called this failing "a cynical lack of respect toward another's love" ("tsinichnoe neuvazhenie k chuzhoi liubvi").[14] More seriously, by openly celebrating "untruth" (*nepravda*) *Strolls* violated an ancient Russian tradition: that of the sacred mission of the word. By this charge, Nepomnyashchy meant not only that the book presented untrue information, but that it "taught one to think in a cunning way" (*uchit lukavo myslit'*).[15] The ecclesiastical tone of this reproach was clear index to the degree of sacralization still in force in secular art—and to the deep differences between these Russian critics in the forum (some of Russia's best) and their compatriot Andrei Sinyavsky, on the nature of the divine, the obligations of literary criti-

---

[12] Bocharov, "Obsuzhdenie," 80.

[13] Vail and Genis, "Obsuzhdenie," 123, 124.

[14] Tertz, *Strolls with Pushkin*, 151.

[15] Tertz, *Strolls with Pushkin*, 152.

cism, and the dynamics of the creative process. Meanwhile, in Paris, Sinyavsky's wife Maria Rozanova fretted against all parties. She reminded the belligerents that Pushkin's "skinny erotic legs"—for the worst uproar in the book had been caused by the delightful line: "Pushkin ran into great poetry on skinny erotic legs and created a commotion"—was simply a metaphor. The *real* genre of the Pushkin book, she insisted, was a love letter to her.[16]

Questions of genre do receive some attention in that forum, however, and here Vasily Rozanov and the concept of parody come into play. Bocharov, in his quasi-defense of Tertz, acknowledges that *Strolls* is a literary as well as a critical work—and thus it resembles the criticism of creative writers such as Tsvetaeva and Rozanov, from whom, he said, we do not expect scholarly objectivity but "lively wilfulness" (*iarkoe svoevolie*).[17] Dmitry Urnov, who thoroughly disliked Tertz's book, also compares it with Rozanov, whom he calls the "methodological source" for *Strolls*. But Urnov prefers Rozanov. Unlike Tertz, Vasily Rozanov was sincerely committed to an "inconsistency principle"; upon its contradictory foundation he builds his case for the spontaneous and uncoordinated virtues of the home, for compassion toward small and pitiable things, for the unfinished, "manuscript-like" quality of the soul, and for the unsystematizable—and thus maximally honest—personality. Sinyavsky–Tertz imitates Rozanov in his "ruses and grimaces" but lacks Rozanov's originality, his "keenness of wit and shrewd insight (*ostrota i pronitsatel'nost'*)."[18] Since one of Rozanov's goals had been the destruction of literariness, it was fully appropriate for him to parody literary form and compare human thought to fallen leaves—vegetable matter once organic, now dead, gathered up not in books but in bushels (the Russian word *list* means both a page in a book and a leaf on a tree, distinguished only by different plural forms; so the ambiguity works in Russian as it does in English). Rozanov's strategy was that of an anti-aesthete. When applied to Pushkin, however, this same casualness,

---

[16] See Maria Rozanova, "On the History and Geography of this Book," *Russian Studies in Literature* 28, no. 1 (Winter 1991–92): 89–98; original in *Voprosy literatury* (October 1990): 154–60.

[17] Bocharov, "Obsuzhdenie," 78.

[18] Urnov, "Obsuzhdenie," 140.

glorification of random, undisciplined proliferation, and disdain for literary perfection was simple blasphemy.

These references to Vasilii Rozanov in the debate over *Strolls with Pushkin* are intriguing. For the attention was not, as it were, reciprocal. Sinyavsky's own "straight" academic lectures on Rozanov, delivered at the Sorbonne in the mid-1970s, deal with Rozanov's attitude toward a host of writers—Gogol, Dostoevsky, Leontiev, Shestov, Tolstoy, Blok, Rousseau—all of whom, to varying degrees, were tormented by their writerly profession and by the ethical costs of "literariness." But curiously, the lectures avoid serious discussion of Rozanov's reverential relation with that originary master who never once doubted his poetic calling or the adequacy of the literary word: Aleksandr Pushkin. ("Pushkin...," Rozanov writes in *Fallen Leaves*, "I *ate* him... It entered into me, it courses through the blood, freshens the brain, cleanses the soul from sins."[19]) Sinyavsky's lectures on Rozanov were gathered together into a book and published in 1982, with absolutely no scandal at all. And thus a strange symmetry emerges. Sinyavsky on Rozanov turns out to be much less scandalous than Rozanov (an infuriating, self-styled paradoxicalist) had been as a writer in his own time; as I will argue below, Sinyavsky takes considerable care in these lectures to smooth out and reconcile Rozanov with himself. In contrast, Tertz on Pushkin created an instant and wide-ranging scandal. Indeed, the scandal was of such gargantuan proportions that the long canonical, iconographic Pushkin could never have triggered it on his own—even though Pushkin, in his own time, was keenly alert to both scandal and theatricality and understood their creative potential.

The Rozanov connection is interesting for yet another reason, however. Tertz's persona as a critic, when not dismissed with disgust by Russians protective of their Pushkin and Gogol, has been defined rather simply: as a mask, as welcome buffoonery or comic relief from the stifling style of the academic researcher, as a miscreant and mocking double. Sinyavsky himself has publicized this image. "He's considerably younger than me," Sinyavsky testified. "Tall. Skinny. Little moustaches, a cap. Walks about with his hands in his trouser pockets, with a swaying gait. At any moment he's ready to slash out, only not with a knife but

---

[19] Vasilii Rozanov, *Opavshie list'ia* (Moscow: Sovremennik, 1992), korob vtoroi, 255.

with a sharp little word that overturns received opinion, with a comparison.... This matter with Tertz is more complicated than the simple history of a pseudonym. Tertz is my fleshed-out style, how its carrier would
look."[20] Sinyavsky's portrait of his *alter ego* is more cunning than it at
first appears. For what, after all, is meant by the "look" and "behavior"
of a style? A style is not applied to a creative work at the end of its
making, as polish or glaze is applied to a pot; it is an energy that perme-
ates the work throughout, and from the first word it pulls the reader
into special, active relations with the consciousnesses depicted within.
When the style in question animates a literary critic rather than a primary creator, the precautions and responsibilities proliferate. For the
world of literary criticism (like that of documentaries or historical novels) cannot be wholly arbitrary or imaginary; it is constructed along borders not entirely of its author's making, and there are givens to which it
must be accurate. How "creative" can criticism become and still retain
credibility?

Here, surely, is the nub of the conflict. Conventional criticism, applied as an act of interpretation to literary works or documented biography, must consider the world of the work (and the life) largely crys-
tallized, closed, and decipherable from traces left in the text or in the
world; Tertz's "fantastic," more psychological approach parodies this
convention. Literary scholarship is "fantasticheskoe" when it promises
not a reading of fixed texts but something more dynamic: the cultivation
of a "style" of critical behavior, one based on a fantasized personal
friendship and an almost voyeuristic access to the subject. If it works—
that is, if it is sensed as authentic, if Pushkin comes alive and the reader,
along with the critic, senses his energy and unpredictability—then this
type of criticism has achieved its goal, which is nothing less than a
glimpse of the poet in the grip of creative process. Since this process
(especially in a genius) is itself never arbitrary, the hope is that once its
dynamics are grasped by the critic the method will generate a discipline
and a precision on its own.

---

[20] Cited in the editorial preface to the two-volume *Collected Works of Abram
Tertz*, Vladimir Novikov, "Siniavskii i Tertz," in *Abram Terts* [*Andrei
Sinyavsky*]: *Sobranie sochinenii v dvukh tomakh* (Moscow: SP Start, 1992), 1: 3–
12, esp. 4.

Why do I suggest that this ambitious program may indeed underlie "fantastic literary criticism"? Because the debates surrounding *Strolls with Pushkin* have failed, on balance, to account for the fact that the overall image of the poet and his works in that book is not all that fantastical. As criticism it gets many things *right*; it strikes many lovers of Pushkin as an unexpectedly accurate (although impudent) portrait of certain genuine sides of the poet, and it prompts the reader to further interpretations of Pushkin's works that are fully compatible with traditional scholarship. It is as if Tertz, with his hand on the truth, twists that truth in such a way that the reader senses its potential rightness but at the same time recoils from its excesses, protests its insolence and brazenness—and thus participates actively in the shaping of that truth. Tertz would have us also at risk, and thus he encourages us, as readers of his criticism, to imitate his own critical persona.

Some of Tertz's current admirers seem to agree (albeit cautiously) that such indeed might be the psychological strategy. In his editorial preface to the 1992 Russian collected works of Abram Tertz, Vladimir Novikov (sidestepping, again, the issue of positive content or critical insight) remarks that the purpose of *Strolls* is "to awaken in each reader a lively interest in Pushkin" and to provide the sort of "readerly pleasure" (*chitatel'skoe naslazhdenie*) that one rarely expects from traditional critical practice. Like the writings of Vasily Rozanov at their most polemically intimate, and like the behavior of the precocious Alexander Pushkin at its most eccentric, "fantastical criticism" is sane enough to take seriously, crafty enough to fascinate us, and just bizarre enough to resist.

For analysts of literature, I believe, this faintly bewildering mix of perspectives can be a worthy position to occupy vis-à-vis our subject matter. For part of our job as critics and close readers is to seek out fresh, yet still respectable means of access to the creativity of great literary and critical minds; and although a marvelous Pushkin opens up in Tertz's book, every strategy has its cost. What does this approach allow us to see, and what is closed to it? Might there be a larger rationale behind this genre that is more durable than the limited, early-Formalist shock value of breaking apart a beloved, partly automated thing? Is Tertz's fantastical variant of literary criticism merely a comic debunking parody of an authoritative genre, or does he intend a more *creative* parody? With these questions in mind, I will now, in the remainder of this essay, juxtapose Tertz's book on Pushkin with Sinyavsky's book on Rozanov's *Fallen Leaves*.[21]

Readers familiar with both texts will easily detect some kindred emphases and values. Sinyavsky–Tertz grounds both Rozanov and Pushkin in oral genres, either of the intimate salon or of the intimate family hearth (Sinyavsky stresses the *rukopisnost'* (manuscript-like quality) of Rozanov's creativity, his hostility to the printing press, and the fact that a formal book suited him far less than "fallen leaves" produced physiologically, like "saliva out of salivary glands";[22] in the same spirit, Tertz stresses the transitory, trivial, impulsive and "societal" origins of Pushkin's poetic genius. Both writers are partial to the fragment and to the illusion of unfinishedness. Each is an innovator who disdains official rank and state service, who mocks *ploshchadnost'* (the spirit of the public square) and its fickle crowds, who cultivates prosaic detail and delights in little things. (Here, Sinyavsky's portrait of Rozanov has received solid support recently from Stephen Hutchings, who argues that Rozanov's rehabilitation of *byt* [the tedium of everyday life]—his insistence, against the grain of the early Symbolists, that *byt* could be invested with value-bearing *sobytiia* [events]—was more profoundly important to Russian culture than Rozanov's better known, and less original, rehabilitation of the family and of sex).[23] Both Sinyavsky's Rozanov and Tertz's Pushkin strive toward *pustota* (emptiness or the void); both do battle with the bad habits of accumulation and "heaviness" (in literary genres and in life); and both understand the positive value of a negated plot. But the differences between the two portraits are arguably more interesting than the similarities.

My comparison of the two genres is Bakhtinian in its inspiration. What is the relationship, in each instance, of the author-critic to his hero-subject? Tertz is on intimate terms with his Pushkin from the very first pages; he crosses over into his hero's chronotope, spies him up

---

[21] Subsequent page references are made to these editions: Tertz, *Strolls with Pushkin*, trans. Nepomnyashchy; and A. Siniavskii, *"Opavshie list'ia" V.V. Rozanova* [V.V. Rozanov's fallen leaves] (Paris, Sintaksis, 1982).

[22] Siniavskii, *Opavshie list'ia*, 113.

[23] Stephen C. Hutchings, "Breaking the Circle of the Self: Domestication, Alienation and the Question of Discourse Type in Rozanov's Late Writings," *Slavic Review* 52, no. 1 (Spring 1993): 67–86.

close where the energy of artistic creation is at its most raw—and in so doing, fulfils many of Bakhtin's requirements for a polyphonic novelist. (In the *Voprosy literatury* forum of 1990, the Gogol scholar Iurii Mann links Tertz's book with the "sacral nature" of Bakhtinian carnival, which, in its combination of "seriousness and laughter, the lofty and the travestied," casts an "estranged and refreshing glance" on Pushkin.)[24] Akin to Bakhtin's beloved rogues and fools, Tertz as narrator-critic exploits in full his outsiderly—yet maximally invasive—perspective; although he knows only what he sees (his wisdom is of the passing moment, not of the ages), he sees everything. Thus our initial acquaintance with the poet in *Strolls* is faintly illicit. Pushkin races around not yet canonized, not yet whole, never fully dressed. The effect is that of a fast-moving blur, a sassy lightness, trustful, superstitious toward fate, lazy, indifferent to rank, whom Tertz himself has trouble getting in focus. *Strolls* has footnotes, but not many: for who needs them, when the critic does the poet the honor of assuming he's still alive, still writing, and what he writes every reader knows by heart?

The critic Irina Rodnianskaia, in her entry for the 1990 forum, called this image a "Tertzized, but still authentic Pushkin" designed to be glimpsed in "instantaneous leaps." According to her, the montage approach governs the organization of the critical argument as well: "from Pushkin's 'frivolity' to eroticism, from eroticism to the Muse, from the Muse to Tatiana, from Tatiana to Fate, from Fate to Chance and the anecdote, from the anecdote to all-embracing good will, from good will to that 'emptiness' (already so familiar), from 'emptiness' to vampirism, from vampirism to an enthusiasm for enumeration and quantity, from this cataloging of the world to the 'insignificance' of Pushkin's details, from them ... to Pushkin's classicism, from classicism to aristocratism and the idea of the nobility...."[25] Rodnianskaia notes that these categories would never "fit" under a single principle if taken as a simultaneous cluster of values; only step by step (only following Pushkin's steps) can one see the connections, and in Tertz's meticulously-woven context, these rapid transitions obey "their own sort of logic." She is right. Just as a life only coheres after it is dead and over, so the "Tertzized" Pushkin is driven less by logical argument than by nervous energy. The

---

[24] Mann, "Obsuzhdenie," 89.

[25] Rodnianskaia, "Obsuzhdenie," 88.

resultant Pushkin is revealed as not only generous, kindhearted, curious, playful (the pious virtues of his Mozartian genius), but also unexpectedly profligate and "crooked"—where before he had been magisterially, classically, canonically smooth.

The best defense for this approach to Pushkin is one that Tertz himself does not bring forward. Tertz's image of Pushkin *as poet* is in fact very much in the spirit of Pushkin as *literary critic*. By and large, Pushkin neither respected nor trusted others' criticism of his work in the press; as a critic of others, he was often prescient, incisive, and usually of few words. He did have a "philosophy of criticism," however, and those Russians who have been scandalized by *Strolls with Pushkin* (Valentin Nepomnyashchy cited earlier, and more famously, Alexander Solzhenitsyn) would benefit by recalling it. Pushkin's levelheaded, lighthearted, self-respecting philosophy can be found in his "Second Missive to the Censor" (1825): "Be strict, but intelligent," the poet addresses the censor in that poem. "Observe your rights as duty requires. / But do not put obstacles willfully in the way / of modest Truth, of peaceful Intelligence / even of innocent Stupidity...." And if at times you fail to find a "great good" in one of our "idle scribblings," then never mind; as long as you see in it no special dissoluteness or danger to the throne, just "wish the author all the best from the bottom of your soul, / Give up on it, my friend, and boldly sign your name."[26] In a more serious vein, Pushkin wrote the following in 1830 as part of a set of jottings entitled "Refutations of Criticism": "An immoral work is one whose aim or effect is to subvert the rules on which societal happiness or human dignity are based. Poems whose aim is to fire the imagination with sensual descriptions can only debase poetry... But a joke inspired by heart-felt gaiety and the momentary play of the imagination can seem immoral only to those who have a childish or obscure concept of morality; they confuse it with moralizing, and see in literature only a pedagogical function."[27] At any point, the Pushkin of *Strolls* could have uttered this wisdom to Tertz's enraged critics.

------

[26] "Vtoroe poslanie tsenzoru (1825)," in A. S. Pushkin, *Polnoe sobranie sochinenii v desiati tomakh* (Leningrad: Nauka, 1977), 2: 198–99.

[27] "Refutations of Criticisms," in *The Critical Prose of Alexander Pushkin*, ed. and trans. Carl R. Proffer (Bloomington: Indiana University Press, 1969), 114. Translation adjusted.

If Tertz's "fantastical" Pushkin is above all an open-minded, parody-ing energy, then Sinyavsky's Rozanov, presented in a "non-fantastical" critical genre, comes across as quite the opposite. The author of *"Opavshie list'ia" V.V. Rozanova* (*V.V. Rozanov's "Fallen Leaves"*) smooths over and straightens out that most contradictory and contro-versial of writers. "Rozanov," Sinyavsky writes—in a sentence that doubtless would have horrified its subject—"was an honest and consis-tent thinker ... and, like all great Russian thinkers, in his consistency he was inclined to go all the way to the end, to extreme conclusions in or-der to explain what seemed to him true...."[28] From the very first pages of his monograph, Sinyavsky strives to fix his subject in an accessible and sensible way. To be sure, given the context and audience of the Sorbonne lectures, there is much to recommend this approach that would not have applied to Abram Tertz. The camp inmate Tertz had been entirely at home with Pushkin; he could "stroll" with his subject, whom all literate Russia loved and knew by heart; a casually dropped word or phrase would open up in every reader whole poems and famil-iar plots. With Rozanov the matter was different from the start. Here, Professor Sinyavsky was lecturing on a little-known turn-of-the-century writer at a French university; since he was introducing what was in effect a primary text, he could not seed his narrative with efficient allusions but had to quote large chunks of *Fallen Leaves* verbatim. In short, Sinyavsky was obliged to be a bit schoolmasterish. Even as he dealt with Rozanov's stubborn, shapeless fragments and recalcitrant personality, he exploited his position as professional outsider and mediator of con-flicts. He was obliged to bestow integrity. Otherwise, one could argue, his students would have had no chance of assimilating the text; only af-ter that familiarity is achieved might they participate in it.

This domestication of Rozanov, putting him in order and reconciling his opposites, is sustained throughout the ten lectures. By the end, we feel that we know the man well—but it comes at the price of being un-moved, almost, to pry further or to reopen awkward questions. Let us consider Sinyavsky's handling of only a few of the familiar charges. Rozanov was "inconsistent"? But Sinyavsky assures us that in this case the very criteria for consistency should be removed: "Rozanov was not a teacher of life, not a preacher of first one and then another idea; he was

---

[28] Siniavskii, *"Opavshie list'ia,"* 49.

simply a human being, transferring his natural, human doubts and hesi-
tations into the sphere of his own writerly 'I'."[29] Or the fact that
Rozanov was both anti-Semitic and a semitophile, a man who admired
Jews for their patriarchal family principle and yet despised them for
their revolutionary sympathies? That was because the Jewish people, so
profoundly attracted by the idea of clan, were dazzled by the "illusory,
forced brotherhood" of socialism.[30]

Do the Jews and the Egyptians compete in Rozanov's thought as
chosen peoples? If so, it does not matter, because "for Rozanov, all reli-
gions of the ancient world were at their base unified."[31] Although
Rozanov appears to be a Russian patriot, in fact he curses out the
Russian people at every possible opportunity; but that is perfectly consistent, because Rozanov considered the cursing-out of someone a sign
of intimacy, *domashnost'* (the principle of the family hearth); and in any
event he always preferred the weak, the humiliated, those in the *wrong*,
to the strong and the triumphant who basked in the right. Did Rozanov
succeed in transcending literature? Yes—but this was a pyrrhic victory,
for in the process he became thoroughly literary himself.[32] In
Sinyavsky's book on Rozanov, it is almost impossible to find a hypocrisy
without its healing seam. And for those stubborn contradictions of content and style that simply cannot be resolved, Sinyavsky resorts to culturally domesticated precedents, proffered as role models freely chosen
by Rozanov and thus not subject to ethical judgment by the critic:
Dostoevsky's Underground Man (a paradoxicalist on principle) and the
figure of the holy fool.[33]

Doggedly, Sinyavsky fills everything in. The final verdict on
Rozanov is that he was "not unprincipled, but irresponsible":[34] believing in contradiction, he was true to this belief—but he ignored the consequences of those contradictions in the real, political, ideological lives
of human beings. Yet even here, Sinyavsky intimates that those ignored
consequences do not really matter and should not really scandalize us,

---

[29] Siniavskii, *"Opavshie list'ia,"* 73.

[30] Siniavskii, *"Opavshie list'ia,"* 98.

[31] Siniavskii, *"Opavshie list'ia,"* 100.

[32] Siniavskii, *"Opavshie list'ia,"* 123.

[33] Siniavskii, *"Opavshie list'ia,"* 175–78.

[34] Siniavskii, *"Opavshie list'ia,"* 290.

since Rozanov himself felt no allegiance to the world of civic institutions. And thus, although the penultimate chapter of Sinyavsky's book is entitled "Paradoxes and Polemics," the ultimate picture we receive of the subject is not stressfully paradoxical at all; it is well-balanced, the product of a strong, sympathetic, and distanced intelligence, and its parts fit together.

We might now begin to sum up these two critical genres. In *Strolls with Pushkin*, the keys to the hero are swiftness, penetrability, and gratitude. Tertz introduces Pushkin as a gifted adolescent who "thought mainly in fragments,"[35] who could "transmute one energy into another" with "amorous mimicry"; a man for whom trustfulness and belief in fate were the signs of special grace and who appreciated even laziness and lolling about in bed as "a type of humility, the grateful receptivity of genius to whatever falls into its mouth."[36] In contrast, Sinyavsky recreates Rozanov—the *theoretician* of sex, the doctrinaire advocate of bedroom slippers and hot tea—as a dour, ponderous and consistent thinker; in the Sorbonne lectures, Rozanov sounds like an old man. To be sure, the experienced reader is prepared for this maneuver, which is very much Sinyavsky's trademark. In both his critical personae, Sinyavsky/Tertz is drawn to uncouple, to mismatch, the critical technique with the received or canonical reputation: if art is an act of transgression—a credo dear to Sinyavsky's heart—then criticism, to some extent, is as well. But is the spirit of Rozanov's thought indeed served by diminishing its exuberant, willed irresponsibility? Is this the way Rozanov himself would have wished to be explicated? I suspect not. As a thinker and critic devoted to destroying the "literariness" of literature and the integrity of any intellectual position over time, Rozanov wished to challenge and shock his readers—and yet the effect of Sinyavsky's monograph is progressively to remove this possibility. His book is academic literary scholarship at its neutral and integrating best, tested against the most recalcitrant, covertly *un*academic material.

Thus our juxtaposition of these two images, Tertz's Pushkin and Sinyavsky's Rozanov, gives rise to a final paradox. In the best traditions of creative parody, Tertz's irreverent image of Pushkin praises the poet's multiplicity and brings the force of the poet's own "lightness" and

---

[35] Tertz, *Strolls with Pushkin*, 100.
[36] Tertz, *Strolls with Pushkin*, 53, 60. 61, 65.

"casualness" to bear against the Pushkin industry, pious and overly protective. In real life, however, the enlightened conservative Pushkin—presented by Tertz as a scapegrace and a scamp—was devoted to "literariness"; he was a writer who (of course) "panted for long hours over drafts,"[37] who felt keenly the need for personal privacy and professional autonomy, and who insisted that literature and criticism serve as guarantees of "societal happiness" and "human dignity." These were the authentic values of the authentic Pushkin, scapegrace or no. Any attempt, however, to endow *Rozanov's* writings or personality with such mature wisdom would be akin to blasphemy, and would have been taken as such by Rozanov himself. Laura Engelstein has summed up the matter well. "Underlying the many paradoxes [in Rozanov] there is one consistent theme," she writes, "—the wholesale rejection of liberalism, with its defense of the coherent, autonomous self, its distinction between public and private, and its striving for civic equality and rational standards of truth and social value."[38] If one matches human subject to methodology, which of these two types of criticism produces the more fantastical image, the one least tethered to reality?

That question has no easy answer, but these two books, side by side, do suggest two different paths for the critic and two ways to open up the complexity of a literary subject for one's readers. Both strategies have their proper time and place. The "professional" literary scholarship exemplified by Sinyavsky's book on Rozanov makes us intimate with Rozanov—but unproblematically so. The further we read in it, the more we know the man, the more completely his contradictions are explained, and the less we feel the need to interrogate the subject himself. Throughout, Rozanov remains tightly in the grip of the critic. The "fantastic literary scholarship" of *Strolls with Pushkin* works by quite a different logic, one might even say by a sort of seduction. But this seduction, I suggest, is not of the easy erotic type that had so scandalized Russian readers and critics. Most of the scandal, among emigrés and then in Russia in 1989, was triggered by a very small amount of excerpted text taken from the beginning of the book. The initial image

---

[37] Tertz, *Strolls with Pushkin*, 53.

[38] Laura Engelstein, *The Keys to Happiness: Sex and the Search for Modernity in Fin-de-siècle Russia* (Ithaca: Cornell University Press, 1992), chap. 8, "Sex and the Anti-Semite: Vasilii Rozanov's Patriachal Eroticism," 333.

provided there is indeed picaresque, focusing more on escapades than on art. Tertz is after larger game. For by the second half of the book, these so-called "aimless strolls" begin to go somewhere.

When that happens, in Tertz's plan (as in Dostoevsky's before him), the "fantastic" becomes profoundly, immortally real. Pushkin begins to bifurcate—coldly and austerely—into ordinary man and super-ordinary genius, a prophet who bears not the trivial, but the terrible, marks of grace. As Bocharov noted in the 1990 forum, Tertz's text contains both mockery and "ecstatic dithyramb"; in portraying Pushkin, the author slips back and forth from a caricatured woodcut image (*lubochnyi obraz*) to a "marvelous original" (*prekrasnyi podlinnik*).[39] I would argue, however, that this "slippage" has a definite cumulative direction. By the final third of the book, Pushkin the poet (who, tomfoolery aside, is the person Tertz really wants us to know) is being compared with Peter the Great, with Saint Petersburg, with the majestic and merciless Flood.[40] And by this time, the reader—so important in the opening scenes as co-stroller, eavesdropper, drinking partner— has become irrelevant. Pushkin is now a tsar, following his own advice to poets, "*zhivi odin*" (live alone);[41] he no longer needs to stroll with anyone. Tertz now tells us that Pushkin, as poet, has "no face…. Just try to approach the Poet—Hello, Aleksandr Sergeevich!—he won't answer, he won't understand that you are talking to him—to this effigy that sees no one, hears nothing, holding a stone lyre in his hands."[42] The whimsical, naughty, personal tone of the earlier pages has largely subsided, replaced by distance and awe. The poet is contemplating *pure art*. And Tertz's last-minute attempt to loosen up this austere vision, to revert to his opening image of Pushkin as gambler and playboy, to return in his final pages to the idea that "art strolls" and that he, Abram Tertz, can again go strolling with Pushkin, is to my mind an unpersuasive and already transcended moment of self-parody. *Strolls with Pushkin* is best read as the birth and maturation of a poet, a one-way vertical trajectory

[39] Bocharov, "Obsuzhdenie," 80.

[40] Tertz, *Strolls with Pushkin*, 122–29.

[41] From Pushkin's 1830 poem "Poètu" ("To the Poet"), whose second stanza begins: "You are a tsar: live alone. Take the free path, wherever your free intelligence attracts you…."

[42] Tertz, *Strolls with Pushkin*, 119.

from unholy scamp to God's chosen mouthpiece. This mature poet is renunciatory, ascetic, and by the end largely autonomous of both Tertz and the reader.

As critical strategies, then, the Rozanov book is academically responsible, the Pushkin book is breathtaking. It would seem that those scandalized by the latter's treatment of Russia's greatest poet did not read far, or carefully, enough. More reasoned critics, with Tertz's entire book in mind, have sensed its shift away from freedom as the portrait matures. Iurii Mann, for one, acknowledges in the 1990 forum that the overall impression is not one of "lightness" or of "scapegrace" but of a well-anchored, deadly serious adult, the "self-sacrificing servant of art, its captive ... a captive of honor" (*samootverzhennyi sluzhitel' iskusstva, ego nevol'nik ... nevol'nik chesti*).[43] As is proper to Pushkin's exuberant energy and disdain for preachiness, this image develops only fitfully, haphazardly. Tertz begins by drawing us in the back door, promising us the fruits of best-friendship, a private stroll with a genius who invites us into his study to watch him flirt, doze, scribble. He makes us intimate with Pushkin the man—and then, as the image matures, withdraws the man and leaves us largely the Poet. "Art becomes a temple for solitary, spiritually gifted individuals who gather around them a generous and grateful flock."[44] This withdrawal of the Poet into pure art leaves us thirsting for further contact, for something that Tertz *cannot* tell us; and that "beyond," which Pushkin as poet has now fixed his eyes upon, is something that we cannot see. There is nothing "fantastical" about this sequence at all. It does serve its purpose, however, which is to cast us out of Abram Tertz and back into Pushkin's writings themselves. And this, certainly, is the most responsible service that even the soberest, most old-fashioned literary criticism could ever hope to accomplish.

---

[43] Mann, "Obsuzhdenie," 98.

[44] Tertz, *Strolls with Pushkin*, 145.

Josephine Woll

Kitchen Scandals: A Quasi-Bakhtinian Reading of Liudmila Petrushevskaya's *The Time: Night*

All readers of Petrushevskaya's prose are struck by the Dostoevskian flavor of her prosaics. Her narrators, like so many of Dostoevsky's, feverishly spill their torrents of words on us, at once pushing us underwater and holding us up by the hair in triumph. They deliberately conceal and inadvertently reveal, construct elaborate masks and strip them away, consciously manipulate the stories of their lives and do their best to manipulate those of us who eavesdrop on those stories. Petrushevskaya, as Helena Goscilo notes, employs "complex narrative strategies à la Dostoevsky, particularly the *skaz* of [her] preponderantly female narrators, which derives from the Underground Man's dialogized monologue inasmuch as it proceeds by allusion, irony, self-contradiction, flaunted omissions, defensively misplaced emphases, red herrings and purple patches, in an unstoppable logorrheic flow calculated to affront and arouse suspicion."[1]

Because of the similarities between Petrushevskaya's prose and Dostoevsky's, particularly between their exceedingly self-conscious narrators, it is helpful to consider the one in light of the other. And the Bakhtinian lens that has afforded so much insight into Dostoevsky can be, indeed has been, usefully trained on Petrushevskaya as well.[2] Two contrasting Bakhtinian conceptual prisms, the "idyll chronotope" and

---

[1] Helena Goscilo, "Petrushevskaia's Vision: No Ray of Light in the Kingdom of Darkness." Paper delivered at the American Association for the Advancement of Slavic Studies Conference in Tucson, AZ, 1992; published in Russian translation by Ural Pedagogical University in Ekaterinburg, 1996; ms. p. 2.

[2] See Goscilo, "Speaking Bodies: Erotic Zones Rhetoricized," and Natalia Ivanova, "Bakhtin's Concept of the Grotesque and the Art of Petrushevsakaia and Tolstaia," both in *Fruits of her Plume*, ed. Helena Goscilo (Armonk, NY: M.E. Sharpe, 1993). Ivanova discusses Petrushevskaya's prose within the framework of Bakhtin's carnival theories but minimizes the depth of despair and the destructiveness of Petrushevskaya's "carnivals."

Janet Tucker, ed. *Against the Grain: Parody, Satire and Intertextuality in Russian Literature*. Bloomington, IN: Slavica, 2002, 185–95.

crisis-time, are particularly relevant in considering *The Time: Night*, and especially the role of its proliferating scandal scenes.[3]

Bakhtin identifies as a characteristic feature of idylls the special relationship of time and space:

> an organic fastening-down, a grafting of life and its events to a place... Idyllic life and its events are inseparable from this concrete, spatial corner of the world where the fathers and grandfathers lived and where one's children and their children will live. This little spatial world is limited and sufficient unto itself, not linked in any intrinsic way with other places, with the rest of the world. But in this little spatially limited world a sequence of generations is localized that is potentially without limit... Love, birth, death, marriage, labor, food and drink, stages of growth—these are the basic realities of idyllic life. They are brought into close proximity in the crowded little world of the idyll...[4]

In the "crowded"—not to say cramped—"little world" of Anna Adrianovna, the narrator of *The Time: Night*, and her immediate family—daughter Alena, son Andrei, grandson Tima, mother Sima—the basic realities are in close proximity indeed. As in the sub-genre Bakhtin designates as "family idylls," Petrushevskaya's characters share food and drink "around the table"; food and children are associated in terms of both the nourishment of new growth and the sublimation of sexual activity. And yet we never doubt that Petrushevskaya is creating a parody of the idyll, an idyll at least violated, if not indeed perverted and overturned. Petrushevskaya achieves this grotesque inversion mainly by means of scandal scenes and devises a uniquely female view of the defiled, profaned idyll.

---

[3] The first is part of "Forms of Time and Chronotope in the Novel," in M. M. Bakhtin, *The Dialogic Imagination*, trans. Caryl Emerson and Michael Holquist (Austin: University of Texas Press, 1981), 224–36 *passim*. The second is developed in "Characteristics of Genre and Plot Composition in Dostoevsky's works" and "Toward a Reworking of the Dostoevsky Book," both in *Problems of Dostoevsky's Poetics*, ed. and trans. Caryl Emerson (Minneapolis: University of Minnesota Press, 1984). My thanks to Dr. Emerson for her suggestive comments on Bakhtin's relevance to Petrushevskaya.

[4] Bakhtin, "Forms of Time and Chronotope in the Novel," 225–26.

Within the generally overwrought tone that characterizes most of the text of this short novella, nine discrete scandal scenes can be identified:

1. The first scene in the novella, when Anna Adrianovna and her grandson Tima are ostensibly on a purely social visit to her old friend Masha. In fact they are hungry and visit in hopes of being invited to eat with Masha's family. The children's quarrel over toys sparks a nasty verbal brawl among the adults and Anna Adrianovna and Tima are in effect kicked out.

2. Anna Adrianovna's daughter Alena visits with her new baby, Katia. Furious name-calling seems to end with reconciliation: mother, daughter and grandson all eat together in the kitchen. Actually, as we later learn, Alena stomps off in a rage.

3. Anna Adrianovna alludes casually to an argument: "As usual after a major set-to we all disappeared to our respective corners" before emerging to reengage; Alena bursts into tears "once again"; Alena insults her mother. The fight ends when Anna Adrianovna "walked off, locked myself in my room and wept long and bitterly."

4. Anna Adrianovna recalls a scandal scene that occurred twenty years earlier, when Anna Adrianovna, her husband and her mother Sima were visited by the husband's ex-wife and son. The ex-wife slapped Anna Adrianovna's face, broke a window, slashed her wrist with a shard of glass. Subsequently Anna Adrianovna's husband left her and returned to his former wife and their son.

5. Anna Adrianovna's son Andrei completes his prison term and comes to his mother's apartment to demand money. She and Tima remain inside in the kitchen, he stands outside on the staircase; they scream at each other through the door. The scene ends inconclusively, but we later learn that Anna Adrianovna gives him money she can ill afford.

6. Anna Adrianovna reads a ten-year-old entry from Alena's diary recording a scandal scene in which Anna Adrianovna and her mother Sima rage at each other.

7. Anna Adrianovna "invents" a scandal scene in Alena's *persona*, in which both women and Tima participate in a hysterical emotional tug of war.

8. Anna Adrianovna creates a public scandal on a tram, accusing a man who has been kissing and tickling his small daughter of sexual molestation.

9. The final scandal scene of the novella occurs when Alena arrives at her mother's apartment, daughter Katia and new baby in tow, to move in. The scene appears to end in a relatively peaceful conversation; in fact, Anna Adrianovna comes home to find the rest of them gone.

We immediately observe that every one of these scenes, with the single exception of the tram, takes place indoors. We are deep within that limited spatial world of the idyll, whose "unity of place ... contributes in an essential way to the creation of the cyclic rhythmicalness of time."[5] Here, however, the cyclic rhythm is one of tears and slammed doors, of insults repeated and refined over years of battle. Although they stage their scenes in small and overcrowded apartments, far from the Dostoevskian drawing rooms where scandals usually occur in the presence of a crowd of guests, Petrushevskaya's characters live in buildings that smell no better than Dostoevsky's Haymarket slums; a century on, they live as poorly as Dostoevsky's low-level Petersburg *chinovniki*, four flights up without an elevator.

We are in a twentieth-century Soviet woman's world, though we should remind ourselves of its fictional dimensions: the real world of Soviet women would necessarily include a great many other sites, such as work places and the crowded public transportation required to get there, lines outside state stores, clinics with and without children, parks and playgrounds with children, etc. Petrushevskaya's characters inhabit a claustrophobic world. Their hallways and kitchens sag with the moist air of drying laundry; their bathrooms reek of the camphor smell of the vaporizing steam needed to clear a child's congested chest. The ornate samovar of a spacious nineteenth-century parlor is degraded to a teapot broken by Anna Adrianovna's mother; the delicacies scraped together

---

[5] Bakhtin, "Forms of Time and Chronotope in the Novel," 225.

for Marmeladov's funeral feast transmogrify into bread with perhaps a bit of butter, at best some soup.

The specific spaces themselves may have changed, accomodating shifts in class, lifestyle, gender, etc. Relational space, however, remains much the same as it is in Dostoevsky. Bakhtin draws attention to "up, down, *the stairway, the threshold, the foyer, the landing*" that map the territory of Raskolnikov's dreams.[6] Such interstices and portals, separating and connective spaces, play no less critical a role in Petrushevskaya's fiction than they do in Dostoevsky's. Three of the eight interior scandal scenes explicitly involve boundaries: twice (episodes 2, 9) Alena appears "on the doorstep," once (episode 5) Andrei hurls his insults through the locked door. Several others indirectly involve traversing barriers, whether by snooping behind closed doors, coming out of one's own room to do battle in the boxing ring of the living room, using the phone either to cross borders (by speaking) or to create them (by hanging up).

Bakhtin, in the discussion of Raskolnikov's dreams just cited, explains that the threshold spaces in which Dostoevsky's scandals occur are far removed from the "comfortably habitable interior spaces [where] people live a biographical life in biographical time: they are born, they pass through childhood and youth, they marry, give birth to children, die. This biographical time Dostoevsky 'leaps over.' On the threshold and on the square the only time possible is crisis time, in which a moment is equal to years, decades."[7] Petrushevskaya distorts time in a similar fashion, eschewing ordinary biographical and historical temporal markings, but she does so along gendered fault-lines.[8] *The Time: Night*, like most of her work, exists in what feels like an almost permanent state of crisis time, defined by Bakhtin as the time when "the forbidden line is overstepped."

---

[6] Bakhtin, "Characteristics of Genre," in *Problems of Dostoevsky's Poetics*, 169.

[7] Bakhtin, "Characteristics of Genre," 169–70.

[8] The narrator in "Our Crowd" makes casual reference to "Polish, Czech, Yugoslav … events," and to "such and such trials…, then the trials of the people who'd protested the results of the first trials …" These are the reader's only chronological markers in what seems, until its last pages, an aleatory story of betrayal and cynicism. Lyudmila Petrushevskaya, "Our Crowd," in *Glasnost: An Anthology of Russian Literature under Gorbachev*, ed. Helena Goscilo and Byron Lindsey (Ann Arbor: Ardis, 1990), 9.

Time in *The Time: Night* is not a matter of logical sequence, chronological ordering, or—least of all—public event. It most certainly *is* a matter of biology. Virtually all of Petrushevskaya's narrators, and certainly Anna Adrianovna, construe time as a necklace of births, nursing, childhood illnesses, men loved, men lost. As Anna Adrianovna muses, interpolating her thoughts into the recollected scandal with her ex-husband's ex-wife (episode 4), "You look back on your life and the men run like milestones through it. Jobs and men, with children for chronology, just like in Chekhov."[9] In Petrushevskaya's scandal scenes, the shift in location involves a change in personnel. The cast of characters, unlike Dostoevsky's, almost never includes outsiders: no nosy lodgers, no servants or students, no town society or audience to snigger or guffaw. With the exception of the tram scene, the participants are almost always members of the family, immediate, extended (ex-spouses and lovers) or symbolic (Masha and her crew).

At the same time, the characters who "act out" the scandal scenes in *The Time: Night* appear to be playing to an unseen audience, and the scenes themselves often involve the inversion—from "feast" to "antifeast"—characteristic of Dostoevsky's scenes.[10] Thus when Anna Adrianovna and her mother fight, recalled by Alena in her diary (episode 6), they are playing not only to the gallery beyond the kitchen wall—that is, Alena herself, in the other room—but to a much larger house. The tears, shouts and moans over a broken tea cup and broken teaspout climax as Sima/Granny—with an effort both patent and patently theatrical, Alena notes dryly—falls to her knees in supplication and cries out, "Save me! Lord, people, save me!" The Lord may hear her, but nobody else is around to help. When Andrei brings home two

---

[9] Anna Adrianovna refers to Chekhov's 1885 story, "Living Chronology" ("Zhivaia khronologiia"), in which an elderly husband socializes with a friend and dates events by the ages of his children. He is oblivious to the fact that each of "his" children was fathered by a different celebrity who visited his town and became a "friend of the family." As the final paragraph—and his youngest child's age—reveals, these "family friends" include the friend with whom he is conversing. I am grateful to the anonymous reader who drew my attention to this story.

[10] I am borrowing from Renata Lachmann, who writes of "Feste" and "Gegenfeste" in *Gedächtnis und Literatur: Intertextualität in der russischen Moderne* (Frankfurt: Suhrkamp, 1990), 269–73.

"sluts" (recalled by Anna Adrianovna in the midst of episode 5), he takes them into his mother's room and locks the door. For one full hour he stays inside, ostentatiously prolonging their love-making as Anna Adrianovna raps persistently and impotently on the door. She is an audience of one—but she's the one who counts.

Outside the confines of her home, in a world that operates with a different scale of time and space, scandals don't work out quite the same way. Men apparently dominate this world, but even when women are involved (in, for instance, the hospital where her mother resides), the rules are different, and Anna Adrianovna can't control them the way she can at home. She succeeds in humiliating the father in the tram by eroticizing his affection toward his daughter (Petrushevskaya avoids clarifying whether his caresses are actually suspect), but genuine outsiders are present, and they turn on her as a meddling old bitch. While she pats herself on the back for diverting the father's unhealthy love for his daughter into hatred for herself—thereby "saving another child," as she puts it—the reader is entitled to question her reading of the episode.

She has even less control in the final sequence of the novella, when she at first attempts to bring her incontinent, psychotic mother home from the mental hospital and then relinquishes her to the ambulance drivers. In that scene outsiders actually control her: she can't even manage to provoke a proper scandal, let alone achieve the results she claims to want.

For Petrushevskaya's characters, then, scandals can only properly occur within this grotesque parody of idyllic space, the intimacy of family hell. In home/hell, as Malcolm Jones says, "the threat of scandal is heightened by being set in a context where anything improper is likely to disturb a precarious emotional equilibrium, and the slightest tremor is likely to bring down the whole structure of order and propriety."[11] Thus the scandals in *The Time: Night*, located in the privacy of home, populated by one's kin, resemble one another, and fundamentally parallel Dostoevsky's scandals in both their nature and function. Petrushevskaya's scandal-scenes flay decency, respectability, the outward forms and rituals of family life and bonds to reveal the underlying reality. Digressions, episodes, remarks, memories within memories, anecdotes punctuate the scandal scenes and contribute to what Jones

---

[11] Malcolm Jones, *Dostoevsky: The Novel of Discord* (London: Elek, 1976), 48.

calls the "sensation of disharmony," since the reader continually feels "delayed, waylaid or diverted," unclear on how, if at all, one will get back to the point.[12]

All of them involve speech or actions that produce tension, embarrassment, anarchy. Petrushevskaya's characters, like Dostoevsky's, yell, shriek, curse, blaspheme. Physical violence—in *The Time: Night*, at any rate—is generally restricted to histrionic gesture rather than actual abuse. Characters hurl tablecloths, slap faces, beat at the door; unlike the *dramatis personae* of other Petrushevskaya stories, they don't pummel one another. Still, the impetus exists. Anna Adrianovna recalls the scandal created by her former husband's ex-wife with admiration: "Clever lady. A woman with a thirst for destruction can accomplish a great deal!"[13]

She herself prefers emotional destruction, and she is past mistress of verbal insult. She, her son and her daughter adroitly target one another's fears and vulnerabilities; taking careful aim, they hit bull's eye after bull's eye. Thus Andrei curses vilely during his fights with his mother, repeating the phrase "fucking mother" and "mother fucker" in order to violate her most dearly-held self-image as iconic maternal principle. Both he and Alena call her "mad," a "mad old bag," "off her rocker," "completely bonkers," etc., exploiting her fear of inheriting her mother's illness.

To be sure, Anna Adrianovna reciprocates in kind, and her years of practice often give her an advantage. She harps on Andrei's lack of cleanliness, his fear of arrest, his greater fear of his criminal cronies. She alludes to his homosexuality and calls him a lunatic. But partly because she fears him, partly because of his gender, she is at less than her vengeful best with him. She reserves her cruellest venom for her daughter Alena. Alena, after all, is female and will continue to repeat her own patterns; Alena provides Anna Adrianovna with the next generation of children.

This mother drills relentlessly at the caries in her daughter's neurotic psyche: Alena's slovenly appearance, Alena's inability to hold onto a man. The second scandal scene, for instance, seems to end in

---

[12] Jones, *Dostoevsky*, 42–43 *passim*.

[13] All citations are from Ludmilla Petrushevskaya, *The Time: Night*, trans. Sally Laird (New York: Pantheon, 1994), 62.

reconciliation, a peaceful meal at the kitchen table. But we later read that, as they were sitting over their bowl of soup, Anna Adrianovna could not resist needling her daughter: "I said, 'You should keep a better watch on yourself, look what's become of you!' She looked away and her eyes filled with tears, she was seething with hatred for me again. She got up without so much as a 'thank you' or 'piss off,' not even a word to Tima."[14]

Similarly, the scandal imagined by Anna Adrianovna in her daughter's persona (episode 7) follows and responds to a phone conversation that, like the meal mentioned above, seemed to end in conciliation. Mother advised daughter, daughter heeded the maternal counsel: "Then I'll do what you say, Mum..." The truce hardly endures, however. When Alena belatedly asks about Tima, her mother replies triumphantly: "What's that to you?" and hangs up. In two other scandal scenes mother goads daughter to tears by saying that no one could live with her, and cites as evidence Alena's abandonment by husband Sasha.

Anna Adrianovna is a classic Dostoevskian character, a female hybrid of Fyodor Karamazov and the Underground Man, part buffoon, part truth-teller, her voice "unstable, equivocal, full of muffled ambivalence, ... internally dialogized and shot through with polemic," as Bakhtin wrote of "Bobok's" narrator.[15] Like the Underground Man, Anna Adrianovna embodies *ressentiment,* uniting "a maddening sense of impotence ... to a dæmonically obsessive total recall, until the sufferer's entire consciousness is like an open sore whose sight evokes only disgust in both the victim himself and those around him."[16]

In her assumption of the sadistic clown mask, the buffoon who mocks, Anna Adrianovna most resembles Fyodor Karamazov. Harriet Murav aptly notes that Fyodor Karamazov makes himself into a buffoon "in order to inflict and suffer insult: the role of buffoon allows him to stage the insult himself, thus providing him with a constant flow of

---

[14] Petrushevskaya, *The Time: Night*, 32.

[15] Bakhtin, "Characteristics of Genre," 138.

[16] Michael Andre Bernstein, "Poetics of Ressentiment," in *Rethinking Bakhtin: Extensions and Challenges*, ed. Gary Saul Morson and Caryl Emerson (Evanston, IL: Northwestern University Press, 1989), 205.

pain and pleasure."[17] So does his female avatar a hundred years later. Monster mother to Fyodor Karamazov's monster father, no less "theatrical, provocative and scandalous" (in Murav's words) in her behavior, she is intent on creating crises in which, as Bakhtin writes, "one is renewed or perishes."[18] Ultimately, Petrushevskaya's scandal scenes serve the traditional purposes of such scenes as designated by Bakhtin, "to snap or at least weaken the rotten cords of the official and personal lie" and to lay bare 'human souls' "outside the usual conditions of their life ... opening up another—'more genuine'—sense of themselves and of their relationships to one another."[19] But they also subvert that purpose, insofar as what remains after the human soul is "laid bare" are open wounds, vulnerable to infection, and dripping with blood, pus, and tears. No antiobiotic or clean bandages are available. We are in the domain that Bakhtin, rethinking his reading of Dostoevsky, designated as "catastrophe":

> Catastrophe is not finalization. It is the culmination, in collision and struggle, of points of view... Catastrophe does not give these points of view resolution, but on the contrary reveals their incapability of resolution...; catastrophe is the opposite of triumph and apotheosis. By its very essence it is denied even elements of catharsis.[20]

When Anna Adrianovna recalls the scandal her ex-husband's ex-wife created, she shifts to speaking about herself:

> She'll smash herself to pieces and then look what happens—it all starts fresh, some new destructive impulse gets going—and once again she'll have to pick up the pieces and start all over from scratch, that's how it goes—at least that's what happens to me, that's just how I am, just how I am with others.[21]

---

[17] Harriet Murav, *Holy Foolishness: Dostoevsky's Novels and the Poetics of Cultural Critique* (Stanford: Stanford University Press, 1992), 138.
[18] Bakhtin, "Characteristics of Genre," 169.
[19] Bakhtin, "Characteristics of Genre," 145.
[20] Bakhtin, "Toward a Reworking of the Dostoevsky Book" [Appendix 2], 298.
[21] Petrushevskaya, *The Time: Night*, 62.

It is indeed how she is, with herself and with others. She offers neither them nor herself a cathartic release, let alone a genuine chance at renewal, only a repetition. *The Time: Night* is *Notes from Underground* without Liza. Petrushevskaya provides not even a possible or hypothetical alternative to the bitter cycle of hurt-and-be-hurt, no way of breaking the closed circle of resentment and humiliation. Scandal scenes are the weapons Anna Adrianovna uses to destroy her family; they are the literary devices that Petrushevskaya uses to stir the elements of "family idyll" into the parodic stew that is *The Time: Night*.

Notes on the Contributors

AMY SINGLETON ADAMS is an associate professor of Russian at the College of the Holy Cross in Worcester, Massachusetts. Her recent work includes *Noplace Like Home: The Literary Artist and Russia's Search for Cultural Identity* (SUNY Press). Professor Adams received her doctorate from the University of Wisconsin.

⊕   ⊕   ⊕

JULIE CASSIDAY, whose Ph.D. is from Stanford University, is an associate professor of Russian and Chair of the Program in Comparative Literature at Williams College. She is the author of *The Enemy on Trial: Early Soviet Courts on Stage and Screen* (Northern Illinois University Press). Professor Cassiday has published articles on Soviet literature and presented papers at the American Association for the Advancement of Slavic Studies, the American Association of Teachers of Slavic and East European Languages, and the California Slavic Colloquium. Her essay in this volume, "Flash Floods, Bedbugs and Saunas: Social Hygiene in Maiakovskii's Theatrical Satires of the 1920s," previously appeared in *The Slavonic and East European Review* 76, no. 4 (October, 1998): 643–57.

⊕   ⊕   ⊕

CARYL EMERSON is A. Watson Armour, III University Professor of Slavic Languages and Literatures at Princeton University. She is a translator and critic of the Russian literary critic and philosopher Mikhail Bakhtin and has published widely on nineteenth-century Russian literature, on the history of literary criticism, and on Russian opera and vocal music.

⊕   ⊕   ⊕

Janet Tucker, ed. *Against the Grain: Parody, Satire and Intertextuality in Russian Literature*. Bloomington, IN: Slavica, 2002, 197–200.

HELENA GOSCILO, UCIS Research Professor of Slavic at the University of Pittsburgh, writes on gender and culture in Russia. She has authored and edited more than a dozen books, including *Balancing Acts* (1989, 1991), *Skirted Issues: The Discreteness and Indiscretions of Russian Women's Prose* (1992), *Fruits of Her Plume: Essays on Contemporary Russian Women's Literature* (1993), *Dehexing Sex: Russian Womanhood During and After Glasnost'* (1996), *TNT: The Explosive World of T. Tolstaya's Fiction* (1996), and *Russian Culture in the 1990s* (2000). She currently is working on a cultural study of the New Russians (with Nadezhda Azhgikhina) and a volume on Russian book illustrators (with Beth Holmgren).

⊹　　⊹　　⊹

JERZY KOLODZIEJ—Ph.D., Indiana University—is an associate professor of Slavic languages and literatures at Indiana University and director of the Summer Workshop in Slavic, East European, and Central Asian Languages. He is the author of "Iuliia Voznesenskaia's Women: With Love and Squalor," in *Fruits of Her Plume: Essays on Contemporary Russian Women's Literature*, "Wladislaw Reymont," in Magill's *The Nobel Prize Winners: Literature*, and "Elements of the Petersburg Theme in Olesha's *Envy*," in *Festschrift for Vadim Liapunov*. He has contributed a number of translations to Ardis Publishers.

⊹　　⊹　　⊹

DEBORAH MARTINSEN, who received her Ph.D. from Columbia University, is the Assistant to the Director for the Core Curriculum and an adjunct assistant professor at Columbia University. She is the editor of *The History of Russian Literary Journals* (Cambridge University Press) and the author of "Dostoevsky's *Diary of a Writer*: Journal of the 1870s" (included in the above volume) and "The Cover–Up: General Ivolgin and Corporal Kolpakov" (in *The Slavic and East European Journal*). She has published a number of essays and review articles on Dostoevsky and has presented numerous conference papers in the United States and Europe on Dostoevsky.

⊹　　⊹　　⊹

DEREK MAUS received his Ph.D. from the University of North Carolina at Chapel Hill; his dissertation was entitled "Cold War Satire in Russian and American Fiction, or How We Learned to Start Worrying and Hate the Bomb Again." An assistant professor of English and communications at SUNY College in Potsdam, he is the author of the forthcoming "Another Roadside Epiphany: Flannery O'Connor's *Wise Blood* and Nikolai Gogol's *Dead Souls* as Religious Satires," in the *Southern Quarterly*, and "The Devil in the Details: The Role of Evil in the Short Fiction of Nikolai Vasilievich Gogol' and Nathaniel Hawthorne," which appeared in *Papers on Language and Literature* in Spring 2002. He has also published "Space, Time and Things Made 'Strange': Andrei Belyi, Pavel Filonov, and Theory of Forms" in *Studies in Slavic Culture*.

✧   ✧   ✧

ALEXANDER PROKHOROV completed his Ph.D. in Slavic Languages and Literatures at the University of Pittsburgh. He teaches at the College of William and Mary and does research in film, literature, and cultural studies. He has published numerous articles on both literature (Derzhavin, Dovlatov, Vasily Kamensky) and linguistics and has presented papers on subjects as wide–ranging diverse as film, dance, and literature.

✧   ✧   ✧

JANET TUCKER has her Ph.D. from Indiana University and is a professor of Russian language and literature at the University of Arkansas. She is the author of *Innokentij Annenskij and the Acmeist Doctrine* (Slavica Publishers), *Revolution Betrayed: Jurij Oleša's* Envy (Slavica Publishers, 1996), and co–translator, with Robert Schoenberg, of Anatolii Gladilin's *Moscow Race Track* (Ardis Publishers). She has recently published essays on Pushkin, Dostoevsky, and Babel'.

✧   ✧   ✧

JOSEPHINE WOLL, professor of Russian and Russian literature at Howard University, received her Ph.D. from the University of North Carolina. She is the author of numerous works on contemporary

Russian literature and culture, including *Invented Truth: Soviet Reality and the Literary World of Iurii Trifonov* (Duke University Press, 1991), *Soviet Dissident Literature: A Critical Guide* (G.K. Hall, 1983), *Repentance* (with Denise Youngblood) (I. B. Tauris, 2000), and *Real Images: Soviet Cinema and the Thaw* (I. B. Tauris, 2000).

Bibliography

Afanas'ev, A. N. *Narodnye russkie skazki.* Vol. 1. Moscow: Akademiia, 1936.

———. *Narodnye russkie skazki v trekh tomakh.* Vol. 2. Moscow: Goslitizdat, 1938.

———. *Narodnye russkie skazki v trekh tomakh.* Vol. 1. Moscow: Gosudarstvennoe izdatel'stvo khudozhestvennoi literatury, 1957.

Agranovskii, A., Iu. Alevich and G. Ryklin. *Liudi-vrediteli: Shakhtinskoe delo.* Moscow and Leningrad, 1928.

Alpers, B. "'Klop' v Teatre imeni Vs. Meierkhol'da." In *Teatral'nye ocherki v dvukh tomakh.* 2 vols. Moscow: Iskusstvo, 1977, 130–32.

Babel', Isaak. *Konarmiia.* 3rd ed. Moscow: Gosudarstvennoe izdatel'stvo, 1928. Reprint, London: Flegon Press, n.d.

Bachelard, Gaston. *The Poetics of Space.* New York: The Orion Press, 1964.

Bakhtin, M. M. *The Dialogic Imagination: Four Essays by M. M. Bakhtin.* Translated by Caryl Emerson and Michael Holquist. Edited by Michael Holquist. Austin: University of Texas Press, 1981.

———. *Problems of Dostoevsky's Poetics.* Edited and translated by Caryl Emerson. Introduction by Wayne C. Booth. Minneapolis: University of Minnesota Press, 1984.

Baratoff, Nathalie. *Oblomov: A Jungian Approach. A Literary Image of the Mother Complex.* Berne: Peter Lang, 1990.

Barratt, Andrew. *Yurii Olesha's "Envy."* Birmingham, England: Birmingham Slavonic Monographs, 1981.

Bayley, John. *Tolstoy and the Novel.* London: Chatto and Windus, 1966.

Beaujour, Elizabeth Klosty. "Architectural Discourse and Early Soviet Literature." *Journal of the History of Ideas* 44 (July–September 1983): 477–95.

Janet Tucker, ed. *Against the Grain: Parody, Satire and Intertextuality in Russian Literature.* Bloomington, IN: Slavica, 2002, 201–12.

————. "On Choosing One's Ancestors: Some Afterthoughts on *Envy*," *Ulbandus Review* 2, no. 1 (Fall 1979): 24–36.

Beaujour, Elizabeth Klosty. *The Invisible Land: A Study of the Artistic Imagination of Iurii Olesha*. New York: Columbia University Press, 1970.

Belinkov, Arkadii. *Sdacha i gibel' sovetskogo intelligenta: Iurii Olesha*. Madrid: Ediciones Castilla, 1976.

Belinsky, Vissarion. *Sobranie sochinenii v 3-kh tomakh*. Moscow: Khu-dozhestvennaia literatura, 1948.

Bely, Andrey. *Petersburg*. Letchworth, England: Bradda Books Reprint, 1967.

————. *Petersburg*. Translated by Robert A. Maguire and John E. Malmstad. Bloomington, IN: Indiana University Press, 1978.

Benjamin, Walter. "The Work of Art in the Age of Mechanical Repro-duction." In *Film Theory and Criticism*. 5th edition. Edited by Leo Braudy and Marshall Cohen, 731–51. New York: Oxford University Press, 1999.

Berlin, Sir Isaiah. *The Hedgehog and the Fox: An Essay on Tolstoy's View of History*. New York: Simon and Schuster, 1953.

Bethea, David, ed. *Pushkin Today*. Bloomington, IN: Indiana Univer-sity Press, 1993.

————. *Realizing Metaphors: Alexander Pushkin and the Life of the Poet*. Madison: University of Wisconsin Press, 1998.

Blium, V. "Vozroditsia li satira?" *Literaturnaia gazeta*, no. 6 (27 May 1929): 2.

Bloom, Harold, ed. *Modern Critical Views: Isaac Babel*. New York: Chelsea House Publishers, 1987.

Borden, Richard. "The Magic and the Politics of Childhood: The Child-hood Theme in the Works of Iurii Olesha." Ph.D. diss., Columbia University, 1987.

Borowec, Christine. "Time After Time: The Temporal Ideology of *Oblomov*." *Slavic and East European Journal* 38, no. 4 (Winter 1994): 561–73.

Brodskii, Iosif. "O Serezhe Dovlatove." *Petropol': Pamiati Sergeia Dovlatova* 5 (1994): 167–73.

Broich, Ulrich. *The Eighteenth-Century Mock-Heroic Poem*. Cambridge: Cambridge University Press, 1990.

Brown, Deming. *Soviet Russian Literature Since Stalin.* Cambridge: Cambridge University Press, 1979.

Brown, Edward J. *Mayakovsky: A Poet in Revolution.* Princeton: Princeton University Press, 1975.

———. *Russian Literature Since the Revolution.* New York: Collier Books, 1963. Rev. and enl. ed. Cambridge, MA: Harvard University Press, 1982.

Busch, Robert Louis. *Humor in the Major Novels of F.M. Dostoevsky.* Columbus, OH: Slavica Publishers, 1987.

Chapple, Richard L. *Soviet Satire of the Twenties.* Gainesville, FL: University Press of Florida, 1980.

Chizhevsky, Dmitry. "Gogol: Artist and Thinker." *The Annals of the Ukrainian Academy of Arts and Sciences in the U.S.* 4 (1952): 261–78.

———. *History of Russian Literature from the Eleventh Century to the End of the Baroque.* 's-Gravenhage: Mouton, 1962.

Chudakova, Marietta O. *Masterstvo Iuriia Oleshi.* Moscow: Nauka, 1972.

Clyman, Toby W. "Babel' as Colorist." *Slavic and East European Journal* 21, no. 3 (Fall 1977): 332–43.

Connery, Brian A. and Kirk Combe. *Theorizing Satire: Essays in Literary Criticism.* New York: St. Martin's Press, 1995.

Cornwell, Neil. "The Principle of Distortion in Olesha's *Envy.*" *Essays in Poetics* 5, no. 1 (1980): 15–35.

Curtis, J. A. E. "Down with the Foxtrot! Concepts of Satire in the Soviet Theatre of the 1920s." In *Russian Theatre in the Age of Modernism,* edited by Robert Russell and Andrew Barratt, 219–35. New York: St. Martin's Press, 1990.

Denitskii, V. A., ed. *Izbrannye stat'i po russkoi literature XVIII-XIX vv.* Moscow: Akademiia nauk, 1958.

Derzhavin, Gavriil. *Sochineniia.* Moscow: Pravda, 1985.

Dobroliubov, N. A. *Sobranie sochinenii.* Moscow: Khudozhestvennaia literatura, 1987.

Dostoevsky, Fyodor. *Polnoe sobranie sochinenii v tridtsati tomakh.* Leningrad: Nauka, 1972–90.

———. *Demons.* Translated by Richard Pevear and Larissa Volokhonsky. New York: Vintage Classics, 1994.

Dovlatov, Sergei. *Ours: A Russian Family Album.* Translated by Anne Frydman. New York: Weidenfeld and Nicolson, 1989.

———. *Sobranie prozy v trekh tomakh.* Vol. 2. St. Petersburg: Limbus Press, 1993.

———. *The Invisible Book.* Translated by Katherine O'Conner and Diana L. Burgin. Ann Arbor: Ardis, 1979.

Draitser, Emil. *Techniques of Satire: The Case of Saltykov-Ščedrin.* Berlin: Mouton de Gruyter, 1994.

Durova, N. A. *Izbrannye sochineniia.* Moscow: Moskovskii rabochii, 1983.

Ehre, Milton. *Oblomov and His Creator: The Life and Art of Ivan Goncharov.* Princeton: Princeton University Press, 1973.

Eliade, Mircea. *Cosmos and History: The Myth of the Eternal Return.* Translated by Willard R. Trask. New York: Harper and Brothers, 1959.

Elliott, Robert C. *The Power of Satire: Magic, Ritual, Art.* Princeton: Princeton University Press, 1960.

Engelstein, Laura. *The Keys to Happiness: Sex and the Search for Modernity in Fin-de-siècle Russia.* Ithaca: Cornell University Press, 1992.

Erlich, Victor. *Russian Formalism: History – Doctrine.* 3rd ed. New Haven: Yale University Press, 1981.

Ermilov, V. "O nastroeniiakh melkoburzhuaznoi levizny v khudozhestvennoi literatury," *Pravda,* no. 67 (4512) (9 March 1930): 4.

———. "O trëkh oshibkakh Meierkhol'da," *Vecherniaia Moskva* no. 63 (1876) (17 March, 1930): 3.

Evdokimova, Svetlana. *Pushkin's Historical Imagination.* New Haven: Yale University Press, 1999.

Fanger, Donald. "Conflicting Imperatives in the Model of the Russian Writer: The Case of Tertz/Sinyavsky." In *Literature and History: Theoretical Problems and Russian Case Studies,* edited by Gary Saul Morson, 111–24. Stanford: Stanford University Press, 1986.

Fanger, Donald, ed. *O Dostoevskom: Stat'i.* Providence: Brown University Press, 1966.

Friedberg, Maurice. "Yiddish Folklore Motifs in Isaak Babel's Konarmija." In *Modern Critical Views,* edited by Harold Bloom, 191–98. New York: Chelsea House Publishers, 1987.

Frye, Northrup. *Anatomy of Criticism*. Princeton: Princeton University Press, 1957.

Genis, Alexander. *Dovlatov i okrestnosti*. Moscow: Vagrius, 1999.

Gerould, Daniel, guest ed., Jeanine Parisier Plottel, ed. *Melodrama*. New York: New York Literary Forum, 1980.

Gerould, Daniel and Julia Przybos. "Melodrama in the Soviet Theater 1917–1928: An Annotated Chronology." In *Melodrama*, edited by Daniel Gerould and Jeanine Plottel, 75–92. New York: New York Literary Forum, 1980.

Ginzburg, Mirra, ed. and trans. *A Soviet Heretic: Essays by Evgeny Zamyatin*. Chicago: The University of Chicago Press, 1970.

Gogol, Nikolai. "The Nose." *The Overcoat and Other Tales of Good and Evil*. Translated by David Magarshack. New York: W.W. Norton & Co., 1965, 203–33.

———. *Sobranie sochinenii v semi tomakh*. Moscow: Khudozhestvennaia literatura, 1960, 1966–67.

Goncharov, I. A. *Sobranie sochinenii*. Moscow: Khudozhestvennaia literatura, 1952–55.

Goncharova, N. "'Bania' V. Maiakovskogo." *Rabochaia gazeta*, no. 65 (2414) (21 March 1930): 7.

Goscilo, Helena. *Fruits of her Plume*. Armonk, NY: M.E. Sharpe, 1993.

Goscilo, Helena. "Petrushevskaia's Vision: No Ray of Light in the Kingdom of Darkness." Paper presented at the American Association for the Advancement of Slavic Studies Conference in Tucson, AZ, 1992; published in Russian translation at the Ural Pedagogical Institute in Ekaterinburg.

Goscilo, Helena and Byron Lindsey, eds. *Glasnost: An Anthology of Russian Literature under Gorbachev*. Ann Arbor: Ardis Publishers, 1990.

Greene, Thomas. "The Norms of Epic." *Comparative Literature* 13 (1961): 193–207.

Griffiths, Frederick T. and Stanley J. Rabinowitz. *Novel Epics: Gogol, Dostoevsky, and National Narrative*. Evanston, IL: Northwestern University Press, 1990.

Guilhamet, Leon. *Satire and the Transformation of Genre*. Philadelphia: University of Pennsylvania Press, 1987.

Harper, Kenneth. "Text Progression and Narrative Style." In *American Contributions to the Eighth International Congress of Slavists, Za-*

greb and Ljubljana, September 3–9, 1978, edited by Victor Terras, 2: 223–35. Columbus, OH: Slavica Publishers, 1978.

Harrison, Ellen Jane. *Aspects, Aorists and the Classical Tripos.* Cambridge: Cambridge University Press, 1919.

Hartwig, Joan. *Shakespeare's Analogical Scene: Parody as Structural Syntax.* Lincoln: University of Nebraska Press, 1983.

Hedges, Christopher. "Jokes from Underground in Morocco." *The New York Times* (21 January 1995), A4.

Henry, Peter. *Modern Soviet Satire.* London: Collet's, 1974.

Highet, Gilbert. *The Anatomy of Satire.* Princeton: Princeton University Press, 1962.

Holquist, Michael. *Dostoevsky and the Novel.* Evanston, IL: Northwestern University Press, 1977.

———. "St. Petersburg: From Utopian City to Gnostic Universe." *The Virginia Quarterly Review* 48, no. 4 (Autumn 1972): 537–57.

Hutcheon, Linda. *A Theory of Parody: The Teaching of Twentieth-Century Art Forms.* New York: Methuen, 1985.

Hutchings, Stephen C. "Breaking the Circle of the Self: Domestication, Alienation and the Question of Discourse Type in Rozanov's Late Writings." *Slavic Review* 52, no. 1 (Spring 1993): 67–86.

Iakubovskii, G. "O satire nashikh dnei," *Literarturnaia gazeta*, no. 11 (8 July 1929): 3.

Ingdahl, Kazimiera. *The Artist and the Creative Act: A Study of Jurij Oleša's Novel "Zavist'."* Stockholm: Minab/Gotab, 1984.

Ivanov-Razumnik. *Vershiny.* Petrograd: Kolos, 1923.

Jones, Malcolm. *Dostoevsky: The Novel of Discord.* London: Elek, 1976.

——— and Robert Feuer Miller, eds. *The Cambridge Companion to the Classic Russian Novel.* Cambridge: Cambridge University Press, 1998.

"'Klop.' Novaia p'esa Vl. Maiakovskogo." *Vecherniaia Moskva*, no. 1 (1513) (2 January 1929): 3.

Koehler, Ludmila. "The Grotesque Poetry of Dostoevsky." *Slavic and East European Journal* 14, no. 1 (Spring 1970): 11–23.

Kornblatt, Judith Deutsch. *The Cossack Hero in Russian Literature: A Study in Cultural Mythology.* Madison: The University of Wisconsin Press, 1992.

Lachmann, Renata. *Gedächtnis und Literatur: Intertextualität in der russischen Moderne.* Frankfurt: Suhrkamp, 1990.

Lauer, Reinhard. "Zur Gestalt Ivan Babichevs in Olešas *"Zavist'."* *Die Welt der Slaven* 7, no. 1 (June 1962): 45–54.

Lenin, V. I. *Polnoe sobranie sochinenii.* Moscow: Politicheskaia literatura, 1975–78.

Loseff, Lev. *On the Beneficence of Censorship: Aesopian Language in Modern Russian Literature.* Munich: Verlag Otto Sagner, 1984.

Lunacharsky, Anatoly. *Byvshie liudi: Ocherk istorii partii es-erov.* Moscow: Gosudarstvennoe izdatel'stvo, 1922.

———. *O teatre i dramaturgii.* Moscow: Iskusstvo, 1958.

———. *Sobranie sochinenii.* 8 vols. Moscow: Khudozhestvennaia literatura, 1963–67.

———. "What Kind of Melodrama Do We Need?" Translated by Daniel Gerould. *Slavic and East European Performance: Drama, Theatre, Film* 14, no. 3 (Fall 1994): 60–64.

Luplow, Karen. "Paradox and the Search for Value in Babel's *Red Cavalry.*" In *Red Cavalry: A Critical Companion,* edited by Charles Rougle, 69–93. Evanston, IL: Northwestern University Press, 1996.

Lyngstad, Alexandra and Sverre Lyngstad. *Ivan Goncharov.* New York: Twayne Publishers, 1971.

Maguire, Robert A. and John E. Malmstad. Notes to *Petersburg* by Andrei Bely. Translated by Robert A. Maguire and John E. Malmstad, 294–356. Bloomington, IN: Indiana University Press, 1978.

Margolin, Samuil. "Vesna teatral'noi chrezmernosti." *Vestnik rabotnikov iskusstv,* nos. 10–11 (1921): 122.

Martinsen, Deborah. "Dostoevsky and the Temptation of Rhetoric." Ph.D. diss., Columbia University, 1990.

Mathewson, Rufus. *The Positive Hero in Russian Literature.* Stanford: Stanford University Press, 1975.

Mayakovsky, Vladimir. "Klop. Novaia p'esa Vl. Maiakovskogo." *Vecherniaia Moskva,* no. 1 (1513) (2 January 1929): 3.

———. *Polnoe sobranie sochinenii.* Moscow: Khudozhestvennaia literatura, 1959.

McLean, Hugh. "Satire." In *Handbook of Russian Literature,* edited by Victor Terras, 385. New Haven: Yale University Press, 1985.

———. "Skaz." In *Handbook of Russian Literature,* edited by Victor Terras, 420. New Haven: Yale University Press, 1985.

Meerson, Olga. *Dostoevsky's Taboos.* Dresden: Dresden University Press, 1997.

Meierkhol'd, V. E. "Vystuplenie v Tsentral'nom dome VLKSM Krasnoi Presni, 12 ianvaria 1929 goda." In *Stat'i, pis'ma, rechi, besedy,* 176–78. 2 vols. Moscow: Iskusstvo, 1968.

Merezhkovskii, Dmitrii. *Polnoe sobranie sochinenii.* St. Petersburg, 1912.

Miatlev, I. P. *Polnoe sobranie sochinenii.* Saint Petersburg: Apollon Fridrikson, 1957.

Mokul'skii, S. "Eshche o 'Klope.'" *Zhizn' iskusstva,* no. 13 (24 January 1929): 10.

Moore, George. *The Book Kerith.* New York: MacMillan, 1917.

Morson, Gary Saul. *The Boundaries of Genre: Dostoevsky's "Diary of a Writer" and the Traditions of Literary Utopia.* Austin: University of Texas Press, 1981.

———, ed. *Literature and History: Theoretical Problems and Russian Case Studies.* Stanford: Stanford University Press, 1986.

———. *Narrative and Freedom: The Shadows of Time.* New Haven: Yale University Press, 1994.

———, and Caryl Emerson, eds. *Rethinking Bakhtin: Extensions and Challenges.* Evanston, IL: Northwestern University Press, 1989.

Morson, Gary Saul and Caryl Emerson. *Mikhail Bakhtin: Creation of a Prosaics.* Stanford: Stanford University Press, 1990.

Murav, Harriet. *Holy Foolishness: Dostoevsky's Novels and the Poetics of Cultural Critique.* Stanford: Stanford University Press, 1989.

———. *Russia's Legal Fictions.* Ann Arbor: University of Michigan Press, 1998.

Nabokov, Vladimir. *Nikolai Gogol.* New York: New Directions, 1961.

Nepomnyashchy, Catharine Theimer. "An Interview with Andrei Sinyavsky." (Arlington, VA, January, 1990). *Formations* 6, no. 1 (Spring 1991): 6–23.

———. "Notes on the Context of Siniavskii's Reception in Gorbachev's Russia." *Russian Studies in Literature* 28, no. 1 (Winter 1991–92): 3–11.

———. *The Poetics of Crime: An Approach to the Writings of Abram Tertz.* New Haven: Yale University Press, 1995.

"Obsuzhdenie knigi Abrama Tertsa 'Progulki s Pushkinym.'" In *Voprosy literatury* (October 1990): 77–153. Partially translated as "A

Discussion of Abram Tertz's Book *Strolls with Pushkin.*" *Russian Studies in Literature* 28, no. 1 (Winter 1991–92): 63–88.

Olesha, Iurii. *Povesti i rasskazy.* Moscow: Khudozhestvennaia literatura, 1965.

Orwin, Donna Tussing. *Tolstoy's Art and Thought, 1847–1880.* Princeton: Princeton University Press, 1993.

Othow, Helen Chavis. "*Roots* and the Heroic Search for Identity." *College Language Association Journal* 26, no. 3 (1983): 311–24.

Paglia, Camille. *Sexual Personae: Art and Decadence From Nefertiti to Emily Dickinson.* New York: Vintage, 1991.

Peace, Richard. *Dostoevsky: An Examination of the Major Novels.* Cambridge: Cambridge University Press, 1971.

———. *"Oblomov": A Critical Examination of Goncharov's Novel.* Birmingham Monographs, no. 29. Birmingham: University of Birmingham, 1991.

Pereverzev, V. F. "Sotsial'nyi genezis oblomovshchiny." *Pechat' i revoliutsiia* 2 (1925): 61–78.

Petrushevskaya, Ludmila. *The Time: Night.* Translated by Sally Laird. New York: Pantheon, 1994.

Piper, D. G. B. "Yuriy Olesha's *Zavist'*: an Interpretation." *Slavonic and East European Review* 48 (1970): 27–43.

Pisarev, D. I. "Oblomov." *Rassvet (St. Petersburg)* 10 (1859): 5–21.

———. "Zhenskie tipy v romanakh i povestiakh Pisemskogo, Turgeneva, Goncharova." *Russkoe slovo* 12, no. 2 (1861):1–53.

Poggioli, Renato. *The Phoenix and the Spider.* Cambridge, MA: Harvard University Press, 1957.

Preminger, Alex, ed. *Princeton Encyclopedia of Poetry and Poetics.* Princeton: Princeton University Press, 1974.

Proffer, Carl, ed. and trans. *The Critical Prose of Alexander Pushkin.* Bloomington, IN: Indiana University Press, 1969.

Propp, V. Ia. *Morfologiia skazki.* 2nd ed. Moscow: Nauka, 1969.

Pushkin, Aleksandr. *Polnoe sobranie sochinenii v desiati tomakh.* Leningrad: Nauka, 1956–58, 1977–79.

———. *Sobranie sochinenii v desiati tomakh.* Moscow: Khudozhestvennaia literatura, 1959–62.

Rado, Alexander. *A Guide-Book to the Soviet Union.* New York: International Publishers Co., 1928.

Riasanovsky, Nicholas V. *A History of Russia*. 4th ed. Oxford and New York: Oxford University Press, 1984.

Rimmon-Kennan, Shlomith. *Narrative Fiction: Contemporary Poetics*. London: Methuen, 1983.

Rogi, M. "Puti sovetskoi satiry." *Literaturnaia gazeta* 14 (22 July 1929): 3.

Rose, Margaret A. *Parody//Meta-Fiction: An Analysis of Parody as a Critical Mirror to the Writing and Reception of Fiction*. London: Croom Helm, 1979.

———. *Parody: Ancient, Modern, and Post-Modern*. Cambridge: Cambridge University Press, 1993.

Ross, Rochelle H. "The Unity of Babel's *Konarmija*." *South Central Bulletin* 41, no. 4 (Winter 1981): 114–19.

Rowe, William W. *Leo Tolstoy*. Boston: Twayne, 1986.

Rozanov, Vasilii. *Opavshie list'ia*. Moscow: Sovremennik, 1992.

Rozanova, Maria. "On the History and Geography of this Book." *Russian Studies in Literature* 28, no. 1 (Winter 1991–92): 89–98. Translation of original in *Voprosy literatury* (October 1990): 154–60.

Rudnitsky, Konstantin. *Russian and Soviet Theatre: Tradition and the Avant-Garde*. Translated by Roxane Permar, edited by Lesley Milne. London: Abrams, 1988.

Russell, Robert and Andrew Barratt, eds. *Russian Theatre in the Age of Modernism*. New York: St. Martin's Press, 1990.

Ryan-Hayes, Karen. "Narrative Strategies in the Works of Sergei Dovlatov." *Russian Language Journal* 45, no. 153 (1992): 155–78.

———. *Contemporary Russian Satire: A Genre Study*. Cambridge: Cambridge University Press, 1995.

Salomon, Roger B. *Desperate Storytelling: Post-Romantic Elaborations of the Mock-Heroic Mode*. Athens, GA: University of Georgia Press, 1987.

Scheffler, Leonore. "Jurij Olešas Roman *Zavist'*—ein Kommentar zur Zeit [Skizze zum Missverständnis der Kritik]." *Zeitschrift für slavische Philologie* 36 (1972): 266–95.

Serman, Il'ia. "Teatr Sergeia Dovlatova." *Grani* 140 (1985): 138–62.

Setchkarev, Vsevolod. *Ivan Goncharov: His Life and Works*. Würzburg: Jal-Verlag, 1974.

Sibley, Gay. "*Satura* from Quintilian to Joe Bob Briggs: A New Look at an Old Word." In *Theorizing Satire: Essays in Literary Criticism*, edited by Brian A. Connery and Kirk Combe, 57–72. New York: St. Martin's Press, 1995.

Sicher, Efraim. *Style and Structure in the Prose of Isaak Babel'.* Columbus, OH: Slavica Publishers, 1986.

Simmons, Ernest J. *Introduction to Russian Realism.* Bloomington, IN: University Press, 1965.

Sinyavsky, Andrei. *"Opavshie list'ia" V. V. Rozanova.* Paris: Sintaksis, 1982.

Sokolov, Yu.M. *Russian Folklore.* Translated by Catherine Ruth Smith. Hatboro, PA: Folklore Associates, 1966.

Steiner, George. *No Passion Spent: Essays 1978–1995.* New Haven: Yale University Press, 1996, 116–21.

Stenbock-Fermor, Elizabeth. *"The Master and Margarita* and Goethe's *Faust." Slavic and East European Journal* 13, no. 3 (Fall 1969): 309–25.

Sukhikh, Igor'. *Sergei Dovlatov: Vremia, mesto, sud'ba.* St. Petersburg: Kul'tInform Press, 1996.

Sukhovo-Kobylin, Alexander. *The Trilogy of Sukhovo-Kobylin.* Translated by Harold Segel. New York: Dutton, 1969.

Tal'nikov, D. "Novye postanovki: 1. 'Klop.'" *Zhizn' iskusstva,* no. 11 (10 March 1929): 10.

Terras, Victor, ed. *Handbook of Russian Literature.* New Haven: Yale University Press, 1985.

Tertz, Abram [Andrei Sinyavsky]. *Fantasticheskii mir Abrama Tertza.* Paris: Inter-Language Literary Associates, 1967.

———. *Strolls with Pushkin.* Translated by Catharine Theimer Nepomnyashchy and Slava I. Yastremski. New Haven: Yale University Press, 1993.

———. *V teni Gogolia. Sobranie sochinenii v dvukh tomakh.* Moscow: SP Start, 1992.

Test, George. *Satire: Spirit and Art.* Tampa, FL: University of South Florida Press, 1991.

Tolstoy, Leo. *Hadji Murad. Great Short Works of Leo Tolstoy.* New York: Harper and Row, 1967.

———. *I Cannot be Silent: Writings on Politics, Art and Religion.* Bristol, U.K.: Bristol Press, 1989.

———. *Polnoe sobranie sochinenii.* Vol. 2. Moscow: I. D. Sytina, 1912.

Tolstoy, Leo. *The Sebastopol Sketches*. Translated by David McDuff. London: Penguin Books, 1986.

———. *War and Peace*. Translated by Aylmer Maude, Louise Shanks Maude, and George Gibian. New York: W. W. Norton and Co., 1996.

Toporov, Viktor. "Dom, kotoryi postroil Dzhek. O proze Dovlatova." *Zvezda* 3 (1994): 174–76.

Tseitlin, A. G. *I. A. Goncharov*. Moscow: Akademiia nauk, 1950.

Tucker, Janet. "A Re-examination of Jurij Oleša's *Envy*." *Slavic and East European Journal* 26, no. 1 (Spring 1982): 56–62.

———. *Revolution Betrayed: Jurij Oleša's "Envy."* Columbus, OH: Slavica Publishers, 1996.

Tseitlin, A. G. *I. A. Goncharov*. Moscow: Akademiia nauk, 1950.

Tynianov, Iu. *Arkhaisty i novatory*. 1929. Reprint, Ann Arbor: Ardis, 1985.

———. "Dostoevskii i Gogol': K teorii parodii." In *O Dostoevskom: Stat'i*, 153–96. Edited by Donald Fanger. Providence: Brown University Press, 1966.

———. *Poetika, istoriia literatury, kino*. Moscow: Nauka, 1977.

Vanchu, Anthony. "Jurij Oleša's Artistic Prose and Utopian Mythologies of the 1920s." Ph.D. diss., University of California, 1990.

Vishevsky, Anatoly. *Soviet Literary Culture in the 1970s: The Politics of Irony*. Gainesville, FL: University Press of Florida, 1993.

Wilson, A. N. *Tolstoy*. London: Hamisch Hamilton, 1988.

Wilson, Wayne P. "The Objective of Jurij Oleša's *Envy*." *Slavic and East European Journal* 18, no. 1 (Spring 1974): 31–40.

Woroszylski, Wiktor. *The Life of Mayakovsky*. Translated by Boleslaw Taborski. New York: Orion Press, 1970.

Zamyatin, Evgeny. *We*. Translated by Mirra Ginzburg. New York: Bantam Books, 1972.

Zaslavskii, L. "Vrediteli." *Pravda*, no. 115 (3947) (19 May 1928): 3.

Index

Janet Tucker, ed. *Against the Grain: Parody, Satire and Intertextuality in Russian Literature.* Bloomington, IN: Slavica, 2002, 213–24.